CU00923398

Managing stress

Ifor Capel and John Gurnsey

Managing Stress

Constable · London

First published in Great Britain 1987
by Constable and Company Limited
10 Orange Street, London WC2H 7EG
Copyright © 1987 by Ifor Capel and John Gurnsey
Set in Linotron Plantin 11pt by
Rowland Phototypesetting Limited
Bury St Edmunds, Suffolk
Printed in Great Britain by
St Edmundsbury Press Limited
Bury St Edmunds, Suffolk

British Library CIP data
Capel, Ifor
Managing stress
1. Medicine, Psychosomatic   2. Stress
(Psychology)   3. Stress (Physiology)
I. Title   II. Gurnsey, John
616.8   RC455.4.S87

ISBN 0 09 467260 1
ISBN 0 09 468010 8 Pbk

Contents

Acknowledgements

Any book of this type owes a great deal to many people. We have read literally hundreds of books, articles and reports on the topics of stress, disease and brain neurochemistry. Much of this data forms the basis of this work and our thanks are due to the many authors involved. Thanks are due also to the librarians and their staff who helped us track down much of the information; the library staff at the North East London Polytechnic, the King's Fund Centre, Northwick Park's Clinical Research Centre, LSE's British Library of Political and Economic Science and Harrow Reference Library are particularly acknowledged.

A number of friends and colleagues also gave time to read various drafts and make comment. Particularly acknowledged are Helen Dorrell and Edgar Spencer of North East London Polytechnic's Bio-Electric Therapy Research Laboratory, who have read and lived with the project throughout. Their support and encouragement have been unfailing, and their comments both sensitive and constructive. In the conventional medical area, Dr David Donaldson, Consultant Chemical Pathologist at the Crawley Hospital, West Sussex and the East Surrey Hospital, Redhill gave important help, not least in the fields of drugs and neurochemistry. Dr Ronald Davey of the Blackie Foundation helped to give what we hope is balance and perspective to our examination

I

of alternative medicine, although this remains one of the book's most complex and difficult areas.

Also gratefully acknowledged are the self help groups who gave time and made various documents available, particularly Action on Alcohol Abuse and Joan Jerome at TRANX, the UK's National Tranquilliser Advisory Centre. Both groups do outstanding work, and deserve to exist in a far more secure economic environment than appears possible at present.

At a personal level our wives Madeline Capel and Anne Gurnsey read and re-read various drafts and corrections. Their help throughout was positive and encouraging accompanied only occasionally by dark murmurings about husbands who failed to take their own advice. Margred Capel also gave time from her track and field activities to read the book in full. Her comments were welcome, often perceptive beyond her years, and certainly she takes much of the credit for removing some of the grosser grammatical errors.

To all these, and many more, our thanks are due, though the blame for any errors or omissions must lie firmly with the authors.

Introduction

This book is about human stress, how well we cope with it, and the diseases which may follow if we cope badly. From the beginning we must recognise that human stress is difficult to define. Many, if not most, definitions fall back on analogies with engineering stress. This suggests that a limited number of forces acting on an object will bring a precise response. Such a definition is useful, and does have parallels with the human condition, but is far too limited. Thus when engineers express shear stress in mathematical terms, like:

$$\tan \quad 2\theta = \frac{S_{xy}}{(S_x - S_y)}$$

– the first and last formula to appear in this modest volume – they are identifying and quantifying the three or four variables which lead to their exact response. No such precise, comfortable formula exists for the human condition.

In biological or human terms, stress cannot be represented by a limited number of variables. Here, when we talk of stress, we mean our response to a wide and varying range of external pressures. Where engineering stress can be represented by four or five parameters, in human beings the factors which cause stress [stressors] may number dozens. While engineering stress is acting on an object whose re-

3

sponse is precise and predictable, biological variability ensures that the reaction of human beings is notoriously imprecise and uncertain. As if this were not enough we know that many other factors, like fitness, tiredness and ill health also influence our response to stress – and largely determine our ability to cope. What we are looking for is a formula which allows us to represent the action of the unquantifiable on the infinitely variable, clearly a mathematical impossibility.

Despite this difficulty, before we begin we need a definition of human stress. It is an indication of the complexity of the subject that we have a great many to choose from. Among the best is one that states that stress is 'the physiological, psychological and behavioural response of an individual seeking to adapt and adjust to both internal and external pressures'. This definition is good because it clearly distinguishes between the stress itself, which is essentially our response, and the stressor, which is the agent which brings about that response. It also serves to indicate the far reaching nature of stress, and does not concentrate solely on the negative aspects. In this respect, we must recognise immediately that not all aspects of stress are undesirable. Indeed, in the early stages the body does not distinguish between stress which is positive and stress which is adverse or damaging. Thus a kiss or a slap may initially evoke a very similar stress response, with much of the real distinction coming later.

Inevitably, this book will concentrate on the more deleterious aspects of stress. We must, however, recognise that stress is also a vital – and positive – ingredient of our daily lives. Without the drive which stress provides we achieve nothing. The problems arise when the body's ability to respond to stress becomes disrupted and does not allow an individual's metabolism to revert to its original state. Then, instead of stress being a positive force, its effects can become extended and damaging, leading eventually to disease and even death. One problem is that our stress response is as deeply rooted as our emotions. It is the sum of numerous variables and as such its effects may be difficult both to predict and to isolate.

One spin-off from the engineering approach to stress has been a constant drive to quantify the various aspects of stress. This led many writers to assign certain stress loadings to various jobs and positions. In this book we have avoided such an approach, not because we do not believe it is valid, but because we are far more concerned with stress as it affects the individual. Simply expressed, this means we are less concerned with what job an individual does, than what effect that job has on the individual. This approach we believe is important, because we know that stress is intensely personal and highly specific. What stresses one individual will leave another virtually untouched. Similarly, as individuals we may, indeed almost certainly will, find some forms of stress more difficult to handle than others. This makes a personal approach to stress essential, there are very few general rules.

We have also turned away from the concept that each individual has an optimal level of stress outside which problems may occur. This is an attractive idea, not least because we know that both too little and too much stimulation can be harmful. In this respect we must recognise that boredom and too little stimulation evoke a stress response very similar to, and just as harmful as, that produced by prolonged pressure and tension. Man is indeed a very complex animal. Such a pattern means that any optimal level of stress must be elastic, changing as a result of a host of factors including the time of day, the nature of the stress, the effectiveness of our coping mechanisms and any other stressors we concurrently face. The idea of an optimal level of stress might work if we faced our stressors singly, but this is not the case. In any situation we are stressed by a number of factors, each acting singly and also combining to orchestrate our cumulative response. In such a situation the isolation of any optimal stress level is to our minds impossible.

In coming to write this book we had to define closely our own objectives. A great deal has been written already about stress, and we wanted a different approach. We have also become tired of reading self-help health manuals which are full of gloom and despair. Such books lecture and hector the reader and, in our opinion, often provide more worry than benefit. What we have sought to do is to place the facts in front of the reader. The action taken on those facts must be largely determined by personal objectives and circumstance. We have also kept absolute 'do nots' to the minimum. In this context, we recognise that many self-help books leave little in life to enjoy. The gurus in these areas may seek to live for ever, but like Methuselah they get damn little pleasure out of life. A long time ago the pop song complained that everything in life we enjoyed was 'illegal, immoral – or it makes you fat'. The objective of this book is to help make us more aware of and resistant to stress so we can enjoy life to the full.

This book has drawn heavily on the latest research, particularly in brain neurochemistry. This is essential, because we now know that our response to stress is framed very much in the behaviour of the nerve cells and endocrine centres of the brain. This should not intimidate the reader who lacks any background or scientific training. One thing which angers both authors is the way clinicians, scientists and others use technical language to isolate themselves from the population at large – or from those whose skills lie in other disciplines. This is particularly unforgivable with doctors, who often fail to understand that patients have a right to have their condition explained in something which resembles English. Where technical terms are used in this book they are explained, and readers with no scientific training should have little trouble understanding the text which follows.

Much of this book is based on the research into biolectric therapy undertaken by Ifor Capel in Houston and London. This technique is reviewed elsewhere, but essentially it uses minute electrical charges – really below the level of sensation – to stimulate the release of specific brain chemicals. As we will see in Chapter 3, the chemicals in question lie at the heart of our response to stress. By the control of their release, and indeed their level, we can go a long way towards controlling the nature of our response to stress; this be it noted via a non-invasive technique which utilises the body's own biochemistry and does not resort to the use of drugs.

Throughout this book we have been cautious in our claims for bioelectric therapy – and probably far more cautious than we need to be. It seems to have immense potential both in the treatment of pain and in the whole sphere of symptoms associated with withdrawal. Already controlled bioelectric therapy has shown outstanding – and repeatable – results in the treatment of addiction. This is not always the case with less exact attempts to harness electric impulses, often at far higher energy levels. By closely analysing feedback, in the form of blood biochemistry, Capel's progress is slower but more exact than some other researchers. Where TENS (trans-cutaneous-electrical-nerve-stimulation) and other electrical therapy methods may sometimes get a result, the basis of this result is often unclear. What Capel is seeking, and is close to finding, is a very precise bioelectric science. Once we have this, it will almost certainly revolutionise our treatment not only of stress, but also of a range of conditions – not least addiction – which are closely associated with stress.

Despite the hope bioelectric therapy brings, we must recognise that there is no simple answer to stress. We live in a rapidly changing society and for all of us change is stressful. Similarly, modern life styles play havoc with our body's natural reaction to stress. Much of this natural response lies in physical effort, yet modern life has removed the physical dimension from much of our work and play. We need therefore to replace this element if our stress response is not to turn inwards on ourselves and cause damage and disease. The old adage says that 'for every complex problem, there exists a number of simple solutions – all of them wrong'. Nowhere is this more true than with stress, although it is amazing how simple the most effective stress therapy may be, once we have identified the problem.

When we began this book we were concentrating primarily on the business sector. Our main aim remains to provide a comprehensive and up-to-date manual for senior managers in industry and commerce. We believe this is essential because poorly understood stress-related conditions cost industry millions each year in sickness, lost production, staff who drop out and increased militancy on the part of the workforce. Work occupies a major place in our lives. It is the source of our livelihood and from it we draw much of our status in society. Yet it is also a major cause of stress, a fact compounded by the ever changing nature of modern industry. For this reason we have tried to provide information by which senior staff can identify and seek to control stress in the work-place. Many of these techniques are new but have often proved more effective than those introducing them had anticipated. At times we have drifted over into more general discussion. Man does not work, or live, in isolation. Stress which affects us at home will influence our performance at work – and vice versa. Indeed if one general criticism can be levied at industrial stress programmes, it is that they try to look at work in isolation. We do not believe that such a separation is either valid or possible.

It is inevitable that conventional medicine bears much of

the brunt of the rise in stress-related disease in modern society. During the course of this book we will examine, sometimes critically, the role of conventional medicine in the treatment of such disorders. While it is not our intention to be unduly critical, it must be said that modern medicine, with its emphasis on high technology and drug-based therapy, is not ideally suited to the prevention, diagnosis and treatment of stress. Stress conditions are notoriously difficult to isolate, so the temptation is to embark on drug treatments which act on the symptoms, but do nothing to treat the root cause of the condition. We know that many stress conditions respond well to counselling and advice, yet this is often lacking in our time-conscious health units. One aim of this book is to help the readers individually to identify and tackle stress problems at an early stage. This may involve the intervention of conventional or alternative medical practitioners. In each case our recommendation is the same. Demand an explanation and an understanding. It is your body and your condition, and we know that in terms of stress we gain comfort from understanding and knowledge, because we fear nothing more than the unknown.

So what do we seek to achieve by this slim volume? We already know that stress is linked with a number of diseases both as a primary cause and as a factor which makes other conditions far harder to treat. As our understanding grows, it seems certain that stress will become associated with many more disorders, some of them grave and even terminal. Stress related disorders have shown a startling rise over the last ten years as our adaptive processes have struggled to find balance in a society which grows ever more stretched and pressurised. Medical science alone cannot find the answer, and a great deal must depend on the individual. If we wish to remain healthy, successful members of our modern society, we must individually find ways to adapt – or pay the consequences. If we regard stress as a force, a form of energy in fact, then we must try to harness that energy. We may develop techniques which deflect some of the more harmful aspects of stress, but we must still live in a society which is essentially stressful. We said earlier that stress is a potent force which also provides much of our creative drive. We must seek to make this aspect of stress work for us, while developing our own personal coping mechanisms for the rest. The alternative is a massive expansion in stress related disease for which society and the medical professions are very ill prepared.

John Gurnsey
London, October 1986.

—1—

The origins of stress

The late 1970s and early 1980s have seen a rapid upsurge of interest in stress, particularly in relation to health. This has given rise to a spate of journal articles, books, TV programmes and even courses aimed at identifying and limiting the effects of stress. Despite this often unbalanced and hysterical interest, stress is not a new phenomenon. It is a biochemical and behavioural reaction which has its origins very firmly in the 'fight or flight' response of our remotest ancestors. What changes is not so much man as the society which surrounds him. By limiting or inhibiting man's natural response to stress, what our urbanised and industrialised societies have done is to change the way in which stress manifests itself.

It must be emphasised that stress is not purely a product of Western society. Stress is present in all societies no matter how limited or how primitive. Whenever man interacts with the environment or other people, a degree of stress is bound to exist. What man has created in Western society, and particularly the cities, is an artificial environment in which stress is present but our ability to mitigate that stress is limited. As a result, it is not surprising that numerous studies have shown that a migration to the cities is associated with a rise in stress related conditions. This applies both in the West and, it seems, in more primitive Third World societies. A recent study of Kenyan tribes with a historically low blood pressure level which changed little with ageing, showed startling adjustments among those members of the tribe who moved to the cities. Here not only did blood pressure rise significantly, but it showed a steady move upwards consistent with the ageing of the individual. As we will see elevated blood pressure (hypertension) is one of the conditions most closely associated with stress.

One of the factors undoubtedly causing the rise in blood pressure among urbanised Kenyans is change, and we know that change is one of the most powerful stressors of all. This is crucial because change is a feature of modern society. We now live in an environment where changes to our work, our home life – and even our leisure – appear constant and never ending, and if anything the pace of change is accelerating. Although some change clearly brings benefit it is still a stressful experience. Modern society is to some extent characterised by the subordination of the individual and this in itself causes problems. We are essentially individuals, not groups or city totals. Within fast moving societies, we demand the right of self expression or else we feel swamped and anonymous. This is correct – even vital – but it also adds to our stress levels. By demanding the right of self-expression, and limiting the role of the State in determining our lives, we are more fulfilled but we also take upon ourselves some of the stress which would otherwise be borne by the State.

This book is about stress and the work-place, although we must recognise from the start the impossibility of isolating one section of our lives from any other. Man is a complex animal, and nowhere is this better demonstrated than in our response to stress. Different stressors bring a different response – of that there is no doubt. Thus a senior executive who copes adequately with a heavy and varied workload may finally snap not because of overload at work, but because of extra problems at home. The book will therefore also touch on the vital support provided by a stable home life and outside leisure interests.

The universal and complex nature of stress does not alone account for the current interest in the subject. This comes from a greater awareness of the link between stress and disease, and the belated recognition of the economic cost to industry of stress related disorders. Stress, as we will see, has already been linked with a number of diseases and is implicated in a great many more. It is without doubt a major cause of heart disease, much mental disorder, ulcers, headaches, hypertension, some cancers, skin disorders – and a range of other perhaps less devastating conditions. As well as diseases directly attributable to stress many existing conditions may be made worse by its presence. These include arthritis, asthma, diabetes, migraine and some gastrointestinal conditions. This means that, if stress did not actually cause your gastric ulcer, it will certainly not make the condition any easier to treat. Some measure of the problem can be seen from the fact that one recent review of UK general practitioners estimated that between 60 and 70 per cent of patients seen came as result of stress related conditions.

Our linking of stress and disease is not new. When Plato suggested that medicine's greatest mistake was 'separating the soul from the body', he was acknowledging the role stress plays in the disease process. In the last century at least one clinician linked the incidence of breast cancer to what he called 'melancholic women'. Only now do we know that prolonged stress, by depressing the immune system, may well create exactly the environment in which the neoplastic (cancer forming) process can thrive. What is new, both in this book and as a result of new research is the range of diseases which are now linked with stress. This is growing all the time, and is certainly far wider than many had originally anticipated.

Neither is disease the limit of stress's involvement in our health problems. It is also strongly implicated in the rise of abuse-related disorders in Western society. Under stress many turn to drugs, tobacco, alcohol – or even food – as an outlet. While in some cases these may give a short-term relief from the effects of stress, in the long-term their effect may be devastating to health. Substance abuse, both in its effect on health and the society in which we live, is now a major problem in the West. Similarly, as much of the world starves, obesity and its associated health problems continue to rise in the West. Both forms of abuse owe much of their origin to our response to stress.

Over the last few years there have been many attempts to quantify the cost to industry of stress related disorders. Because of the wide ramifications of stress none has proved entirely satisfactory. In the US recent figures suggest that stress costs industry at least $30 billion a year – nearly 80 per cent of it spent on replacing burnt-out executives. In the UK, official figures suggest that stress might cost as much as 3.5 per cent of the GNP. The answer is that nobody knows, and the real costs of stress both in human and economic terms are incalculable. Not surprisingly concern over the effects of stress is now bringing some response from industry. As of mid-1985, around 20 per cent of the companies listed in the US's Fortune 500 had some form of stress management programme. What is surprising is not that the figure is so high, but that it is still so low. More worrying is the fact that it is certainly far lower among Europe's major companies.

One factor inhibiting the introduction of stress management programmes is that there is still a certain stigma attached to stress related disorders. This applies both at a corporate and personal level. Many companies fail to set up programmes because they do not wish to acknowledge that stress is a problem within their organisation. They see its presence as some sort of management failure. Such an attitude is unrealistic. Stress is present in all spheres of human contact and activity. It need not be destructive, and indeed is a very important part of the creative process. As stress is highly personal and specific, it is hardly surprising that within any large organisation there will be those who are pushed too far – and those who are stimulated too little. There is no stigma in this, though as we progress there may well be in the failure to perceive the problems posed by stress and set up programmes to limit its worst effects.

In terms of stress, man's interaction with his place of work is complex. Whereas biochemistry, pharmacology and to some extent medicine are very exact quantitative sciences, the study of human behaviour is far more complex, and based largely upon descriptive evaluation and experimentation which can be fraught with difficulties. This is not a criticism of the psychologists and behavioural scientists involved, rather another acknowledgement of man's complexity. There is also a massive difference in our personal attitudes to work and this influences our response to stress in the workplace. When at the beginning of this century Freud talked of work in terms of 'satisfaction' and 'creativity for the individual' he was talking of the privileged few. Certainly there can have been very little creativity or satisfaction in the sweatshops of the late Victorian era.

It is a sad fact of modern life that, for many, work holds very little personal satisfaction. As C. W. Mills suggested graphically 'each day men sell little pieces of themselves which they buy back at night and weekends with the coin of fun'. Recent trends in automation have reduced work satisfaction still further. In the past machines needed tending, adjusting; an element of skill was required. Much modern equipment is self-regulating and self-pacing, with man only intervening on the rare occasions when anything goes wrong. As a result modern automated factories have very low manning levels and it is entirely possible for an individual to work a full shift and never see another human being. He could not be more alone if he were on the moon; and we know that for man, by nature a gregarious animal, loneliness is a major cause of stress. Not surprising then if Studs Terkal talks of modern work in terms of 'daily humiliation' where survival is the only objective, rather than in Freud's more gentle terms.

Despite being often boring and repetitive, work plays a very important part in man's existence. We spend nearly one-third of our lives working – some 100,000 hours in all. As well as providing the means by which we purchase our home, food, consumer goods and leisure, work is associated with our status in the community. In any conversation one of the first questions asked is 'what do you do?' This makes unemployment even harder to bear. No matter how dull the work, most workers prefer it to the spectre of unemployment, and not just because they fear a reduced income. Loss of job also implies a loss of status in society, which may be harder to bear than financial deprivation.

Where work is unduly boring or unfulfilling, many seek to find their satisfaction in highly developed diversionary or escapist activities. Wage slaves by day, they concentrate their real lives elsewhere. Despite the efforts of industrial psychologists to limit the effects of stress at work, much of this pattern is likely to remain. Manufacturing industry is committed to automation levels which must continually reduce the role of the work-force. Indeed such a pattern is spreading from the blue collar sector into the junior and senior executive levels, and even quite senior staff now have to seek their real satisfaction in activities outside work. In the case of older people this may prove difficult and stressful in itself, because they are less well equipped for such an approach than their blue collar colleagues, who had always expected a limited degree of satisfaction from their work.

In this chapter on the origins of stress, we have paid considerable attention to the work environment. This is necessary because recent research has suggested that stress at work may be far more damaging than stress in other parts of our lives. Stress at work is also particularly 'harmful because it may appear inescapable. As we will see, few things are more damaging than the inability to influence our situation. As society's attitude changes, and the job market contracts, it may be far easier to walk away from an unhappy marriage than change a promising career in mid-stream. As we work we get locked into financial commitments such as mortgages and school fees. If we are also unhappy in our work, then these may become a different burden from the one we had originally anticipated.

We have talked generally about stress, and clearly we need to identify some of its major causes. This is not as simple as it may sound. The causes of stress are intensely personal. Many factors which one person may find acutely distressing will not affect another. Despite this a number of stressors have been identified, and for convenience these can be categorised into four main areas covering the environment, job design, contractual factors and personal relationships. This is a division of convenience, and the examples given are not meant to be exhaustive – merely indicative. They include:

Environmental factors
Noise; poor lighting; poor ventilation and temperature control; fumes and/or smoking; overcrowding; isolation; vibration; static; badly designed furniture or machines; inadequate canteen or childcare facilities.

Job design factors
Poor job design and conflicting objectives; role conflict; too much or too little work; monotonous and repetitive work;

under utilisation of skills; too little or too much supervision; lack of job control; lack of involvement in decision making; constant sitting; inadequate breaks; constant use of machines, including VDUs.

Contractual factors
Low pay; shift work; unsocial hours; excessive hours or overtime; job insecurity; poorly thought out or unfair promotion procedures; lack of recognition.

Relationship factors
Poor relationships with colleagues at any level; impersonal treatment; sexism or racism; ageing; poor communication; client/customer complaints.

Some of these factors are faced by all of us at some time. The global presence of stress deserves emphasis, because far too many books on industrial stress concentrate on one sector of the work-force – management. It is long overdue that we recognise that stress is not the remit of one sector of industry, be that management or the shop floor. It may be a far more serious problem among junior or manual workers, not least because they can exercise less influence over their circumstances. One US study of 2,000 top managers concluded that they showed far fewer adverse stress reactions than had been expected, despite the fact that their positions were highly responsible and demanding. In the UK a more pragmatic study by the British Institute of Management concluded that there is 'no discernible occupational hazard associated with being an executive'. These findings could in part be due to a natural weeding out process in which the weak fall by the wayside. Modern industry may not be as crude or cruel as survival of the fittest, though it may well demand survival of the most adaptable.

The changing role of management is one reason why many

recent stress studies have concentrated on this group. Gone, in many industries, is the comfortable long-term pattern of management development. Where we once trained our managers through their twenties and thirties to reach maturation during their forties and fifties, this is no longer possible in many high-tech areas. As we grow older we become less receptive to innovation both in psychological and biochemical terms. In many industries it is now common to talk of a manager's creative life being finished in his early thirties, leaving the problem of what to do with a host of young surplus executives. In no sector of commerce is such a pattern more noticeable than in the foreign exchange markets. Here the work is so demanding that three years is typically seen as the limit of human endurance. Assuming they make no killing, such individuals face either a bleak future, or a dramatically reduced role in life.

High technology is also affecting the conventional management role. Where once computing was the job of the specialist, we now see the ubiquitous microcomputer and software package penetrating all levels of management and financial control. This requires re-training for which many managers in mid career are ill prepared. A changing job pattern accompanied by re-training can be a stressful experience, not least for those who expected an unhindered, undemanding route to the top. Neither, it is clear, can management expect the degree of security it once enjoyed. Job insecurity and the fear of redundancy are a major cause of stress among both junior and senior executives. The fact that many are highly specialised, and virtually unemployable elsewhere, merely adds to their concern. We are living in a harsh economic environment, which affects all levels of industry.

While we can understand why many stress studies concentrate on management, there is considerable evidence that top management is cushioned from some of the worst effects of stress by the staff beneath them. The fact that stress-related disorders are often more common in intermediate rather than top managers appears to confirm this view. In 1977 one study in the UK confirmed that deaths from stress-related diseases were far more prevalent among manual and unskilled workers than among the professional and managerial classes. A similar study of 270,000 workers in the US showed that disabling coronary disease was two and half times more common among manual workers than executives. Although such statistics should be used with care, because other factors including nutrition, smoking, drinking, access to medical facilities and home life may intrude, they do suggest that the significance of stress as a cause of disease in non-management sectors has been sadly neglected.

Some indication of the pattern of disease among various sectors of the work-force is shown in table 1. While not all the disorders shown are stress-related, many are, a damning indictment of the ability of stress to cause disease. Such figures also put in question much of management's hardline approach to absenteeism amongst manual and unskilled staff. Other figures produced by Social Trends would appear to show a much closer link between the incidence of disease and time lost than many unsympathetic managers might have expected. Using the same key groupings, Social Trends in 1977 showed that professional staff have the lowest absence rates, at 3.9 days per year, followed perhaps more surprisingly by skilled non-manual staff at 6.7 days. Management staff came third with 7.2 days, closely followed by skilled manual staff (9.3 days). The highest absence rates of all were found amongst the partly skilled (11.5) and the unskilled or manual workers (18.4).

In terms of stress in the work-place a great deal can also be read into these figures. It is known that stress is related to job satisfaction. While top management might be expected to gain a good deal of satisfaction from their work, it is clear that other groups including professional and skilled non-manual staff achieve the same. These groups often have a great deal of control over their work, or may be very close to a recognisable end product. One of the most dehumanising and stressful aspects of working for a large company, or on a production line, is that the worker is seldom associated with a complete entity or end product. This can result in feelings of isolation and alienation. Indeed the feeling of being merely a cog in a larger whole, makes it difficult for any worker to sustain the self respect which is essential to all of us.

A major problem for those trying to tackle stress, whether at home or in the work-place, is identifying the condition – and its cause – at an early stage. By the time the physical manifestations of stress begin to appear the condition is already well advanced. For this reason any effective stress control programme must aim at identifying the likely causes of stress, rather than waiting until the first harmful effects appear. This may not be easy; stress is seldom caused by a single isolated incident, but more typically builds up over a series of what may appear unrelated events. Also the early signs of stress are varied and very specific to the individual concerned. They include irritability, depression, apathy, headaches, backache, lassitude, changes in eating or smoking patterns, insomnia – and many more. It is also typical that in the early stages of stress, the sufferer is the last person to perceive he has a problem. For this reason support programmes aimed at recognising stress in others are vital.

In the work-place, it is important that management recognise the hidden nature of stress in its early stages. Experienced management negotiating staff are accustomed to work-force representatives putting forward minor problems which may hide beneath them a series of deep seated and serious grievances. In much the same way complaints about

Managing stress

Table 1 UK deaths by major cause and social class.
1970–72. [15 to 64 year old males only.] Standard
mortality rates to 100.

	1	2	3	4	5	6
Trachea, bronchial & lung cancers	53	68	84	118	123	143
Prostate cancer	91	89	99	115	106	115
Ischaemic heart disease	88	91	114	107	108	111
Cerebrovascular disease	80	86	98	106	111	136
Pneumonia	41	53	78	92	115	195
Bronchitis/ emphysema	36	51	82	113	128	188
Accidents [not motor]	58	64	53	97	128	225
Car accidents	77	83	89	105	120	174
Suicide	110	89	113	77	117	184
All causes	77	81	99	106	114	137

Key 1 – Professional. 2 – Managerial.
3 – Skilled non-manual. 4 – Skilled manual.
5 – Partly skilled. 6 – Unskilled manual.
Source. Social Trends 1977.

new equipment may hide, not difficulties with the equipment itself, but the uncertainty and insecurity which surround its introduction. This is not in itself surprising as insecurity, uncertainty and change itself are known to be major causes of stress. In the UK, the Association of Scientific, Technical and Managerial Staff [ASTMS], a white collar trade union, claimed that the main problem with

VDUs was not the health risk they posed, but the uncertainty and insecurity stemming from the introduction of new equipment, learning to use it and its compulsory imposition. Certainly if one looks closely at the list of minor health problems often associated with VDU use, they bear very close resemblance to the early warning signs of stress.

The fact that the behavioural problems associated with stress are as unspecific as the physical manifestations is an important fact management must recognise. Most studies on the financial cost of stress concentrate far too closely on absenteeism, or the replacement cost of burnt-out executives. Stress is also a major cause of increased labour militancy, a fact even the militants themselves may not recognise. In a strict medical sense stress is not contagious, although some of the attitudes and responses which stem from its presence may appear to be. Also associated with stress may be increased wastage, stemming from a casual or indifferent attitude to company property, and rises in petty pilfering or vandalism. In this respect, it is no coincidence that when the Rover car company in the UK was first taken over by BMC, there was a dramatic rise in cars taken off the production line for remedial attention. Few factors demotivate, or cause the workforce more stress, than uncertainty.

At work and at home we must also consider our ability to evoke stress in others. Senior managers with an erratic personality and temper, far from helping reduce the level of stress within an organisation, can become its prime cause. Stressed senior staff are a menace for any organisation, and not just because of the effect they have on the the staff beneath them. Above all stressed senior staff are unreliable, in both their relationships and the decisions they take. They may appear to work long hours but their output is typically low and erratic. Their relationship with clients may become uncertain or damaging or even catastrophic. The list is endless – but worst of all – it is unpredictable.

So far, this book has concentrated on the negative aspects of stress. Despite the gloomy list of problems given above, we must repeat that we do need the challenge stress provides as an essential part of the creative process. One of the hardest concepts of all to convey is that what stresses one man may actually provide another with exactly the drive he needs to succeed. There is a great deal of truth in the old adage that 'one man's stress is another man's challenge'. It is unfortunate that the term stress has become so closely associated with hard work, because hard work alone is not a cause of stress. The more modern idea that 'hard work never killed anyone; but stress has killed a great many' appears to be true. The human body is designed for work and, in a healthy state, has an immense capacity for it. It is overload, often characterised by unrealistic time deadlines, unclear objectives and poor personal relationships which implies stress. It is a strange fact of human behaviour that when taking physical exercise we accept the need for a period of rest, in fact our bodies demand it, yet we often cannot accept that a similar recovery process is needed when we are faced by mental or emotional demands.

Hans Selye, the founder of much of modern stress theory, recognised that a certain amount of stress is essential both to survival and performance. Certainly without stress, and the drive it provides, mankind would achieve little. Selye also showed that pleasurable events are themselves stressful and indeed physiologically the body does not distinguish between what he called good stress (eustress) and bad stress (distress). What we have to recognise is that stress is present in all human relationships and activities, and only becomes harmful when there is some imbalance and man's natural coping mechanisms come under strain.

Selye's terms have not gained widespread acceptance.

This is rather surprising because the definitions do make a distinction which may be important in health terms. Unfortunately the study of stress is plagued by a host of semi-specialist terms, often used in a very imprecise manner. One such term is 'burn-out', which is used to denote emotional exhaustion and reduced personal achievement, typically in respect of tired executives. While the term itself may be useful, its erratic use is not. Burn-out also tends to imply a degree of passive acceptance and inevitability which is certainly not useful. The stress response is not fixed, and it can certainly be adjusted culturally, educationally or merely by experience. We can in fact do something about stress, if not at the source, then by conditioning our own response to it.

If we reject the inevitability of burn-out then, as indicated earlier, we also largely reject the concept of a rigid personal threshold for stress. The idea that everyone has a fixed level above which the manifestations of stress appear is far too simplistic for a condition like stress, which has many causes. It also does not explain why events which will cause us distress one day may cause us virtually no inconvenience on another. Though we reject fixed personal thresholds, it is clear that individual responses to the same stress vary widely. In Western society we admire those who appear calm under stress, though often this composure is purchased by a devastating effect on the body's internal chemistry. How often do we hear suprise expressed when a seemingly impregnable colleague succumbs to an open show of stress? In this context it should be recognised that there is no super-race who is immune to stress. What differs merely is our initial tolerance level and how well, or badly, we develop mechanisms to cope with the stress we face.

It is clear from this that there is no simple equation of cause plus effect equals response for stress, and we are faced by one of health's most complex disorders. The fact that our response to stress may be remote from its cause merely adds to the problem. Thus a person who expresses violence at home may be having difficulty at work, while problems at home influence our performance and attitude at work. It also appears that stress can cumulate; limited amounts of stress both at home and at work may add up to more than the individual can bear. This is particularly significant in the case of women, who are now employed on a large scale in Western societies. Women, far more than men, bear the problem of a dual role. In the UK, a TUC (Trades Union Congress) study showed that working women spent some 23 hours a week on household duties, compared with only some 12 hours by their husbands. This is a massive extra burden.

Whatever else this book offers, it will *not* offer simple, solutions to the problems of stress. Its aim is to provide an understanding and base from which management can make its own decisions on stress control. So far the most effective stress management programmes have been introduced in the US, and there is no coincidence that here there is a close link between health insurance and industry. Where stress management programmes have been introduced in US industry, they have improved both production and industrial relations. They have had an added benefit in cutting health insurance charges. In Japan the problem of industrial stress has also been long recognised. If some Japanese techniques, like providing a dummy of the managing director for junior staff to assault, look idiosyncratic they appear to be working. The Japanese also recognised early, and sought to tackle, the problems faced by introducing new technology. They even introduced their own word – technostress – for this difficult area.

In Western Europe most companies, with the exception of some multinationals, lag in recognising stress as a major problem. In much of Europe, management's attitude might be characterised by 'it's your problem, don't bring it to work'. This will change, although progress in Europe seems certain to be slower than elsewhere. One factor forcing change will be the wider recognition of the link between stress and individual diseases. Already in the US we have seen litigation in which workers have successfully sued companies over stress-induced disorders. As this practice spreads, as it inevitably will, the creation of stress control programmes will be seen as essential and routine, and stress management will be taught in much the same way that standard safety procedures are taught today.

This chapter is called 'the origins of stress'. In fact it examines much more and identifies what we are trying to achieve in this book. Stress, and its link with disease, is a very complex issue. In the chapters which follow, we will examine the causes of stress, the biochemical implications of that stress, and the manner in which this may bring about disease. This is a very complex pathway and one in which many of the steps are still unclear or unknown. As our understanding grows, it seems likely that many more disorders will show some direct or indirect link with stress. If this is so then our ability to recognise and tackle the root cause of stress may become one of the most pressing health problems of our age.

—2—

Stress, society and the workplace

This book is not a sociology text, but we must examine the part social factors play both in creating stress and in determining our response. Man is a highly conditioned animal, conditioned by cultural factors, experience and the demands of society. Some of these factors create stress, while others may inhibit our natural mechanisms for coping with stressful situations.

Much of the structure of our society, and our attitudes to work, money and family have their origins in the nineteenth century. This period saw the rise of the industrial state and the steady drift away from the land. It also saw significant changes in the nature of man's work. From being largely physical, and closely linked to the seasons, work became sedentary, often conducted in closed artificial environments and above all remote from any movement of the calendar. As we will see, such changes have major implications when we come to consider stress. As work was changing so too was the structure of society. The need to centralise industry, and the services which supplied it, led to the rise of industrial towns and cities, and to the mass movement of populations, a migration which often brought with it isolation, loneliness and alienation.

Where once change had been slow, occurring across generations, now massive disruption was happening in a few years. Rapid change stretches man's adaptive capabilities,

28

and provides a type of pressure which is in itself acutely stressful. The move to the cities also brought a reduction in the mechanisms by which man had traditionally – if inadvertently – countered stress. Rural communities are by nature supportive, but support – vital in the management of stress – is harder to find in cities, which can be cold and impersonal. Whereas in the rural community the Church and the priest had held a central role, religion has failed to have the same impact in the cities on a largely peripatetic population.

The decline of religion in the West is undoubtedly linked with the rise in stress related disease. Not only is religion a support and comfort in time of need, but it can also alleviate uncertainty and insecurity – which we know are acutely stressful. Fundamental religious faith demands a blind acceptance, which some may see as close to fanaticism; the word Islam itself means obedience. Such faith may curtail personal freedom but it reduces uncertainty and therefore stress among the faithful. As the power of religion declines in the West, so too does influence of the priest. It is clear that for many the doctor has now replaced the priest as the first contact in a crisis. This is fine, providing we recognise that their roles – though analogous – are essentially different.

The nineteenth century saw the establishment of many of the attitudes and criteria by which we govern society. These include a heavy emphasis on work, not just for the rewards it brings, but because work or employment is in itself somehow dignified. This attitude still has a major effect on the unemployed, many of whom find their loss of status harder to accept than a reduced income. For those still in employment the constant rat race for success, in which performance and material rewards are the only criteria, may become very damaging in terms of health and personal relationships. It is also clearly the reason why an increasing number of senior executives, recognising some of the risks, are dropping out of business life at the height of their powers.

Nineteenth century thinking also influences the personal qualities by which we set highest store. This is unfortunate because in terms of stress, some of the qualities the Victorian era identified as laudable could not be worse chosen. Self reliance, stoicism, control and above all the refusal to show emotion were – and still are – considered essential attributes particularly in men. In polite society we are even denied the relief of swearing, one of nature's more effective and harmless mechanisms for relieving stress. Whatever the merits of these qualities, they have a devastating effect on our response to stress. As we will see, the presence of stress evokes far-reaching biochemical changes in both the brain and the rest of the body. These changes are not permanent and indeed they must be relieved if their effects are not to become damaging in themselves. Suppressing our reaction to stress, be it in emotional or physical terms, is among the most damaging ways in which we can potentiate [extend and make more potent] the stress response.

This is possibly best illustrated in the belief that *real* men do not cry. Weeping, or a physical expression of distress, is a natural and important part of our response. In many ways it is unfortunate that the last forty to fifty years have seen the decline in the West of socially acceptable death rituals. As death replaces sex and disease as the last taboo, we seem unable to create methods which help us cope with bereavement. There is no doubt that death rituals provide comfort to those who have suffered loss, and limit the period of mourning. There is little difference between the heavy formalised mourning [Shiva] of the orthodox Jewish community and the Irishman's lighthearted drink laden wake; both have been shown to ease the stress and pain of bereavement, and to help those who are left on the path to recovery.

Modern society also separates man from his more natural

instincts in the way it debases sex. Once a source of comfort, pleasure and procreation, sex has now become the province of media hype and pornography, giving to many, and not least the young, a false view of its role. To what extent pornography is behind the rise in sexually transmitted disease and crimes against women is arguable, but it is is evident that by creating ridiculous and unachievable sexual stereotypes, pornography – and a large part of the media – has created a sense of inadequacy in many who are perfectly normal. As a result, instead of being a source of comfort, for many sex itself has become another major cause of concern.

In any consideration of the social background to stress, the media play a major role as the source of most of our information and many of our attitudes. Unfortunately this dependence is often not reflected by a responsible approach on the part of those running newspapers, cinema and television. By concentrating on lurid crimes the media often give a false impression of the frequency of such events, creating a sense of fear, and hence stress, in those who are most vulnerable. One recent survey in London showed that 75 per cent of women were afraid to go out at night, despite the fact that street crime in London is only some 20 per cent of that seen in many US cities and also tends to be very localised. The most likely individual to be assaulted in London, as in most major cities, is a young male who frequents places of entertainment late at night, and usually provokes his attackers. Such facts it seems are not newsworthy.

The media must also bear much of the blame for the sense of division in our society. By showing an almost prurient interest in disputes between black and white, rich and poor, male and female, the media increase hostility. This is a major cause of stress. One area where the media have often proved less than helpful is the growing division between the

31

police and many sectors of our society, now extending well beyond the student groups, ethnic minorities and drop-outs who have traditionally had an uncomfortable relationship with the police. It is, however, far less sinister and incomprehensible than the media might suggest: the changing attitude to the police is symptomatic of a far wider rejection of the intrusion of the State in our daily lives. As centralisation subordinates the role of the individual, it is natural – even laudable – that many will seek to reject this in their quest for personal identity.

The challenge to authority is part of a wider phenomenon characteristic of late twentieth century society. Much of modern life, whether work or play, lacks challenge and an element of physical risk. This has led to a significant rise in dangerous sports like deep sea diving, parachuting and hang gliding. For some, even gambling could come into this category, although this is a different problem. Risk-taking of this type normally occurs in a controlled environment, which means the risks involved are theoretical rather than actual. This perhaps explains why such people may spend a great deal of money on their hobby, rather than simply taking a late night stroll in places like New York's Central Park. More serious are other forms of deliberate risk-taking which involve the use of recreational drugs like tobacco, alcohol, heroin and cocaine. Use of these is often based on our response to stress but can also be regarded as a challenge to society. Few in our society can now be unaware of the risks posed by such products, but the use of alcohol and hard drugs in particular continues to rise, not least among the young.

The implications to health of substance abuse are considered elsewhere. What is relevant here is society's attitude to such problems. This tends to be ambivalent, largely because tobacco and alcohol are now firmly embedded, not just in social custom, but also in the national and international economic framework. Thus, in the UK, the government takes some £50 million *per day* in tobacco taxes, a source of revenue even the anti-smoking lobby acknowledge it would be difficult to replace. A similar pattern exists in the alcohol sector, a fact which has enabled the alcohol industry to exert such pressure that in *real terms*, the cost of alcohol in the UK has declined over the last ten years. This pattern continues despite the fact that both alcohol and tobacco have been identified as a major cause of disease and death in all Western societies.

We said that government attitudes to substance abuse were ambivalent, and this deserves explanation. On the one hand are major tax revenues, on the other must – or should – be concern over health. In the UK alone, tobacco is the prime cause of 100,000 deaths a year, while alcohol is associated with 30,000 more. The figures are even higher if abuse-related complications in other disorders are also considered. Despite this, health education programmes remain underfunded, the Cinderella of the health sector in most Western countries.

Further evidence of ambivalence is seen in the attitude of many Western governments to drug abuse. Unable to conceive measures which wean tobacco and alcohol tax revenues out of the national economic framework, many have given a totally unbalanced emphasis to the curbing of drug abuse. It would be cynical to suggest that this is done to draw attention from their lack of activity elsewhere, but some might draw just that conclusion. This does not mean that this book condones the use of hard – or soft – drugs. It is a question of balance. Where tobacco in the UK kills more than 100,000 people annually, the total number of UK deaths from heroin misuse from 1967 to 1981 was under 1,500 – less than 100 per year. Though figures are not available, the normal pattern of heroin use would suggest that in 70 per cent or more of these cases, death would also be associated with abuse of another substance – most typically alcohol.

So far, this chapter has concentrated on a general social background to the problem of stress. This is justified because, as we have indicated, man is a conditioned animal. He brings to his work attitudes and approaches which are inseparable from his social environment. Thus work becomes a mirror of what is happening outside. It would be foolish, however, if we did not also recognise that work and the whole business environment bring pressures and stress of their own. These cover the four categories mentioned earlier [environment, job design, contractual factors and personal relationships] – although sometimes it may seem that personal relationships dominate the work scene.

The work environment is one of the fastest changing sectors of all, and as change is so closely linked with stress, it is essential that management recognise the full implications of this. The alternative is to risk not just a rise in stress-induced disease, but also an increase in unrest and militancy, and what management literature describes as 'work-force demotivation'. Uncertainty, particularly in a fast changing technical environment, is a major cause of stress. It is amazing therefore, in this age of information technology, how poorly designed are some management structures for communication. This often seems to apply most at times of cutbacks and redundancies, when good communication is vital.

Work, however, is not only about cutbacks and redundancies. It is about the place and environment in which many of us spend a large proportion of our lives. Over the last hundred years work has changed dramatically, but not always for the better from the point of view of stress. While we now have greater control over the quality of the environment in which we work, the nature of work for many has deteriorated significantly. The steady increase in automation, which has long affected the industrial sector and now impinges on the office and junior management, has implications for all of us. Many jobs which once involved an element of skill now amount to little more than machine minding. This is not only dehumanising, it also causes stress and unhappiness, a serious problem for management because the trend to automation is accelerating.

As early as 1895 Max Nordau wrote of industry 'our modern rate of change has exceeded man's power of adaption'. His words were prophetic but how much more serious a problem do we face now. Many believe we are moving into a post-industrial society in which work is undergoing a change even more radical than that seen in the industrial revolution. This looks likely to be a largely communications or information-based industry. Already we see a pattern of workers who move away from their central site and keep in contact via computers, modems and the growing range of communications networks. This pattern is important, and has implications for society as a whole.

Decentralisation may be important, even vital, but it is probably not the major problem posed by increased automation. In terms of stress, this must lie in the way in which automation eliminates interest in the work we do. A review taken in the US in the late 1970s showed that the bulk of the work-force in small industrialised towns and cities did not expect to get satisfaction from their work, despite environmental improvements. Automation is interacting with the four main areas of stress, improving some, while making others far more damaging. Stress in industry is therefore actually rising despite efforts to create pleasant and pollution-free environments.

Recognition that many gain little satisfaction in their work is an important part of management's role in combating stress. Boredom is a major cause of stress, and its effects may be more damaging than those caused by overload. This does not mean that we all have to undertake tasks which are varied and far reaching to gain job satisfaction. It may, however, mean that the soul destroying production line has a limited future – at least where man is involved. At Volvo in Sweden, the old production line has already been largely abandoned. Here workers, operating in teams, take a vehicle right through the production process. Instead of being concerned with one small part of many vehicles' construction, the group handles all aspects of production, and has a close link with an identifiable end product. In economic terms Volvo's experiment has had a major impact. It would be surprising if it did not also have a similar effect on the stress levels of its workers.

The problems of lack of interest and a sense of identity in our work are clearly linked with industrialisation, and have few parallels in rural communities. Studies show that not only do farm workers expect intrinsic satisfaction from their work, but also that this is actually achieved. It is no coincidence that farm workers and, for example, gardeners have always enjoyed low levels of most stress related disorders. These tasks involve a close link with nature and the seasons, and a fine balance between physical and mental effort. The fact that they are not traditionally well paid appears incidental, suggesting perhaps that much of industry is over-preoccupied with money, partly because this is the only form of satisfaction available.

Another trend which adds stress in the work-place is the move towards larger units. Big, often multinational, companies can become remote and impersonal. Within such organisations even quite senior staff can struggle for identity, while junior staff may feel they disappear altogether. It is also difficult for workers to identify with management decisions, when those decisions may be made 10,000 miles away and appear remote and immutable. Even improved communication can be of limited benefit, and the answer would seem to be some maximum size for a company. This appears to have been recognised by some, and recently many multinationals have been broken down into smaller, semi-autonomous units. Such a pattern gives local staff a greater sense of identity, both with the company and its product.

For a work-force nurtured on Victorian values, and raised on Keynesian economics, security in employment has always been important, but within a constantly changing industrial scene has been far harder to provide. Automation, a harsh economic environment, plus the rise in manufacturing power of some Third World countries, have caused a steady increase in unemployment in all Western nations. Because much of this comes from a fundamental shift in the nature of employment, it will clearly be far harder to tackle than any previous recession. In many Western countries, there is a heavy sense of defeat associated with persistent high unemployment levels. This affects not only those who are unemployed but also those who are still in work. Where once a laid off man could hope quickly to find a new job, this is no longer the case, a fact which adds significantly to the sense of insecurity prevalent in much of European industry.

For those in work, security is no longer concerned just with continuing employment, but also with the ability to do a range of tasks within a constantly changing environment. Automation is a major cause of reduced manning levels, but it is also a cause of stress in those who are expected to adapt or change their career in mid-stream. Where for our parents' generation training or an apprenticeship could provide a job for life, in most areas this is no longer the case. Now workers must re-train every few years to adapt to the demands of the newest technology. It is a foolish management that does not recognise the implications such re-training has in terms of stress. Industry has recently become more professional in its approach to training and re-training, partly because of the complexity of much of the new technology. It would seem sensible if re-training also came to include some education in how to handle and limit stress in our fluid industrial environment.

Automation now affects both the shop floor and the office. This sometimes brings bizarre results, with machine design being concerned solely with optimal results and caring little about providing decent or ergonomic working conditions for the staff involved. This is unfortunate, because man still has more to offer than even the most sophisticated of equipment. As Mike Cooley [Lucas Aerospace] put it to graphic effect 'In man–machine interaction the human is slow, inconsistent unreliable but highly creative; whereas the machine is faster, consistent, reliable but totally non-creative.' Strange then that in many of our factories we pay so little attention to encouraging man's creative processes. Even where automation brings with it a decent environment, like the clean rooms used in computing, these are provided more for the machines than the people using them.

Increased automation is also reducing the number of tasks where physical labour is significant. This means that where automation creates employment, it does not necessarily relate directly to those who are unemployed. Such a pattern indicates a bleak future for the manual worker, the unskilled and the poorly educated, who are already among the most vulnerable in our society. It does, however, facilitate the employment of women by eliminating the physical element. In many Western societies 30–40 per cent of women work, while in the UK 50 per cent of all families rely wholly or in part on income brought in by women. Despite such figures, none but the most chauvinist would claim that women have yet found an equal standing with men, or indeed their true place in industry and commerce.

A high percentage of working women imposes stress of

its own, both at home and at work. By working many women adopt a demanding dual role, and we know that such a division can be extremely stressful, especially if any conflict of interest is present. Many entrenched male attitudes add to the working woman's difficulties both at home and at work, despite moves towards equal opportunity legislation in many countries. Not only do men on average earn more than women for the same or similar work, but many promotion procedures favour men. Throughout much of industry, and particularly traditional heavy industry, the insulting attitude that women are more uterine than cerebral persists. As a sense of injustice and unfairness is a major cause of frustration and stress at work, it is hardly surprising that many women are among the prime sufferers.

Neither if women are successful is the problem necessarily over. Many women in senior positions are resented by the men beneath them, and they may even suffer at home if their career outstrips that of their husband. The bread-winning concept is ingrained into the male ego, and many men may see little more in their wife's success at work, than the loss of a hostess and support for their own work. The fact that some companies recruiting senior or management staff still check the wife's credentials suggests that the idea of the wife merely as an adjunct dies hard. If such attitudes do not change willingly, they will soon be removed by force.

The last twenty years have seen a rise in female militancy, with clear implications for the work-place. Gone is the willingness of women to accept patently unfair career structures, and to tolerate blatant sexual discrimination and harassment. For management, and indeed our consideration of stress, such attitudes are important. As we have already indicated, unfairness is a major cause of stress. So too is harassment be it based on sexual, ethnic, religious or any other grounds. In many ways harassment in the work-place is more offensive [and stressful] than in the community at

large, because it may appear inescapable, particularly if
the offender is more senior than the staff member being
harassed. It follows that it is vital that we create management
and work structures in which harassment and discrimination
have no place.

The increasing presence of women in industry has important implications in our consideration of stress. We now
know that there are significant differences between men and
women in the way they respond to stress, with corresponding
differences in the type of disease which may result from
continued stress. Thus a woman under pressure who turns
to alcohol faces greater risks than a male colleague who does
the same. Recent research has shown that a woman's tolerance to alcohol damage is far lower than that of a man. This
means that cirrhosis can be induced in women by lower
levels of alcohol and the disease develops far faster. This is
due entirely to human biochemistry, and has nothing to do
with male chauvinism. In this book we will examine many
of the different ways stress manifests itself in men and
women. As women come to play a greater role in industry,
not least in senior positions, it is vital that management
recognises the implications of such differences. This must
be done objectively: it would be unfortunate here if radical
feminism prevented a clearer understanding.

In this chapter, we have been at pains to emphasise the
responsibility of management in the field of stress. This
covers the nature of work, the physical environment, communication, fair promotion practices and – we hope – the
creation of stress management and control programmes.
Though comprehensive this is not the total of management's
responsibility, which covers everything from siting the
work-place, to ensuring the provision of adequate breaks –
and making sure these are taken. One simple device shown
to have a significant effect on stress, is the introduction of
flexible hours. This allows workers to avoid the worst rigours

of commuting, to work [within reason] when they feel most productive, and takes away some of the pressure associated with working very rigid hours. Flexible hours should also be attractive to management. Though often introduced primarily for the benefit of travelling staff, they have been shown to have a more significant effect on production than had been anticipated.

We must also consider the responsibility of the workforce. Many managers pride themselves on the long hours they work, while the presence of overtime may encourage others to work hours far beyond the norm. Such people would be well advised to listen to Bernardino Ramazzini who put it eloquently: 'tis a sordid profit that is accompanied by the destruction of health.' While adverse stress is not synonymous with hard work, working excessive hours (70–80 per week) can bring serious problems. Not only does it reduce skill, but recent research has shown it can also be very harmful to health. Very long hours reduce the body's ability to restore physiological balance, a vital factor in the way we recover from stress. Excessive hours can also affect personal relationships. This is a two-edged sword; healthy personal interactions help us cope with stress, while strained relationships can in their own right become a major cause of stress. Excessively long hours, particularly over an extended period, are not advocated by the authors of this book.

Neither need the long hours be spent at one activity. Recent research at the Bell Telephone Company in the US has shown that men who work by day and study by night are particularly at risk. They show a far higher rate of heart attacks, a condition closely linked with stress. In an interesting aside, this research also suggests that a major contrast between hectic and monotonous periods in the day makes the risk of serious disease far higher. Thus, if an individual has a very boring job followed by a very active and stimulating study period [or vice-versa], damage is far more likely than if he is constantly very active. We are back again to the fact that boredom can be a very serious and damaging form of stress.

This indicates that break periods are essential for everyone, from the managing director to the shop floor cleaner. The same could also be said of holidays, though these need not involve expensive flights to the sun. Indeed one major problem with modern holidays is that they often seem to increase stress rather than to relieve it. Travel itself is stressful, and those planning holidays should take this into consideration. Long-distance jet travel imposes massive pressure on the body's adaptive system. Whilst we accept and understand the phenomenon of jet lag with its effect on sleep and digestion – and its inducement of a general malaise, long-distance travel has also been linked with far more serious heart and digestive disorders. For the business traveller, jet lag poses particular threats. Travelling backwards and forwards across time zones gives the body little or no chance to recover and re-establish equilibrium. It is hardly surprising that some enlightened firms impose a 24-hour moratorium on staff working after a long distance flight. While this is not enough for a full recovery, it can help in overcoming the worst effects of jet lag on mental performance.

In the West, we spend a great deal of money on holidays. In 1984, the West Germans alone spent more than £4,000 million on holidays outside Germany, while both the Americans [£3,000 million] and the British [£1,200 million] spent significant amounts on overseas holidays. Despite this, the holiday letdown syndrome is a well recognised phenomenon. This has several causes including false expectations and conflicts within the family. Holidays are also frequently associated with aggressive behaviour, and even civilised people can show a low flashpoint while on vacation. This is not surprising. Irritability is an early sign of stress, and having spent a great deal of money on a holiday, we can easily become frustrated if we do not feel we are gaining benefit.

Despite such problems, well chosen holidays *can* relieve stress, though it would be false to expect too much from them. If we take our holidays to evade stress at work, then the benefit will be limited if that stress remains unchanged when we return. The most important aspect of holidays could lie in giving the worker a target – a break to look forward to. Here, Karl Neumann's comment after visiting a series of German health spas would seem relevant. He concluded: 'If you remove a person from the everyday stresses of home and work, let him relax and spend time in warm water, that person will feel better – whether the underlying pathological process is altered or not.'

Later in this book we will look at ways in which both the individual and management can minimise the presence and the effects of stress. Throughout, we must emphasise that man does not work in isolation, and the growing pace and pressure of modern life are intrinsically linked with the extra stress we face at work. We live in what W H Auden once described as 'an age of anxiety'. This age is characterised by an unprecedented speed of change and, above all, a society in which material success is often the only criterion by which we are judged. If we accept that this situation is unlikely to change, then it is man who must adapt and find ways to live with pressures which often appear massive and immutable. If we fail, the consequences will be grave, both for industry and the societies in which we live.

—3—

The biochemistry of stress

3.1. Background

To understand stress, and indeed any human disorder, requires a basic knowledge of both physiology and biochemistry; and to understand fully how a disease disrupts the body, we must first be aware of how a body functions when it is well. We can then take steps to curb the impact of the disease. Any study of stress must concentrate on how the body reacts to pressure [or stressors], and how it reverts to a steady state once the crisis is eased. Ideally we would also like to explain how unrequited stress gives rise to disease. Unfortunately the precise nature of many of these mechanisms is unknown. We know that stress is linked with many disorders, and that this link is often specific to an individual. What we do not yet know, although it is the subject of intense research around the world, is how that link is forged, and to what extent we can limit its effect.

One problem we face in dealing with stress is that many of those most concerned with it do not have a medical background. Managers have often trained in accountancy, commerce, economics or perhaps in some other scientific or engineering discipline. Their knowledge of medical terminology, and indeed biochemistry, may be at best hazy. While this is understandable it is also unfortunate, as it means the 'jargon' which surrounds the topic of stress separates them from a more detailed understanding. On the pages which follow we have not sought to compromise the depth of the technology; we have, however, tried to explain the topic in straightforward terms.

3.2. The brain and the nervous system

Any physiological understanding of stress must begin with the brain. This is a highly complex tissue like no other known to man. It comprises at least 100 billion cells – although there are those who put the figure much higher. The bulk of the brain cells are neurones, although the neurones are surrounded by numerous specialist glial cells which provide both nourishment and support. A typical neurone has a large number of short, stumpy processes called dendrites which receive signals. These signals may be combined and integrated within the cell, after which they pass out through a longer single process called the axon. Nerve cells and their fibres [axons] comprise a tightly inter-locking web. The cell processes [axons and dendrites] are not, however, in actual contact, and gaps called synapses or synaptic clefts exist between them. These synapses play a vital part both in passing and modulating nerve impulses.

Within any nerve complex, including the brain, the trans-mission system is double, being both electrical and chemical. Signals pass down the axons electrically, with polarisation and depolarisation being caused by the movement of sodium and potassium ions into and out of the cell. At the synapse, the energy of the impulse stimulates the secretion of chemi-cal transmitters [neurotransitters] which convey the impulse across the synaptic gap. In the receiving cell the signal is facilitated and modulated before being passed on. Some measure of the complexity of the human brain can be seen from a recent estimate which suggested that it contained at least 100 trillion synapses. How close this estimate comes to the truth no-one knows, but it does serve to emphasise the immense complexity of the central nervous system.

Neither is the study of neurotransmitters a simple matter. Some thirty substances are now known, or believed, to be neurotransmitters. Each has a highly specific excitatory or inhibitory effect, which means that a neurotransmitter can either facilitate or prevent an impulse from moving across a synapse. The recent discovery that nerve cells can emit and receive more than one neurotransmitter is an important step forward. It means that excitory impulses, like pain, can be moderated by other transmitters – acting as neuromodulators. In the case of pain this would clearly decrease the transmission of the impulse and hence the perception of pain.

Although a large number of substances are known to be neurotransmitters, these are not randomly distributed throughout the brain. Many are localised in clusters of neurons, with groups of axons which pass into highly specific regions of the brain. The result is a very sophisticated coding system which allows far more than the simple transmission of impulses. It is common to liken the brain to the modern linear computer. This is a vast oversimplication which fails to appreciate the complexity and sophistication of the brain network. If we remove a single relay from the computer it will cease to function. This is not the case in the brain, where major disruptions caused by damage, tumours or strokes can be bypassed. Similarly the computer's function is limited by a strict binary code. This is not the case in the brain where the system of transmission is less precise and exact, but far more flexible. What results is a brain system which modulates, amplifies and interprets signals with a degree of subtlety and control which would be impossible for any man-made machine.

Brain study is difficult and although recent years have seen significant steps forward, we still have a great deal to discover about both its structure and function. One problem is that the brain reveals little when it is dissected. Where the manner of function may become apparent from the gross examination of some other organs like the heart, this is not the case with the brain. Electrical impulse studies may reveal more, but a great deal of our knowledge of the human brain has come from the study of its diseases and abnormalities, and their impact on the individual patient. One problem is that neuronal cells are highly sensitive and easily damaged by toxins. For this reason the brain is isolated from the general circulation by a filtration system known as the blood–brain barrier. This barrier allows the entry of small molecules, like oxygen, but prevents the passage of larger molecules. All larger molecules, including glucose, must be taken into the brain by specialist transport mechanisms, a fact which clearly has implications for the design of drugs which act on the brain.

3.3. Hormones and homeostasis

Not all parts of the brain are protected by the brain blood-barrier. The pituitary, which serves to control the hormonal function of the body, is linked with the general circulation, a connection vital to its main function. In fact we now know a good deal about the regions of the brain and the functions they control. This knowledge is vital to the study of stress, not least because it helps us to identify the action of those neurotransmitters which are localised in specific regions. In man the highly developed fore-brain is the centre of intelligence and reasoning, while the limbic regions of the mid-brain [and particularly the amygdala] are associated with emotion. Various neural pathways pass from the mid-brain through the hind-brain into the spinal cord and are concerned with the central perception of pain. In our study

47

of stress we must pay particular attention to the hind-brain. This primitive region, which includes both the hypothalamus and the pituitary, is concerned with the vital concept of homeostasis.

Homeostasis may be defined as the mechanism by which the body maintains a steady state, a constant internal environment irrespective of external conditions. To perform this function, part of the hind-brain [the hypothalamus] monitors the blood concentration of salts and sugars, and acts to stimulate the release of hormones. In this context a hormone may be defined as a blood-carried internal secretion which acts to stimulate activity in other organs. A vital difference between hormones and transmitter substances is their length of action. Neurotransmitters are, or should be, very short-lived in function. By contrast hormones carried by the blood have a much longer lasting action. This difference is crucial to the understanding of stress. The pituitary hormones, many of which act on other hormone releasing [endocrine] glands, serve to regulate the metabolism of the whole body. The organ's central function can be seen by the nature of the hormones it secretes – and the organs on which they act. They include:

ACTH [adrenocorticotropic hormone]	– acts on the adrenal glands;
TSH [thyroid stimulating hormone]	– acts on the thyroid;
HGH [human growth hormone]	– acts on the bones;
LH [luteinising hormone]	– acts on the sex glands;
FSH [follicle stimulating hormone]	– acts on the sex glands;
PL [prolactin]	– acts on the breasts;
ADH [anti-diuretic hormone]	– acts on the kidneys.

Stress and homeostasis are closely associated, and indeed stress can be regarded as the enemy of homeostasis. In simple terms homeostasis is the mechanism by which the body restores its steady state when subjected to physical or mental pressure. Where for reasons of excessive load, or perhaps over-sensitivity, the body cannot restore that steady state, then some of the more damaging manifestations of stress begin to make their appearance. From this understanding we can examine the way in which the body reacts to stress, how it moderates its response, and what can go wrong.

When confronted by stress, either physical or emotional, the amygdala in the mid-brain is activated. The resulting emotional response is moderated by input from the higher centres of the fore-brain. This means the brain does not respond blindly but exercises a degree of interpretation. The neuronal response from the amygdala is transmitted and stimulates a hormonal response from the hypothalamus. This releases the hormone CRF [corticotrophin releasing factor] which stimulates the pituitary to release ACTH into the blood. The ACTH in turn stimulates the adrenal glands, a composite of small glands situated close to the kidneys. The adrenal glands comprise two distinct regions, the external part or medulla, which secrete adrenaline [also called epinephrine] and noradrenaline [norepinephrine]; and an internal or cortical region which secretes the corticosteroids – including cortisol. All the secretions of the adrenal glands are closely associated with our response to stress.

At the same time as the hypothalamus is acting on the pituitary inducing the secretion of hormones, it also acts directly on the autonomic nervous system to induce an immediate response to stress. This in part comes from the direct autonomic stimulation of the adrenal glands, which results in an increase in heart rate, plus the suppression of the gut. What is happening is that the body is being prepared for 'fight or flight' via a dual reaction: a nervous response which is typically short-lived, and an endocrine [hormonal] response which is far longer lasting. Neither is the overall reaction quite so simple. The pituitary also acts to release vasopressin, a hormone which constricts the artery walls and elevates blood pressure. This helps consolidate some of the effects of the release of hormones like adrenaline. At the same time the pituitary releases TSH which stimulates the thyroid to release thyroxine. This increases the body's rate of metabolism, enabling it to cope in the longer term with any extra demands placed on it by stress. The body is in fact beginning to prepare itself for both an immediate and a sustained response to stress. With this basic understanding of the processes involved, it is perhaps now time to consider some of the hormones and other substances involved.

Certainly the best known of the hormones associated with stress is adrenaline. This is unfortunate because adrenaline is in fact well down the chain of reactions which form our response to stress. We also casually refer to 'adrenaline running' in association with sporting events. Our coaches and trainers insist we take warm-up sessions, akin to the primitive war dance, to get our adrenaline flowing. The warm-up may certainly be useful but not because of the adrenaline it stimulates. A far more valuable function would seem to be that it stimulates the release of beta-endorphin. This recently discovered neuropeptide [the term covers substances comprising a number of amino-acids and exercising a moderating function in neurotransmission] is associated with the suppression of pain. By stimulating the release of beta-endorphin prior to a sporting contest or athletic event, we may help pass the 'threshold of pain' which is the characteristic of any high level of sporting achievement. We will come back to the endorphins as we progress; they form one of the most exciting discoveries in recent years, and certainly look likely to play a major role in our understanding and treatment of stress related disorders.

While often misunderstood, adrenaline nevertheless plays an important role in our response to stress. Carried by the blood to various organs in the body, adrenaline serves to mobilise the body's resources. It stimulates the release of glucose from the glycogen [starch] stores in the liver, as well as encouraging the breakdown and release of fatty acids into the blood. The breakdown of fats is particularly important as, together with changes in cell membrane permeability, it enables these important energy precursors to enter the muscle cells more readily. Within the cell itself, adrenaline spurs the enzyme systems to greater activity, so increasing levels of energy production, and hence the work potential of the cell. As adrenaline stimulates this activity, antagonistic action of hormones, like insulin which removes glucose from the blood, are suppressed.

As adrenaline acts to mobilise the body's reserves, it also functions in association with other hormones like vasopressin to increase both cardiac output and blood pressure. This is a complex processs. Much of the rise in blood pressure results from constriction of the peripheral vasculature [blood vessels] induced by vasopressin. Adrenaline can also cause dilatation rather than constriction of some blood vessels. Those affected include the blood vessels serving the skeletal muscles and the heart. Dilatation enhances blood flow in these vital areas, so improving performance. As blood flow changes, the body's blood coagulation process is enhanced by the presence of adrenaline, so helping to limit any damage caused by injury.

One feature of the stress response, which accounts for some of the more explosive and even spectacular responses to stress, is the oxygen debt. In periods of extreme exercise or fear, this allows muscle cells to continue to function even though the correct biochemical balance of the cell is not maintained. To all intents and purposes, for a short period at least, the cells cease to obey the natural biochemical laws which govern all cellular activity. The result is a build up of potentially harmful substances like lactate, which are then oxidised when the individual has returned to a less stressful state. Clearly such a condition can only last for a short period, a fact recognised by Selye when he propounded his concept of the General Adaptive Syndrome [GAS]. In GAS Selye recognised that an individual cannot continue head-long flight indefinitely. After the immediate explosive arousal, there is a stage of resistance where the body adapts its metabolism to cope with the presence of stress for an indefinite period. This longer term response is mediated by the adrenal glands still under the control of the ACTH secreted by the pituitary. Now ACTH acts on the cortex of the adrenals, stimulating the release of the corticosteroid hormones. These include the hormone cortisol, whose presence has become so associated with stress that its level is often used as a measure of an individual's response to stress.

Cortisol is a complex hormone and certainly no simple description of its action is possible. It has a range of actions all directly or indirectly associated with our response to stress. The fact that cortisol is often used as a measure of our response to stress has to some extent confused its function. This should not be regarded as purely deleterious as the hormone undoubtedly plays an important role in our coping mechanisms. Biochemically cortisol stimulates glucose synthesis, and in this function is particularly active in the liver, muscles and adipose [fat] tissues. The hormone is also responsible for maintaining the integrity of the microcirculation by preventing the leakage of fluid from the capillaries. Similarly, during stress cortisol plays an important role in stabilising other membraneous structures, including the cell membrane itself and the lysosomes [bodies rich in enzymes [catalysts] and thought to be concerned with intra-cellular digestion].

3.4. Stress and the immune function

Cortisol, and the other corticosteroid hormones, are closely linked with the body's response to damage. Some of this action comes from those functions already outlined. More importantly cortisol is involved in a range of anti-inflammatory and anti-allergic responses, which act to counter the adrenaline [adrenergic] response. This action prepares the body for long-term siege rather than a short explosive battle. It also serves to depress the body's immune system, a vital fact if the stress, or our response to it, is sustained. Again this is an example of the body's long-term stress response countering the effects of the immediate response. When stress is first experienced, the immune system is actually enhanced; only when that stress is sustained is it suppressed.

The links between emotional and anxiety-produced stress, cortisol and the immune system have now been clearly demonstrated. During longer term stress both the cell mediated and humoral [circulating] immune responses are suppressed. The exact impact of this in the longer term is not clear, though any suppression of the immune system creates an environment in which disease can thrive. One effect of sustained stress is that it impairs antibody production. This is reflected by reduced B blood cell activity, and changes in the regulating T cell counts. T cells are white blood cells which function to destroy or neutralise invading protein material, like viruses or bacteria. The cells play a vital role in our natural ability to combat disease, and T cell dysfunction is linked with the AIDS disease. The effect of stress on the immune response is now an area of considerable research. Early findings suggest that personality type may be linked with a low reaction by the immune system. If true, this could explain why some individuals tolerate high levels of stress with no adverse effects. The answer is that no-one yet knows – and the search continues.

Although the precise mechanism by which stress causes disease is often unknown, it is clear that the constant presence of cortisol, and other corticosteroids, in the blood creates an environment which at best might be termed 'unhealthy'. The fact that these hormones can be secreted in anticipation, not as the result of the stress itself, is also significant. High cortisol levels have been shown in those anticipating stressful events, like examinations, dental treatment or surgery, as well as in those experiencing the event itself. In the case of surgery such a reaction is important, and may have serious implications for the outcome or the patient's speed of recovery. Some diseases, and particularly cancer, are extremely stressful. With this disease a patient's attitude to treatment is often closely linked to his survival chance. This fact is not coincidental, and appears to be associated with how well the patient copes with stress.

It should be clear that in considering the adverse effects of stress we are looking beyond the body's immediate and natural response to outside pressure. For our own safety, comfort and performance it is essential that we have the ability to respond to external stimuli. The problems arise because, while we have industrialised our society, our bodies' responses are still closely linked with those of our primitive ancestors. In this context, physical activity is a natural response to stress, and one which enables the body to return quickly to a steady state. Unfortunately modern society denies us many of the natural outlets for stress, so our response becomes potentiated and damaging. Many of the stresses of modern society are, or appear, inescapable; a fact which means the stress response is constantly being triggered. In some stressful situations, like driving, we are denied any physical outlet for the stress we incur, and so our response turns inwards. High circulatory levels of these stress hormones are undoubtedly deleterious, and their biochemical effects are certainly linked with some of the early stress symptoms including irritability, apathy, lassitude – and many more.

By now it should be becoming evident that the biochemical response to stress is far from simple. It involves neurochemical, hormonal and immunological activity. These changes do not occur independently: a degree of congruence exists between them. This has led some researchers to the belief that the nervous and the immune systems may be functionally connected [the hormone and nervous systems clearly are]. Whether this is true or not, there is certainly an essential balance between the brain, the peripheral nervous system and the endocrine and immune systems. While the current measurement of stress concentrates on scaling changes induced by the autonomic nervous system or the endocrine system, there are many who feel we could more effectively measure changes in the immune system. Such changes might show not just the presence of stress, but also how well the patient is coping with it.

3.5. Neurotransmitters and stress

Recent years have seen developments in research techniques which have enabled us to gain a far clearer understanding of how the brain functions. Although a great deal remains to be determined, these developments have certainly helped our fundamental understanding of stress. In considering the biochemistry of stress, it is appropriate here to return to our study of the brain and its nerve cells, and above all to consider the bewildering range of substances which have now been shown to have some action within the brain. Such a study is important, because disturbances in the synthesis, release or inactivation of transmitter substances can result in brain disorders. Similarly problems in the sensitivity of the post synaptic receptors can lead to some of the conditions associated with stress.

As stated earlier transmitter substances are not distributed randomly throughout the brain. Most are highly localised in specific centres and pathways. In association with the hormone activities, it is the rise and decline in the activity of neurotransmitters during the day which controls cyclical behaviour like waking and sleeping, as well as such factors as eating. This is important, not least because disruptions here form some of the early manifestations of stress. ACTH, the hormone associated with initiating the adrenergic stress response, is also involved with waking us up in the morning. In times of stress, where ACTH is constantly triggered, it is not surprising that we have trouble sleeping. Similarly, with long-distance jet travel across time zones, the essential balance between the neurotransmitter/hormone and the time of day becomes disrupted. This results in the breakdown in sleep patterns and general malaise familiar to anyone who has suffered jet lag.

Recent research has clarified the biochemical sequence of events involved in synaptic transmission. This has enabled us to begin the development of drugs designed to selectively enhance or block individual stages of the process. Typically, transmitter substances are not manufactured from scratch at the synapse. They are developed from locally held precursors, an important distinction as these precursors may give rise to more than one substance. The fact that ACTH and the neuropeptide beta-endorphin both have the same peptide precursor [beta-lipotropin] appears particularly significant. Beta-endorphin, as we will see, appears to be a naturally occurring opiate which enables the body to overcome some of the pain associated with excessive exertion. Its release in parallel with ACTH would seem to be involved in 'steeling' the body against any exertions stemming from a vigorous stress response.

Transmitter substances are stored in vesicles and released into the synaptic space in response to a nerve impulse. They permeate across the space interacting with receptors in the receiving nerve cell. Many transmitters, like acetylcholine, appear to have more than one type of receptor – so can induce more than one type of response. Once released the transmitters must be inactivated if the response is not to become too prolonged. This is a vital process. Nerve fibres can carry several hundred impulses a second but this is only possible if the post-synaptic [receiving] membranes are allowed to recover quickly. A wide range of biochemical methods are used to deactivate neurotransmitters. In the case of acetylcholine the transmitter is inactivated in the synaptic gap by an enzyme called acetylcholinesterase. In the case of noradrenaline, a transmitter related to the hormone produced by the adrenal gland, deactivation is at the synaptic receptor via a totally different method. In fact a wide range of methods exist for the deactivation of neurotransmitters, the only real link being that each is highly specific to the transmitter involved.

The identification and mapping of brain neurotransmitters is a fairly recent development. Much still remains to be done. Among the best understood transmitters are the monoamines – noradrenaline, dopamine and serotonin. Noradrenaline is implicated in the maintenance of arousal, dreaming, sleep and mood. Where experimental animals are subjected to excessive stress, noradrenaline levels are at first raised but quickly become depleted. Such a reaction, which is clearly to the disadvantage of the animal concerned, appears to be linked not just to the persistence of the stress but also its nature or quality. Such a distinction is important.

It could help explain not only our different responses to stress, but also why some stressors are far more damaging than others.

In fact this noradrenaline dysfunction could account for the biochemical feedback mechanisms which exist during the stress process. Many believe there is a close connection between the noradrenaline pathway and the initial ACTH response to stress. In the ACTH reaction we see a chain of events which lead eventually to the production of cortisol. This series of reactions, sometimes referred to as a hormone cascade, should switch off and not become prolonged and potentially harmful. The mechanism for that 'switching off' is not yet clear. Noradrenaline is implicated in this determinant role, probably via the inhibition of CRF synthesis. When depleted it is clearly not available to function, a fact which in experimental animals has been directly linked with some of the more adverse effects of stress – and most particularly ulcer formation. Others suggest it is more likely that high levels of cortisol are implicated in the switch off of ACTH. Whichever is correct, the fact remains that with no functioning feedback mechanism the individual's metabolic response to stress is impaired, and a state of exhaustion or even death can result.

The essential balance and feedback mechanisms which exist between the neurotransmitters and hormones in the brain are an important part of our understanding of the stress response. One example is the hormone melatonin, which is produced by the pineal body, a small gland emerging from the anterior surface of the brain. Melatonin is released by the pineal at night, but during the day it is converted to serotonin. While melatonin does not actually cause sleep, it acts rather like the pre-med injection used prior to surgery; it induces a relaxed attitude in which sleep is possible. In function melatonin has been likened to the brain's own tranquilliser. This is something of a simplification but there are useful similarities. Unfortunately the action of melatonin, and its conversion to and from serotonin, can be easily disrupted by stress. This may mean both a loss of sleep and a reduced level of calm and tranquillity for those suffering from stress. Also important is the fact that in the presence of chronic pain serotonin levels in some parts of the brain become seriously depleted.

The study of chronic pain and its control and relief provide one of medicine's most active research areas. While, in biological terms, acute pain may serve a function, warning of injury or enforcing immobility, much of the chronic pain associated with cancer, arthritis and other disorders serves no real function. It is merely physically, psychologically and socially destructive. We have now reached the point where the the Chronic Pain Syndrome is recognised not merely as a symptom, but as a disorder in its own right. The close study of many of the hormones, neurotransmitters and neuromodulators involved in stress is also linked with our understanding of pain.

The main transmitter involved with relaying pain is called substance P. Substance P was one of the earliest recognised neurotransmitters, and is present in several brain pathways and the sensory nerve fibres. Although substance P acts to relay the pain impulse, another neurotransmitter met-enkephalin can function to suppress the release of substance P in sensory fibres. This clearly reduces our perception of pain, a fact which may yet have vital implications for the understanding and treatment of both stress and chronic pain. Met-enkephalin is one of a group of substances, including leu-enkephalin and beta-endorphin, generically known as the endorphins. More recently, this group has also become known as the endogenous opiates, because in their sedatory and painkilling effects they mimic the opiates, like morphine, which are widely used in medicine.

The endorphins are difficult to study because they are

quickly degraded once outside the brain. They have, however, analgesic [painkilling] properties many times greater than those of morphine, or any artificial opiate known to man. One problem slowing progress is that when they are injected intravenously, analgesic results with both beta-endorphin and met-enkephalin have been disappointing. This almost certainly relates to the presence of the blood–brain barrier, which prevents the passage of larger molecules. In experimental conditions when the endogenous opiates are given intracerebrally, directly into the brain ventricles, their effect has been shown to be far more pronounced.

The endogenous opiates are now the subject of very active research and it will be some years before their full properties are recognised. It is already known that they can act either as neurotransmitters or neuromodulators, and act directly to induce hormone secretion. The exact nature of their painkilling function is not clear, but it is believed that they bind to the same receptor sites as morphine, so their potential as a naturally occurring, non-addictive opiate could prove a valuable tool in therapy. Although most attention has been directed at the appearance of the endorphins in the brain pathways, their presence has also been demonstrated in other parts of the body, including the gastrointestinal tract. The reason for their presence here has not been fully determined.

One attraction of the endorphins is that we can take action to stimulate their secretion. In the future this may well have implications for the treatment of pain, stress and a range of other disorders. Already some well established procedures like acupuncture, hypnosis and electric shock therapy have been shown to be accompanied by a rise in endorphin levels. A greater understanding of such results, accompanied perhaps by a refining of the techniques involved, could play an important part in the therapy of tomorrow.

Beta-endorphin could also change significantly the treatment of such stress-related problems as overeating and drug abuse. Many of the problems associated with drug withdrawal symptoms come more from the residual effects of the drug on neurotransmitters and neuromodulators, like beta-endorphin, than from abstinence. What results is an uncomfortable imbalance in the body's recovery mechanisms which could be compensated by an increased level of beta-endorphin. The fact that beta-endorphin is naturally regulated is a vital factor in countering addiction. In treating overeating the situation appears more complex. At times of stress beta-endorphin levels rise, a fact which has been associated with increased food consumption. This phenomenon can be countered by using the drug naloxone, an opiate antagonist which occupies the same receptor sites as the beta-endorphin. A good deal of work remains to be done in this area, but certainly beta-endorphin control could prove important in the treatment of some types of chronic obesity.

A greater understanding of synaptic transmission has also brought a greater awareness of how many psycho-active drugs work. Some of these may enhance or inhibit a transmitter, whilst other like naloxone occupy the receptor site blocking entry. One example of a drug often misused is the powerful stimulant amphetamine. This triggers the release of dopamine, a transmitter involved in regulating emotional response and movement control. The too rapid release of dopamine can result in delusions and hallucinations, while long-term overactivity in dopamine secretion is linked with schizophrenia. Not surprisingly drugs which block the dopamine receptors, like chlorpromazine or haloperidol, have been shown to be effective in the treatment of schizophrenia.

In other cases the drug may not act directly on the site of secretion or reception of the transmitter, but indirectly on the agent which reduces the transmitter. The group of enzymes known as the monoamine oxidases function to degrade serotonin, dopamine and noradrenaline. If this enzyme is blocked, by drugs like impromiazid in anti-depressant therapy, then the naturally arousing effects of these transmitters is given free rein. The patient's own natural secretions in fact take over, and should help lift the de-pression. Even more indirect are the methylxanthine drugs like theophylline and caffeine. These act indirectly on what are known as second messenger, energy producing pathways to induce a stimulating effect. Caffeine is an unusual drug because its effect in humans is far more sustained [up to 4 hours] than that demonstrated in most animals. It can also produce effects at very low levels, with doses of only 0.3 mg per kilogram body weight, causing such reactions as anxiety, emotional lability [instability], speeded up thought and diuresis [urine production]. At this level even supposedly decaffeinated coffee could be producing an undesired reac-tion.

The list of psycho-active drugs is growing as a result of our greater understanding of neural transmission and brain pathways. Many of these will be reviewed later when we come to examine the treatment of stress disorders. What we have done here is to review *some* of the transmitters which are linked with the stress response. This is of necessity a selective review as well over thirty substances are now believed to exercise either an excitory or inhibitory role in the brain. Some of these, like the brain's commonest inhibitory transmitter GABA [gamma-aminobutyric acid], are found exclusively in the brain and spinal cord; others may be more dispersed and found elsewhere in the body.

The list appears endless, with the function of some of the newer transmitters being at best poorly understood. The newly discovered substance tribulin is associated with panic and anxiety symptoms, and appears to be directly opposed to the function of the natural neurotranmitter GABA or its synthetic agonist diazepam [Valium]. Certainly tribulin binds to the same receptor sites as Valium, which has spurred a search for some naturally occurring equivalent. Such a discovery could give an important insight into not just the causes of stress, but also some of the problems associated with drug withdrawal. Although tribulin levels are high in those suffering many stress disorders, they are unnaturally low in chronic schizophrenics and heroin addicts suffering withdrawal. This explains the reasons why these disorders are generally not responsive to treatment with diazepam, although the complete significance of this is not clear and research is continuing.

Small, but possibly significant, differences also exist in the male and female response to stress, although this is an area where much work remains to be done. In general males respond to stress most strongly via the sympathetico–adrenal pathway, whilst females respond primarily via their pituitary–adrenal system. The implications of such findings are not clear, although they have been linked with the lower incidence of coronary heart disease in young females. What is known is that tolerance to physical stress involving muscular work is lower in females. This is reflected in a lower oxygen uptake, although the patterns of heart rate adjustment between males and females under stress are very similar. Females also tolerate thermal stress less well then males, although tolerance to cold in women is far greater – a fact reflecting significant differences in sub-cutaneous fat levels.

If our biochemical response to stress is complex, so too are the multiplicity of factors which influence that response. In his writings Hans Selye divided these into two: endogenous and exogenous. Endogenous factors are essentially those we are born with – if you like, our genetic predisposition to a particular stress response. Included in endogenous factors are our natural enzyme levels, age, sex, plus our training or preconditioning. Although we can clearly modify our training in later life, much of our response to stress may be framed in our early experiences, over which we have little control. In our study of the *control* of stress we will concentrate on exogenous factors. These include drugs, nutrition, physical environment and many more, factors over which we have far more control. As this book progresses the significance of this division will become more apparent. So too will the fact that the answers to some of our problems lie firmly in our own hands.

4

Stress, conventional medicine and health

While this book is primarily about stress and disease we must recognise that stress also has implications for our health at what might be termed a sub-disease threshold. This is important, because if we allow minor, day-to-day stress to disrupt our general health, we will cope less well with more serious events. The importance of our general health, as expressed in sensible diet, sleep, exercise and sexual patterns, will be continually emphasised in this book. While we cannot avoid stress totally in our lives, and indeed should not seek to do so, we can certainly do much to limit its more serious effects.

One problem is that the early changes caused by stress are insidious, and may not be recognised either by the patient or the clinician. While some of the more open presentations of stress, like outbursts of temper or headaches may be obvious, changes in long-standing eating, sleeping or sexual patterns may go largely unnoticed, or even be dismissed by an unsympathetic partner. While we do not want a society which is over-preoccupied with studying its health, itself a stressful attitude, we must be aware of the significance of such changes.

Among the earliest and most common ways in which stress affects our general health is the disruption of sleep. This is a two-edged sword. Not only is sleeplessness acutely distressing, and far more distressing than many of those who do not suffer sometimes recognise, but sleep itself is intrinsically linked with both emotional and physical recovery. This leads to a dangerous spiral, where those who react badly to stress are also denied one of nature's most simple and effective mechanisms for relieving it. Sleeplessness is very common. In the UK, 20 per cent of all patients visiting their doctor did so as a result of some form of insomnia. That less than half of these were deemed in need of drug therapy indicates that UK general practitioners at least recognise that a change in habits and life style, rather than chemical intervention, is the answer in most cases.

The link between stress and the disruption of sleep is clear and very easy to recognise. As we have seen, ACTH is at the centre of our response to stress and is also linked both with awakening and arousal. If high levels of ACTH are present, as they are when we are stressed or active, then it is hardly surprising that we have difficulty sleeping. This fact deserves consideration, not least by those who work late and right up to the point of retiring. The answer is to stop work earlier, or retire to bed after a brief period in which we relax and give our bodies' ACTH levels a chance to decline. Even if this means less time spent in bed, the result may be more refreshing than a night spent chasing sleep which refuses to come.

Sleep is now a major topic of scientific study, and this has changed many long-standing attitudes. Where sleep was once regarded as a passive process, it is now recognised by many as an active mechanism by which the body positively reconstitutes itself. Sleep also appears to be closely linked with memory, many researchers believing that short-term electrical memory is converted to longer term chemical memory as we sleep. If true, this would account for the quite startling level of retention we have about things we read or study late at night – a phenomenon known to anyone who has gone through the revision and examination process.

Where early studies emphasised the role of sleep in physical restitution many modern researchers believe this is less important than the climate it offers for emotional and mental recovery. In fact sleep is almost certainly linked with both forms of recovery [emotional and physical], with certain periods of sleep probably having specific functions. Thus, the period called short wave sleep [SWS] is characterised by high plasma levels of HGH [human growth hormone]. This hormone is concerned with, among other functions, protein synthesis – the mechanism by which the body repairs wear and tear. This has led some researchers to suggest that the SWS period is particularly associated with physical recovery. Such a pattern is almost certainly an oversimplification, because while we sleep the general level of our metabolism is reduced, as is the level of protein precursors in the blood. Latest research suggests that the high levels of HGH could be connected to another function – the most likely options being protein preservation or changes in the regulation of the energy substrates. Whatever is true, many still believe that different phases of our sleep are associated with different aspects of recovery.

Although we still struggle to understand the exact process by which sleep aids physical and mental recovery, its bio-chemical basis is better understood. In simplified terms, this comprises two antagonistic systems, one inducing relaxation and sleep and the other stimulating arousal. As mentioned earlier, arousal is closely linked with ACTH levels. These fluctuate significantly throughout the day, maintained naturally by about eight fresh bursts of the hormone. If we work late, or face stress late at night, then this induces a fresh, supplementary burst of ACTH and this will ensure we do not get the sleep we seek.

Also involved with both arousal and sleep is the tiny pineal gland on the roof of the brain. Once thought to be a vestigial [defunct or obsolete] organ, this is now known to play a central role in the body's hormone balance. During the day the pineal body is rich in serotonin, which at night is converted to another neurotransmitter, melatonin. Melatonin does not itself induce sleep, but it is concerned with the process of relaxation which makes sleep possible. Its production is influenced by both noradrenalin and GABA, and the whole complex cycle is readily disrupted by stress. The fact that melatonin, which lies at the core of our ability to relax, does not itself induce sleep, has encouraged researchers to seek another substance which acts more directly. This is usually referred to rather uncertainly as DSIP [the Delta sleep inducing peptide]. Whether DSIP exists or not is far from clear and research on this area is continuing.

It is hard to over-emphasise the vital importance of sleep to our recovery process. This is not, however, the full extent to which sleep affects our general health. It is also closely linked with our day–night [diurnal] rhythms, and perhaps less obviously with our circadian [monthly] and seasonal [infradian] biorhythms. Modern society has done much to try to suppress the significance of the biorhythms, but they remain of major importance. In the US, where SAD [seasonal affective depression] is a recognised disorder, the autumn months have been identified with both reduced creativity and a higher level of depressive illness. Whether such findings are also linked with the high suicide rates in some northern cities, particularly in Scandinavia, is unclear but does look likely. One reason could be the reduced levels of white light in autumn and winter. White light we know stimulates the pineal to release melatonin which, as well as causing relaxation and sleep, affects mood and reproductive behaviour. In therapy, early studies using artificial white light have shown interesting results both in enhancing mood and lifting depression, though much basic, let alone applied, research remains to be done.

Also closely linked with the biorhythms is sexual activity,

another area easily disrupted by stress. Clinicians tell us that physical causes of sexual dysfunctions like impotency are rare, so we must look to psychology and our response to pressure for an explanation. Stress has been directly linked to a wide range of sexual dysfunction including frigidity, impotence, premature ejaculation and imagined inadequacy. This is the tip of the iceberg, with stress being more indirectly linked with, for example, adultery, mistrust, rape – and the total avoidance of sex. We have mentioned elsewhere the sexual preoccupation of much of modern society: this will do little to help those who suffer from sexual problems, merely serving to separate them still further from the comfort and help sex can bring.

Not surprisingly the effect of stress on sexual activity differs widely between men and women. In men, the high cortisol levels found during stress have been linked with low sperm counts. This has implications for fertility. At the same time, achieving an erection is closely associated with parasympathetic and pleasurable stimulation, a fact which may cause problems where stress stimulates the sympathetic nervous system, and so overrides this type of pleasurable activity. The result is the inability to achieve or sustain an erection – itself acutely stressful.

Until recently, in our male orientated society, the study of female sexuality and of women's stress related sex problems had been sadly lacking. This is changing; stress is now known to be a major cause of sexual dysfunction among both men and women. In women, it can cause frigidity, vaginismus [an unnatural contraction of the vagina during intercourse], vaginitis, inadequate lubrication and many more conditions. All these may not merely detract from the pleasures of sex, but make sex itself a traumatic experience and a cause of further stress, not least via disharmony within a relationship. Stress can delay or prevent ovulation, which is not surprising given this process's close link with the hypothalamic–pituitary–gonadal axis. One of the major hormones implicated in delaying ovulation is prolactin, which many researchers claim is as accurate a measure of stress as cortisol. Whether or not this is true, prolactin will undoubtedly serve to delay ovulation and so reduce the chance of conception. This is important both for women striving for a child, and for women in highly stressful occupations. Too little research has been done, but it looks likely that women executives who work under high pressure may have difficulty in conceiving. While this may be acceptable – even desirable – for some, for others it could be an unacceptable price to pay for emancipation.

In terms of stress, many already pay a heavy price for the sexual freedom in our society. While we have succeeded in separating sex from its animal function, it is questionable whether this has helped us find a more balanced approach. In their search for sex, far too many are chasing a non-achievable dream which can only result in frustration and anti-climax – which are acutely stressful. A balanced sex life is important to both our general health and our ability to cope with stress. The aims of such a sex life should be determined by ourselves – and our partners – not by some outside agency. Where the media concentrate heavily on the quantity of sex, and say little about the quality of relationships, they therefore give an unbalanced viewpoint – and one we should reject.

While modern society has separated sex from its original purpose, the same could also be said of our attitude to eating. Appetite operates under elaborate hormonal control in which the sight, smell and presence of food stimulate the brain, the mouth, the gut, etc. While much of the world starves, the ingestion of food in a large part of the West has become debased, resulting in a society in which – depending on the definition used – 30, 40, 50 or even 60 per cent – of the population are overweight. Where obesity was once confined to the affluent and the middle aged, it has now spread throughout society and is becoming an increasing and worrying problem amongst the young. Obesity causes many well recognised metabolic, mechanical and cardio-vascular disorders. Less well recognised perhaps, is the fact that it can also lead to self consciousness, withdrawal and depression.

As we will see, stress and overeating are closely linked. Indeed, in many cases overeating can be regarded as a form of abuse not dissimilar to tobacco or even drug misuse. As a result, much modern research into obesity is concentrating on the role of the neurotransmitters, the study of which offers new hope for what remains a very difficult problem. One of the neuromodulators most under examination in this area is CCK [cholecystokinin] a substance whose neurones and receptors are found both in the brain and in the gut. Though research is still at an early stage, CCK appears to be implicated in the process of satiation, the mechanism by which the body brings eating to a halt. Serotonin also appears to be involved in our choice of food, with particular emphasis on its nutritional content, for example proteins and carbo-hydrates. Clearly such findings are important. It seems possible that CCK and serotonin dysfunction could provide part of the link between stress and overeating, not least because whatever else characterises a stressed individual's eating patterns, it is not a balanced choice of diet.

Beta-endorphin also appears to be involved in overeating. As we have seen this is one of the endogenous opiates, providing a warm comforting sensation when released not unlike synthetic opiates such as heroin. Beta-endorphin levels rise naturally before we eat, a fact which has led some researchers to suggest that stress related overeating is stimulated by a desire to gain the comfort and analgesic effects produced by its release. In such cases, individuals become almost addicted to their own endogenous opiates.

71

If this is true, then it gives real hope for the future. Obesity is one of the major – and seemingly intractable – general health problems of our age. Once we can curb stress-related eating, then we will have a much healthier population, which is more able to cope with stress.

Among the most difficult concepts to convey in this book is the fact that the same stress can create virtually opposite effects in different individuals. Thus, while stress may cause overeating, it also has links with the condition known as anorexia nervosa, in which food is avoided to the point of starvation or even death. Anorexia is not a new condition: its existence has been recognised for more than three hundred years, although only recently has it received the attention it deserves. It is also far more common than many suppose, with one recent US study suggesting that around one in three hundred teenagers will suffer from the disorder – 90 per cent of them female. Such figures are worrying; anorexia has a very high mortality rate, upwards of 10 per cent. This is a devastating figure for a disease which attacks primarily the young. Anorexia nervosa is a complex psychological disorder, whose origins are still largely unclear. Modern theories suggest it is caused by some dysfunction of the hypothalamus, the gland responsible for mobilising the body's resources to respond to stress. Whether this dysfunction is caused by stress alone, or by some other factor or factors, is uncertain. Modern therapy concentrates on drug treatments closely supported by counselling and nutritional rehabilitation. Despite this, follow up studies suggest that 50 per cent of surviving anorexics retain a morbid concern over weight gain well into adult life. A better understanding of the biochemical basis of eating and its possible link with stress could provide a much needed breakthrough in the treatment of this disease.

Eating, sleeping, exercise and sex patterns play an important part in our general health. The human body has a massive – though finite – ability to cope with a wide range of stress. If we undermine this by poor general health, supplemented by the gross abuse of food, drugs, tobacco and alcohol, then we can hardly complain if our bodies fail to cope – or actively rebel. Maintaining good health is part of a positive, almost aggressive approach we can bring to the problems of stress. This approach is vital: if we sit back and let stress just happen to us, its effects can only get worse. From animal experiments, we know that *nothing* is more stressful and damaging than the condition known as learned helplessness, where the animal can do nothing at all to ease its circumstances. This means that in dealing with stress we *must* avoid a passive approach. In this we are helped by a body and constitution superbly designed to cope with the worst stress can offer – provided we give it a chance.

No matter how careful we are in maintaining our general health, stress and pressure can eventually affect all of us. Indeed one objective of this book is to convince senior management that there is no such thing as stress supermen – or women. Though we may cope differently, no one is immune to stress, and the recognition of this is long overdue by some parts of industry. Once stress has taken a hold, it is questionable how effective modern, conventional medicine is. Much of modern medical therapy is preoccupied with identifying and treating symptoms, an approach which can have only a limited impact on stress related disorders. Here there is a need to identify and eliminate the root cause of the condition. If we treat anxiety with tranquillisers, insomnia with narcotics and appetite disturbances with stimulants and depressants, the patient may feel better temporarily, but the cause of their condition remains untreated and unresolved.

It is clear that many people have far too passive an approach to ill-health. They seem to accept that disease is an inevitable part of life, failing to recognise that a great deal of misery can be avoided by changes in life-style and attitude. In part this is due to the emphasis of Western medicine itself, which is preoccupied with disease intervention – though the fundamental cause goes far deeper. Too many individuals seem to feel they can counter a life style of abuse with a few carefully chosen drugs. Once we get such false expectations out of the way, we can begin to draw the correct balance between our general health and conventional medicine. Modern medicine is neither infallible nor omniscient – and it is up to us to consider where our responsibilities end and those of our medical advisers begin.

While the authors do not wish to criticise conventional medical practice, we must recognise that in philosophical terms much of modern medicine is ill equipped to handle complex problems like stress, where education, prevention and counselling must form a major part of therapy. In the West medicine has become too closely associated with disease intervention, and pays too little attention to keeping people healthy. Although most Western countries spend 10 per cent – or more – of their GNP on health, health education and preventive programmes remain underfunded. Even in the US, which spends upwards of US $120,000 million on health, only some 2 per cent is allocated to prevention. In Europe, the figure in most countries is even lower, and made worse by the fact that prevention is an area it appears politically acceptable to cut in times of economic stringency.

All this presents particular problems for the already over-stretched general practitioner, the front line of medical practice in most Western countries. Lacking assistance and support from central services, most GPs now find themselves faced with a massive upsurge in stress-related conditions. These we know can be both difficult and time consuming to isolate. Thus a patient may initially suffer little more than a general and persistent feeling of malaise, which can be episodal and apparently unrelated to any specific disorder. To separate this from any organic cause, and identfy its real origins, takes time.

Time – or rather the lack of it – tends to be a feature of modern medicine. Doctors, and other health professionals, are expected to see the highest possible number of patients, in very brief appointments. In many modern health centres patients may seldom see the same doctor twice, a problem with stress related disorders where it may be as essential for the doctor to recognise the type of patient who has a particular disorder as to identify the condition itself. Clearly such an understanding takes time, and this has been recognised in the stress clinics springing up in the US, UK and Israel. These concentrate on examining and treating stress within small, highly personalised units, in which staff:patient ratios are far lower than those seen in conventional medical practice. Sadly such stress clinics are still few in number.

Although much conventional medical practice struggles to cope with stress, it is nevertheless an area of growing interest and activity. This comes in part from the increased awareness of how much time general practitioners devote to stress related disorders, and also from the belated recognition of the prevalence and significance of such conditions. While figures vary, in both the US and Europe between 50 and 70 per cent of all visits to general practitioners are linked to stress related conditions. This is a massive extra burden for an already overworked section of the medical community. It is hardly surprising if such pressure results in the treatment of symptoms rather than in a holistic approach where all aspects of a patient's condition and life style are examined.

With general practitioners under pressure, other groups such as psychiatrists and psychologists have become involved in the control and treatment of stress. Their approach is very different. Psychiatrists typically use psychoanalysis

or psycholeptic [behaviour controlling] drugs. The significance of these techniques will be touched upon later, but
they will inevitably fail if we do not tackle the root cause of
the problem. Whatever the medical discipline, if we treat
stress symptoms successfully but then return an individual
to the identical life style and environment which caused the
condition, then our hopes for a long term cure are limited.
Too much of modern therapy seems purely palliative, and
can do little more than deflect some of the grosser symptoms
of stress-related conditions.

Recognition of the need to tackle the root causes of stress
lies behind the increased involvement of sociologists and
behavioural scientists in this area. They aim not just to treat
the manifestations of stress but also to reduce the presence
of stress in the environment. This is a complex process, and
it is probably fair to say that so far such groups have had a
limited impact. While they have often been successful in
improving the more obvious environmental factors, like
temperature, noise and pollution, they have been far less
effective in countering the more subtle causes of stress
including personal relationships, ergonomic equipment design and factory sitings. Here work is proceeding, though
progress is slower than many might hope.

One area where behavioural scientists are active is in
trying to identify groups who are particularly susceptible to
stress-related disease. This work is in an early stage but has
already shown interesting results. Probably the best known,
and certainly the most quoted, of these studies is that
conducted by Rosenman and Friedman in the early 1960s,
concerning the prevalence of coronary heart disease among
certain personality groupings. It identified two extremes of
behaviour classified as Types A and B. Type As, who had
a significantly higher rate of coronary heart disease, were
characterised as fiercely competitive, constantly striving for
success, tense, aggressive and impatient. They were highly

committed to their work but often to an extent which was damaging both to their employment and their home life. By contrast, Type Bs were less committed, more patient, less tense – and certainly less striving for success. Such personality traits are clearly extremes, and it is probably best to regard them as the outer parameters of an axis upon which all of us have a place.

Rosenman and Friedman's work is interesting, and we will touch upon it later in the context of cardiovascular disease. Here, it serves to emphasise the pattern and type of thinking with which the behavioural scientist approaches the problems of stress. Clearly, if we can recognise those who are most vulnerable to stress and its disorders, then we can go a long way towards some form of prophylaxis. Behavioural scientists and psychologists are now common in many parts of industry, and in areas like schools and universities. The recent shuttle disaster in the US was immediately followed by the move of a number of psychologists into American schools, a sensible attempt to counter the shock and trauma of what was an intensely personal disaster for many American schoolchildren. Also in the US, there is already a close link between stress control and industrial psychology programmes. As our understanding of the psychological base of disease increases so too undoubtedly will the role of the industrial psychologist.

All this suggests that conventional medicine is belatedly coming to terms with the problem of stress, though much remains to be done. As individuals, we must also avoid expecting too much from our clinicians. The last ten or twenty years have seen a massive and overdue change in public attitudes, both to health and medical practitioners. Patients are now more demanding and aware, prepared to challenge their clinician's decision. This is fine, providing that challenge is not based on either ignorance or misconception. We have a right to be interested in our medical state, though we must be sure of the basis on which we found that interest. Here the media do not always help. By over-generalisation or concentrating on extreme cases, television and newspapers do not always serve the interests of the clinician – or indeed the patient.

Doctors themselves are not immune from the effects of stress. Stress-related disorders are now a major problem among doctors and many other health professionals. This deserves consideration, not least by those seeking to push their own problems on to their clinician. There is no doubt that we expect too much from our doctors – and this is now taking its toll. At a political level, this is typified by a willingness to leave decisions on controversial issues like abortion, child sex and contraception to the clinical judgement of an individual doctor. This is less than fair: doctors have no political mandate to exercise such major decisions and are all too aware of the consequences should they make an error of judgement.

Doctors also work in a constantly changing technical environment and of course change is a major cause of stress. As well as a heavy workload, clinicians must now cope with the steady intrusion into their discipline of other high technology areas like computing, bioengineering and electronics. These impose problems particularly for those who trained in the biological sciences and come uncomfortably to physics and mathematics-based technologies. We know that the need to constantly update our knowledge is stressful but for the clinician the alternative may be even more stressful. The old stereotype of the rural physician who did not update his knowledge after leaving medical school may be amusing but is hardly realistic. If such an unlikely character ever existed, he would certainly not survive long in today's highly technical and litigious society.

The topic of litigation, and the consequent pressure on clinicians, deserves a book of its own. In the US, three times as many clinicians are being sued as ten years ago, with latest figures suggesting that as many as one in six MDs in New York State are currently being sued for malpractice. Even in Europe, where figures are generally far lower, there has been a steady increase both in claims and in the level of awards. If we equate this with the fact that 20 per cent of pregnancies include natural complications which *can* lead to permanent damage in the baby, then clearly doctors are walking a very difficult tightrope. Whatever the cause, stress among physicians is now a recognised and growing phenomenon. As early as 1957, the US Commissioner of Narcotics reported that 1 per cent of all US doctors were addicted to drugs [as compared to 1 in 3000 of the population at large]. By the early 1980s, the US Center for Disease Control reported that 11 per cent of clinicians abused alcohol, drugs or both.

This chapter forms the bridge between the background and technology of stress, and the manifestations of stress in the form of ill-health and disease. In this we must be clear in our claims. We know that life style and our standard of general health have major implications for how well we cope with stress. We are, however, less clear in our understanding of the root cause of disease – and the environmental and stress factors which lead to it. This is not so much an area where medical science has failed as one where its very complexity has held back progress. Even where science suspects a link, this is sometimes difficult to demonstrate, a fact readily used by the tobacco lobby who still question the link between tobacco and disease. We continue to fill our environment with pollutants and radioactivity with little understanding of the long term effects on our health. It is a strange fact that before marketing a drug a company must prove it is safe; yet if the same company wishes to dump drug-related waste into the environment, someone else must show it is harmful.

79

Later we will examine diseases where a link with stress has undoubtedly been demonstrated. Many now believe that, because of its impact on the immune system, stress is implicated in many more disorders and infections. If this is so, then limiting the effects of stress is one of our most pressing health problems. It also requires a different approach from most other areas of medicine. It requires a move away from isolating and treating symptoms to more definition of the underlying cause of disease: a switch, in fact, from pathology correction to health maintenance. In this we cannot expect the medical practitioner to cope alone. A great deal must depend on the individual, both to maintain a good general standard of health, and to introduce personal stress control programmes. It is long overdue that we recognised that the responsibility for our health lies largely with ourselves. On this may depend not just how well we cope with stress but whether we survive.

—5—

The diseases of stress

We shall examine cardiovascular disease and mental disorders in later chapters, because of the volume of the literature and because their link with stress is more clearly understood. In this chapter we will look at other diseases; some whose link with stress is well established and others where it is, perhaps, more tenuous. In all cases we are talking about statistical probabilities. Even where stress has been shown to cause disease, it is typically only one of a number of factors whose significance will vary between individuals. Those reading the following pages should bear this in mind, particularly when drawing parallels with their personal condition.

One of the most important, and exciting, areas of recent research has involved the quest for a link between stress and cancer. Although much of this research is modern, the idea of such a link is not new. In 1885 Willard Parker in the US concluded that 'unresolved grief' was linked with breast cancer in women. His attempt to take this further, and to identify a type of 'melancholic woman', who was particularly prone to the disease, seems to have been unsuccessful. Many studies since have drawn similar conclusions. Again in the US, a careful follow up study on several hundred cancer patients who had been successfully treated over an extended period of up to twenty years, showed that the recurrence of the disease was virtually always associated with a major traumatic experience in the previous six to eighteen months. In 1985, Maier and Laudenslager at the University of Colorado showed that a helpless, passive reaction was implicated in the increased activity of cancer cells. We now appear to have reached the point where virtually all clinicians accept a link between cancer and stress, although its precise nature is more difficult to define.

It has been estimated that around 95 per cent of all cancers are environmental in origin. They are caused by the intrusion of xenobiotics [carcinogens], chemicals which are foreign to the body and cause the growth of tumours. Because these xenobiotics are usually fat soluble, they are able to enter the cell and become involved with its processes and functioning. Unfortunately the elimination of these substances is not a simple matter. To be removed from the cell they must first be made water-soluble, after which they can be eliminated by the body's natural excretory mechanisms – the urine, bile, etc. This conversion is performed by the cell's own enzyme systems, which as we have seen can have an altered rate of activity when we are under stress.

The conversion from fat to water solubility for a carcinogen has its own risks. It involves a series of conversions during which a number of highly chemically active substances may be produced. In such cases, it is not the original chemical which is so damaging, but the products of the body's own attempt to eliminate it. Such a process where a carcinogen is activated almost by accident is known as intoxication – as distinct from detoxication where the effect is more direct.

In fact the situation is even more complex and dangerous. Before being eliminated the carcinogen may link with the nucleic acid [DNA] of the cell. This is the hereditory material which is the basis of both identity and life. If this divides after the intrusion of the carcinogen, then misreading in the DNA being transcribed can occur, resulting in cell aberration. This fact can be compounded by further changes in the cell's enzyme activity. Under stress the action of many body enzymes may be enhanced several-fold. This can have a protective effect, meaning that dangerous compounds are eliminated more readily, or a damaging effect if it helps widen the contact and impact of the carcinogen.

Although carcinogens cause mutation, changing normal cells into aberrant cells, not all these cells go on to cause cancer. The body has a number of well developed mechanisms for dealing with this problem, although again the effectiveness of this process is reduced by stress. Much of the body's response to intrusion is based on the activities of the white blood cells – the leucocytes. In periods of stress leucocyte levels decline significantly, reducing the body's ability to cope with infections caused by bacteria and viruses, and – it is postulated – with cancerous cells.

No-one is saying that stress alone is a direct cause of cancer. The contention is more complex and subtle, suggesting that stress may render the individual less able to deal with the generation of malignant cells. Certainly, where stress disrupts the balance between the neurochemical, hormonal and immune systems, it may well create an environment in which the malignant process can thrive.

One problem facing researchers in this area is the wide range of malignant diseases known as cancer. Much early work has followed Willard Parker, and concentrated on breast cancer. In animals, 60 per cent of females subject to very high stress levels were shown to develop breast cancer, compared with only some 7 per cent in the control groups who were protected from stress. While we must translate such results to the human patient with care, statistical surveys do suggest that many women suffering this disease have experienced major traumatic events in the preceding eighteen months. While the aetiology [origin and development] of breast cancer is complex, many clinicians now believe that stress, and particularly incidents of very high stress, may shorten the latent period of the tumour. This would clearly speed up the growth and spread of the malignancy, though the exact nature and cause of this change is as yet poorly understood.

Stress may have a major influence on the development and outcome of cancer. If the body's resistance is lowered during stress, then it seems reasonable to suggest that cancer will develop faster in those who are continually under stress. This is important because cancer itself is a traumatic and stressful disease. Despite the fact that cardiovascular disease is now the most common cause of death in all Westernised societies, cancer is still the illness which is most feared. Much of this fear comes from ignorance, and continues despite improvements in diagnosis, therapy and clinical outcome. Cancer is now a major taboo, a fact which does not help those who develop it. The rejection of the gravely ill cancer patient by friends, colleagues and even family, is a well recognised phenomenon. If, as seems certain, stress influences the outcome for many cancer patients, such rejection can only do great harm.

The recognition that stress may play a role in the development of cancer is now influencing the nature of therapy. Much of this is directed at reducing the emotional impact of the disease, a difficult problem given the public's emotional reaction. Unfortunately this applies not only to surgery but also to other forms of cancer therapy. Many of the drugs used produce serious side effects, partly because of the narrow divide between the drug destroying cancer cells and attacking the patient's healthy tissue. One effective means of minimising these side-effects is very closely controlled infusion – typically using an electronically driven pump. This replaces the bolus treatments given either in pill form or by injection. In the longer term, the use of monoclonal antibodies to carry drugs solely to the diseased tissue could result in the production of highly effective drugs, with minimal side-effects. In the meantime it is vital, through counselling, advice and related psycho-active drug support, that we seek to reduce the trauma and stress of cancer therapy. On this alone may depend the success or failure of many cancer treatments.

The link between the outcome of cancer and the attitude of the patient is not new: it has been long recognised that patients who are very apprehensive about the disease do worse than those who quickly come to terms with it. This difference applies even where cancer is diagnosed at a very early stage. Although we are still a long way from a full understanding, we now have a base for future research on why some patients do well, and why others go into an immediate decline. If this will not give us a cure for cancer, it could help in developing effective therapies.

The recognition of what might be termed a personality factor in the aetiology of cancer has spurred research into whether certain personality types are more prone to the disease than others. This is still in an early stage, although it has thrown up some interesting results. While sometimes ambiguous, these results suggest that cancer is frequently associated with the inability to express negative emotions. This suggests that a passive attitude, characterised by low levels of aggression and poorly developed emotional outlets, could be associated with both the occurrence and the rapid development of the disease. *If* this is so then some of the supportive measures used in the treatment of depressive illness could be of assistance, though again conclusions must be drawn with great care.

Indeed high aggression levels have been suggested as the reason why paranoid mental patients often show a very slow rate of cancer development. As we have already said, openly expressed anger and aggression are very good for the relief of stress. More puzzling perhaps is the bizarre pattern of cancer development in many schizophrenics. Not only does cancer grow slowly among such patients, but this group is also associated with some of the more remarkable and spontaneous recoveries. Could such facts perhaps stem from a schizophrenic's greater willingness to come to terms with the disease, or is there a more fundamental reason? The answer to such questions could lead to a greater understanding of the link between stress and both the occurrence and development of cancer.

So far we have attempted to give a balanced view of recent thinking on the links between cancer and stress. Although many developments look exciting a great deal remains to be proved. What we can say is that with cancer, unlike many other stress-related disorders, single highly traumatic events, like bereavement, divorce, bankruptcy or job loss, appear to be particularly damaging. What also seems likely is that the way we cope with stress, including the acceptance of the original diagnosis of cancer, has major implications for the success of treatment. In this context, aggression and anger – though not directed at the clinician – are far more helpful than passive acceptance. Many researchers expect to show that stress and cancer are more fundamentally associated. They could well be right!

The links between stress and ulcers in the digestive tract have been recognised for many years. Much work in this area has concentrated on duodenal ulcers. One problem is that, unlike in cancer, the stress which most influences the development of ulcers may be continuous or episodic, rather than one large traumatic incident. This makes establishing a link particularly difficult for the clinician. As we have seen, stress is intensely personal, and what one individual finds stressful, another will not find even mildly inconvenient. In the absence of uniformity, the doctor must make subjective evaluations: an unhappy base from which to draw major conclusions.

While stress in general depresses the activity of the gut, certain emotions are linked with increased gastric activity, blood flow and peristaltic movement. These include hostility, frustration, resentment and guilt. It is also recognised that anxiety can lead to increased and excessive acid secretion, which in turn can lead to ulceration. In animal experiments acute stress has been shown to be highly damaging, inducing the formation of ulcers *in a matter of hours*. In humans, the situation appears even more complex, as the damage caused by this excessive acid secretion may be compounded and, in many individuals, take place several hours after the event which caused the anxiety. This clearly makes taking prophylactic [preventive] measures more difficult.

With established ulcer conditions the pattern and risks are different. Although, in most patients, ulcer *development* is linked with continual stress and maintained high acid levels, this group also appear to be particularly sensitive to single, highly traumatic events. In such cases sudden ulcer perforation can occur, changing a condition which is under control into one of critical dimensions.

While the precise link between stress and ulcers is hard to define, we have shown statistically that many ulcer sufferers are highly sensitive to stress. This seems again to be linked with personality: aggressive, forceful individuals are less likely to suffer than those who are meek and accepting. This has encouraged some to suggest that, in the meek and passive, hostility finds its outlet in bodily dysfunctions like ulcers or cancer. This is almost certainly a vast oversimplification. In the meek and passive, the chemical secretions associated with stress are going to be activated at a lower threshold. Where these secretions are sustained or potentiated we know they are harmful, so it is hardly surprising that we see a higher incidence of physical damage in the hypersensitive. The world can be a harsh place: the old adage that a brave man dies once, a coward many times over may well be significant.

As well as causing the ulcers, and aggravating them, stress can also limit the benefits of therapy. This is hardly surprising if anxiety causes excessive acid secretion. Two substances clearly associated with the aggravation of existing gastric ulcers are histamine and adrenaline, while a third which is strongly implicated is adenosine. This acts on a series of specialist receptors in the gut. Blocking the action of adenosine by antagonistic drugs [drugs which occupy the same receptor sites] like clonidine and the methylxanthines can go a long way to halting or reducing further damage. Although some still doubt the link between stress and ulcers, reduced anxiety levels have been shown to be beneficial both in treating ulcers and in reducing their incidence among susceptible groups. Whether we can take this further via active preventive programmes remains to be seen.

One problem in establishing a precise link between stress and ulcers is that the whole process of ulceration in the digestive tract is poorly understood. It is not sufficient to suggest that high acid levels alone cause ulceration: there is also the question of why the body's natural defence mechanisms fail to cope. One factor linked with stress-induced ulcer formation is the level of brain noradrenaline. This transmitter is linked with our response to stress. Where noradrenaline levels are low, the individual copes well providing no stress is present. If stress is then added, there is a very high chance of ulcer formation, suggesting noradrenaline plays an important part in our natural ability to resist this type of damage.

The sex hormones may also play a role in inhibiting ulcer formation. The occurrence of both gastric and duodenal ulcers is far more common in men than in women who are within their reproductive life span. Following menopause this difference tends to level out, with ulcerative disease being nearly as common in women of late middle age as it is amongst men. In animal studies, stress-induced ulcers have been significantly reduced by the administration of female sex hormones, despite the fact that the presence of the hormone affected neither the acidity nor the volume of the gastric secretions. This suggests an indirect link, triggered by the the presence of the hormone. One theory is that the presence of the sex hormones in some way influences the integrity of the stomach lining. This would enable the stomach to cope with high levels of acid secretion without physical damage. Another theory is that the hormones in some way act on the stress process itself. If this is correct, it could account for other differences in stress-related disease patterns between men and pre-menopausal women.

Recent research studies have also linked zinc levels with both the incidence and treatment of ulcers. Anti-ulcer therapies involving the administration of zinc solution have been highly effective – at least in the trial phase. Apart from enhancing cell division in the gut itself, zinc would appear to enhance the performance of the mucuous membrane lining the gut. This not only has a secretory role, but plays a crucial part in protecting the body from its own secretions. This is important, because we know that zinc levels are naturally depleted during stress.

Although some still doubt the link between stress and ulcers, the evidence for it is clear. What remains to be isolated is the mechanism by which ulceration takes place: what causes a healthy, functioning gut to become diseased in this way. Most now expect stress and the patient's response to stress to be implicated. From such information we should be able to identify those at risk and introduce anti-ulcer programmes.

Cancer and duodenal and gastric ulcers can be life threatening. Stress is also implicated in disorders which, if not life threatening, can certainly drastically affect the quality of life for the sufferer. In this category are many dermatological [skin] complaints. Statistical surveys suggest that 40 per cent of all skin disorders are precipitated by stress, although many of the clinicians most closely involved think the figure is much higher. In some cases, like neurotic excoriations and dermatitis artifacta, stress alone may be the cause. Other conditions, like simplex chronicus and anogenital pruritis [itching], may be partly organic and partly psychological. Many physicians recognise a third category, where emotional factors are a major perpetuating or precipitating factor. This group include urticaria, acne, rosacea [blushing to excess] and herpes simplex.

While the influence of stress varies widely from disease to disease, so does the mechanism by which the disease creates its effect. Stress is clearly implicated in the type of neurological disorder which gives rise to pruritis, as well as in complaints like urticaria which are vascular in origin. Malfunctions of the sweat and sebaceous glands giving rise to disfiguring conditions like acne and seborrhea, if not actually caused by stress, are known to be exacerbated by its presence. It has also been suggested that stress is implicated in the increased fragility of the small blood vessels, characterised by the unsightly fracturing of capillaries in the surface of the skin. And, of course, fear has an effect on the hair follicles: the characteristic piloerection, which involves tingling of the scalp and the sensation of the hair standing on end.

Skin disorders are often embarrassing and acutely stressful. This creates a spiral where the stress produced by the disease actually makes it worse. This applies even in cases where there is no causative link with stress, such disorders as hirsuitism [excessive hair], port wine stains and some forms of eczema, and here doctors may have to recognise that stress is an added problem for the patient.

One skin disease long associated with stress is psoriasis. which appears typically in late adolescence or early adult life and is characterised by raised reddened skin on the elbows or knees. It is not usually serious, though it is embarrassing and unsightly. The link with stress was made because in many patients psoriasis becomes apparent then clears without treatment, its presence being closely associated with the sufferer's state of health. In fact many clinicians now feel psoriasis is no more sensitive to stressful life events than are many skin diseases, including skin cancers, warts and fungal infections. Again the disease acts in an opportunist fashion, moving in when the body's resistance is lowered by stress. In this respect psoriasis is similar to thrush [candida] which, while often making an appearance in those who are under stress, cannot be said to be caused by stress because it is a fungal infection.

In considering the diseases of stress we have concentrated on those where a fairly direct link can be shown or postulated. In other disorders the link is less direct. As we have already said many stressed individuals overeat, eating in most cases an unbalanced diet. This, often coupled with a lack of exercise, leads to obesity – one of the major causes of disease in our over-indulgent society. The health problems posed by obesity are well-documented and understood, and few can fail to recognise the risks. Obesity leads to heart disease and arterial disorders, including hypertension. This link, particularly pronounced amongst men, seems less damaging in women – certainly during their reproductive life. In women, obesity has been linked with higher than average rates of breast and endometrial cancers, though again we are talking of one of many factors. Obesity is also closely linked with a number of mechanical disorders. In diseases like arthritis, while being overweight does not actually cause the condition, it will certainly make it harder to treat. Higher than average rates of chest disorders, liver dysfunction, gallstones, diabetes and varicose veins add up to a heavy price for over-indulgence.

Diabetes is a common condition which we now know has a definite link with stress. This is important because diabetes can lead to other serious disorders. Recent studies in the US have shown that more than 50 per cent of late onset diabetics suffered major trauma – typically characterised by unresolved grief – in the period immediately prior to their condition developing. Furthermore, stress, particularly acute stress, can exacerbate an existing diabetic condition. By lowering blood glucose – while raising ketone – levels, stress causes exactly the rapid changes in insulin requirements that diabetics are unable to meet. This is dangerous and makes it imperative that diabetics develop skills to handle stress. The alternative is to risk health problems even more damaging than the diabetes itself, particularly cardiovascular complications.

Stress is implicated in many food-related disturbances ranging from extreme over-eating, to anorexia nervosa. Mild stress can be linked with finicky eating or the total loss of appetite. One problem here is again the personal nature of stress, the same stress causing one person to fast and another to eat to excess. Many believe the neurotransmitter noradrenaline could have a role in maintaining appetite. This would explain why many lose interest in food when mildly stressed but overeat when under great stress. This pattern closely parallels noradrenaline levels which are heightened when we are mildly stressed, but quickly become depleted and exhausted.

Whatever the cause, being significantly overweight is unhealthy and – for many – embarrassing. Media images are associated with the slim – or at least the healthily voluptuous. This can lead to false expectations in those whose figures do not match, a state of mind which can lead to withdrawal and depressive illness. The treatment of obesity is not simple: it involves counselling and support, as well as a greater understanding of nutrition.

There are other diseases which, while not caused by stress, are made worse by it – and less responsive to treatment. This category includes backache, headaches (including migraine), and even liver cirrhosis. In these, the psychological connection involving the nerves and hormones mediated through the hypothalamus can make the condition worse in the presence of stress. For managers in industry these links between disease and stress should be of particular concern, as the type of stress encountered at work is generally far more damaging to our health.

Behind all this lies the fundamental concept of homeostasis, the intricate, though not particularly sensitive, mechanism by which the body maintains its biochemical balance. Where it is disrupted by stress, we clearly become more vulnerable both to bodily dysfunction and to bacterial, viral and fungal infections. Furthermore, recent research has suggested that mood can have a direct effect on the immune system: we are more resistant to disease when we are content or tranquil. Implicated in this phenomenon is the natural inhibitor substance GABA, acting through peripheral, rather than central [brain], receptors. This induces a sense of well being which is also associated with reduced cortisol levels. Research on this link between GABA and mood is continuing and looks promising. Two areas which could be affected are the treatment of chronic pain with mood enhancers and the important area of placebo therapy.

Research is also continuing on the variations between patterns of disease in men and women, which form an important base for research into why some groups are more prone to disease than others. One problem is that although epidemiological studies may show up differences, these are of little more than passing interest if we cannot understand their scientific cause. A good deal of current research is being directed at the female sex hormones, not least because some of the most startling differences appear in women of reproductive age. Also under scrutiny in men is the hormone histamine, which could play a major role in ACTH secretion – and hence indirectly in our immune response. In women much attention is concentrating on the hormone prolactin although – yet again – work is in an early stage.

Genetic factors may help to explain why some succumb to disease, whilst others go through life unscathed, though their significance varies widely from disease to disease. In heart disorders for example, genetic factors are of major significance. One suggestion is that stress may trigger a genetic predisposition to a disease. If this is so, it could help us identify which diseases are likely to present themselves when an individual is under stress. A great deal of work remains to be done, although – just as there is no super-race who is immune to stress – it appears also that we cannot inherit a greater tolerance to stress.

If all this research appears rather nebulous, it should be made clear that no-one in this area is researching without a purpose. If we can establish a link between stress and a particular disease, then it gives us a better chance of tackling that condition. Even more important, it gives us a better chance of introducing effective programmes for prevention. As we have indicated, most medical treatment in the West is based upon disease intervention. Only more recently, and indeed more slowly, has the concept of prevention begun to take root. In the West, this attitude is probably best developed in Scandinavia, Finland and the Netherlands where the aim is now to prevent people becoming ill. Such a switch of emphasis has massive implications both in social and economic terms. The pace and nature of modern life suggest that the present epidemic of stress-related disorders will continue to grow. Even the politicians may yet come to recognise that prevention is better than cure. Certainly, for those closest to the subject, prevention is essential; our overstretched health services look unable to cope with any further expansion in the incidence of stress-related disease.

—6—

Stress and cardiovascular disease

The disorder whose link with stress is probably least controversial is heart disease. It is also – perhaps more surprisingly – the one where public acceptance of an association is most clear. In a recent UK survey 55 per cent of those asked listed stress as the major cause of heart attacks, with the next highest option [bad diet] polling only some 24 per cent. In this, public opinion is more correct than it often is on health issues. The link between stress and heart disease has been recognised, though not necessarily quantified and understood, for centuries. Indeed one eminent eighteenth century physician, John Hunter, realising the serious nature of his angina condition wrote, 'My life is in the hands of any rascal who chooses to annoy or tease me.' Hunter was acknowledging that his heart condition could be made drastically worse by stress. Sadly, like many physicians, Hunter failed to heed his own advice, and collapsed and died during a heated argument with a medical colleague.

It would be possible to devote a whole book to the connection between stress and heart disease. While research linking other diseases with stress is often very recent, in heart disease we have a long history of often outstanding research. The fact that many of the earlier studies are still quoted and valid also suggests that in this area we are closer to a complete understanding. In this book, we will concentrate on four main areas of disease where a link

96

with stress appears virtually certain: coronary heart disease, hypertension (elevated blood pressure), atherosclerosis (the thickening of the blood vessels), and thrombosis, the condition where clots appear in arteries and veins, leading possibly to strokes and embolism. This it should be noted is a division of convenience: the topics are not mutually exclusive, and there is a close association between them.

In the case of angina pectoris, from which John Hunter died, there appears no doubt about the link with stress. It is characterised by a violent spasm of pain and tightening in the chest, caused by an inadequate blood supply to the heart. This stems in turn from some disorder in the coronary arteries, the blood vessels which serve the heart. Although the causes may be various, typically the lumen [bore] of the artery becomes narrower, so limiting the flow of blood. As we know, during exercise the heart rate increases and blood pressure and cardiac output are increased. At the same time, some arteries become constricted, so compounding in the healthy individual the benefits of such changes. It is hardly surprising that this natural stress response causes problems for those whose coronary artery volume is already reduced. In such cases, the acute stress is not just damaging, it may be fatal.

Numerous attempts have been made to establish psychological links between heart disease and personality type. In many cases such studies produce only vague results, linking a higher incidence of disease to such unquantifiable factors as 'surface calm', 'striving personality' and 'excessive tension'. While such studies may fulfil the researcher's immediate purpose, they are not really helpful in determining the full nature of the link between stress and heart disease. One of the most important studies in this area, already mentioned in earlier chapters, was conducted by Friedman and Rosenman in the USA, and concerned the incidence of coronary heart disease. It identified a series of [Type A] personality

97

characteristics which were particularly associated with a higher incidence of the disease. These characteristics included:

* increased mental alertness;
* an intense drive to achieve often poorly defined targets. Here for Type As self-imposed goals often set greater problems than those set by others;
* a persistent demand both for recognition and advancement;
* an intense and fierce desire to compete. Many Type A characters compete with themselves if no one else is available;
* an involvement in multiple and diverse functions;
* a constant awareness of time, and the propensity to continually accelerate the carrying out of any physical or mental function.

Although many of these qualities appear desirable, we should consider their effects on our endocrine and nervous systems. As we have shown, the continual triggering of the body's mechanisms for dealing with stress can be harmful – particularly where that triggering is not accompanied by any natural outlet for stress. In fact extreme Type A behaviour can be very damaging, both for the individual concerned and for those around him. Even if Type A characters appear to live with their own idiosyncrasies, they can be a major cause of stress in others. In the Friedman and Rosenman study, Type A behaviour linked to other factors, was shown to result in much higher levels of coronary heart disease. In some cases, when linked with, for example, smoking, it was suggested this could increase the risks seven-fold. Given the basis for such findings, it also seems certain that Type A behaviour must affect the incidence of other stress-related disorders.

The Friedman and Rosenman study was a careful one. It took pains to point out that Type A behaviour was only one of many factors implicated in coronary heart disease. The others, together with some findings stemming from the refining of Friedman and Rosenman's work, include:

* parental history *i.e.* genetic predisposition in fact;
* elevated blood pressure;
* smoking;
* elevated serum cholesterol level;
* obesity;
* choice of marriage partner, with some of the highest risk rates being shown by Type *B* men married to highly educated and successful wives.

Once again coronary heart disease shows significant differences in presentation between men and women, with a far lower occurrence in women of reproductive age. Again the basis of this difference is not clear. It may be the sex hormones, or it may be that women of childbearing age are less aggressive: they certainly show a lower incidence of Type A behaviour. Probably many factors are involved.

Many doctors now believe that stress, particularly occupational stress, is the most important factor in coronary heart disease, and indeed in heart attacks generally. If this is so, then perhaps we should pay more attention to limiting stress, and less to emphasising the importance of factors like obesity and smoking. If by smoking someone lowers their stress level, this could superficially at least, be beneficial. Unfortunately, the other effects of smoking are so devastating on health that no responsible individual could make such a recommendation. Coronary heart disease is typically associated with many factors, and all we can do at present is to crudely seek to limit the effect of *all* of them. Only when we have a better understanding of the link between stress and disease can we assign weightings to the individual elements in the connection.

It is not hard to see why continual and unrelieved stress could impose a strain on the heart. As we have seen, during stress adrenalin levels are raised. This not only causes the heart to quicken and increase output, but also some peripheral blood vessels to contract. This is accompanied by the release of sugar, which is normally stored in the liver in the form of glycogen [starch]. At the same time, adrenalin stimulates those enzyme systems concerned with energy production, whilst inhibiting the antagonistic systems which reduce the level of sugars and fats in the blood. This includes inhibiting the role of insulin, the major hormone by which the body removes sugar from the blood. As the flow of sugar increases, so too does the level of free fatty acids. Under the influence of adrenalin these fatty acids are broken down from complex lipids or glycerol, in which form they can be rapidly metabolised for energy production.

Such a natural response is perfectly structured and designed if the stress with which we are faced is mainly physical. If we are taking part in a sporting event, or being chased by an angry crowd, our response to stress is closely in balance with the nature of the stress. The increased energy precursors, the fats and sugars, will allow both an immediate and violent physical response. They will be quickly assimilated and utilised by the muscle tissue, during which process they will be steadily degraded and reduced to carbon dioxide and water. In terms of damage to our cardiovascular system, much of the trouble comes when we have no physical outlet for stress. In such a situation we see the same rise in the levels of fats and sugars, but no complementary increase in exercise to remove them. This results in the build up in the blood of substances like cholesterol, which have been shown to be highly damaging to the integrity of the body's blood vessels.

Unfortunately much of the stress of modern life has no physical link. If we are driving and involved in a near accident, or inconvenienced by another motorist, we have no physical outlet for the energy precursors which are released. It might be better if we got out and started a fight, though this is unacceptable for other reasons. Similarly at work, if we operate under continual pressure or are the type who makes their own pressure [Type As], then we will live with continually high fat and sugar levels. In the case of the sugars, in the short term this is not a major problem, although in later life such a pattern can lead to problems like diabetes. In the healthy individual, high sugar levels are readily utilised by the body, the potential killers being the fats. These may be converted into a substance called triglyceride in which form they can become deposits in the liver and on arterial walls.

The fatty degeneration of the middle coat of the artery wall is called atherosclerosis. This is one of a group of diseases known collectively as arteriosclerosis in which artery walls become fundamentally changed. This typically includes a hardening and rigidity, accompanied by a reduction in the size of the lumen. The result is a rise in blood pressure – itself potentially damaging. Very closely implicated in the creation of atheromatic plaques, the mechanism by which fat is deposited on the artery wall, is the stress hormone adrenalin. This binds to receptors on the blood platelets [small spherical bodies in the blood involved with clotting]. This binding induces the release of a second messenger hormone which causes the platelets to clump together, in which form they can become deposited on the artery wall or lead to clot formation.

In such a mechanism it is clearly not merely stress which is implicated, but unrelieved stress. If we have a physical element by which we can release stress, then the long-term effects are undoubtedly less damaging. Unfortunately most of us now have sedentary occupations in which the physical release of stress is difficult. Social norms also demand that we do not make a physical response, like fighting or jumping up and down, to express our frustration and irritation. If we turn again to the example of driving, we can see why cab drivers in all countries show a higher than average incidence of cardiovascular disease. Though most seem to develop verbal methods to relieve their frustrations, these are not enough to remove the products of what is an extremely stressful occupation.

Changes in the nature of the peripheral blood vessels are only one cause of hypertension, the commonest cardiovascular disorder in Western society. In the US, more than 10 per cent of the population is believed to suffer from hypertension – much of it untreated. In Western Europe such figures are not readily available, but the World Health Organisation [WHO] estimates the total at not less than 25 million people. One major problem in obtaining precise figures is the changing base of what we define as *high* blood pressure. This was originally considered to be a diastolic [resting pressure between beats] in excess of 100 mm. This was subsequently changed, by WHO, to anything above 95 mm diastolic, with many clinicians recommending and using in therapy an even lower figure of not more than 90 mm.

In general attempts to link stress and hypertension directly have proved equivocal. Although adrenalin induces an immediate, and necessary, rise in blood pressure, this is certainly not the same as a condition where this elevation is sustained. As we have already said, the changes induced by the stress hormones are transient, designed to revert to normal once the initial stress is past. This is part of the process of homeostasis, in which the body processes will always strive to revert to a steady state. Although hypertension and arteriosclerosis often occur together, in the vast majority of cases the real cause of hypertension is never known. Only in some 20 per cent of cases is a pathological cause identified, and then it is invariably one of the more extreme causes, like a renal or vasomotor failure, or some significant malfunction of the endocrine system.

Although no direct link between stress and hypertension has been shown, many clinicians believe one must exist. Certainly we know that a tendency to hypertension is inherited, and that in the offspring of many hypertensives stress will bring about the type of changes in blood flow which are associated with elevated blood pressure. This suggests that it might be stress which triggers an already present genetic predisposition to hypertension. Environmental stress has also been shown to be closely associated with a rise in blood pressure. In the early 1970s, a US study showed significant differences in hypertension rates amongst various income groups, which were most pronounced amongst men aged thirty-five to forty-nine. Here raised blood pressure was three times more common amongst the lowest paid, a group in which many would be raising young children in strained and financially stringent conditions. These, and many other facts, do imply a link between stress and hypertension, and this is now an area of considerable research.

Much current research into hypertension is concentrating on the central [brain] and peripheral neural mechanisms, which might underlie the relationship between stress, genetic factors and raised blood pressure. This is not a simple matter as blood pressure is maintained by a number of related factors. If one of these is disrupted, as by drug therapy, it may lead to a compensatory response from the body, and the continuation of the problem. Various ideas have been put forward linking hypertension and our body's response to stress. These include hyperactivity of the sympathetic–adrenal axis, as well as problems with central adrenergic and cholinergic receptor sites. Some of these systems and pathways were discussed in Chapter 3. As yet no one can show a direct link, and the immense complexity of this area suggests that any precise link may be very difficult to find.

While we struggle to identify the link between stress and hypertension, the risks posed by the disease itself are all too clear. These are widespread and often devastating. They include:

* heart failure, and in particular left ventricular failure, [the left ventricle is the heart's most muscular chamber, responsible for maintaining the peripheral circulation];
* arteriosclerosis and atherosclerosis;
* kidney failure;
* strokes;
* eye damage – typically causing the rupture of small blood vessels.

Particularly damaging is the link between high blood pressure and atherosclerosis. Hypertension can lead to an increase in atheromatic plaque in arteries, giving a downward spiral in which blood pressure rises steadily against an increase in peripheral resistance. In the end something must give, typically either the wall of the blood vessel or the heart itself.

Although in most cases the cause of hypertension is unknown, a number of high risk factors have been identified. These often relate closely to those identified with stress disease. They include age, lack of exercise, alcohol abuse, smoking and being overweight. Again in the absence of any real understanding, all modern medical treatment seems able to do is to seek to reduce these high risk factors, and treat the underlying condition with drugs. In fact many clinicians believe that, because of the potentially damaging nature of the condition, we often resort far too quickly to drug therapy in hypertension. Certainly many cases of mild hypertension seem more suited to changes in diet, weight, exercise patterns and salt intake than to a virtually permanent regimen of anti-hypertensive drugs.

One problem with hypertension is that in the early stages the condition is asymptomatic. The patient does not feel ill, and the idea that raised blood pressure causes headaches or giddiness is certainly not true in most patients. Given this there is considerable resistance to drug therapy, which may appear long-term or even permanent. Blood pressure drugs also cause side-effects and in many cases make the patient feel worse than the condition itself. For this reason, the treatment of blood pressure may involve the clinician experimenting with several drugs before one suited to the patient is found. We have a wide range of anti-hypertensive drugs, and these differ very widely in their manner of operation. Most act upon one or more of the elements which go to maintain our blood pressure, and the drugs involved include diuretics, beta-blockers, vasodilators, angiotensin agents and calcium antagonists.

In addition to hypertension, stress is also implicated in the condition known as coronary spasm, an important factor both in angina and infarction [heart attacks]. This spasm, which involves a sudden, involuntary and acutely painful contraction, has been linked with both psychological and physiological stress. In its early stages coronary spasm is reversible, as is seen in angina. If the spasm persists, however, the condition becomes far more serious and life threatening, with thrombosis eventually occurring and grossly reducing the blood flow to the heart.

Although coronary spasm is thought to be important in angina and heart attacks, its precise mechanism is not clear. The presence of large numbers of adrenergic receptors in the coronary arteries themselves suggests it could be mediated by the sympathetic nervous system. If this is so, not only could the condition be made worse by the patient's own response to pain, but it would give a mechanism by which our response to stress could be involved.

A review of heart attack patients shows a close correlation between coronary spasm and the existence of coronary thrombosis. Many now believe that the thrombosis may be secondary, with the balance between death or damage to the heart muscle depending on the extent to which the spasm reduces blood flow. One reason why this theory is not more widely accepted, is doubt as to whether spasm alone would induce a coronary occlusion severe enough to totally block the blood's passage. If it could, then this might explain why someone is said to die of fright or fear. Vasospasm itself is now a recognised condition, which also has major implications in other disorders. Migraine results from constriction and spasm in small arteries in the brain. This is known to be a stress-related condition, suggesting perhaps a wider link between stress and spasm-based disorders.

As we have seen, some of the hormones associated with stress are directly linked with the degenerative damage to the vascular system seen in atherosclerosis. This is not the total picture. During the initial alarm stages of the stress response we know the clotting ability of the blood is enhanced, and the level of serum fibrinogen is significantly raised. This is part of the body's natural response to potential damage. If no such damage occurs, and the stress response is maintained then the blood circulating has a far higher clotting capability than normal. This is dangerous, especially where the blood vessels are already reduced by the presence of atheromatous tissue. The result can be a total thrombosis or stroke, which can be severely damaging – or fatal.

The ability of the cardiovascular system to cope with stress appears to be linked to various structural and functional properties of the system itself. Clearly these vary among individuals. Where a genetic disorder is already present, or there is a predisposition to a particular disease, then it seems likely that this will be heightened by the presence of stress. The ability of the cardiovascular system to adapt to stress also declines with age. Although this is a natural part of ageing, it can can accelerate in the presence of disease – or an erratic life-style.

The changes in the stress response of the elderly are now the subject of considerable research, and from this could come a better understanding of our whole response to stress. As we get older maximum cardiac output and oxygen consumption during exercise both decline significantly. Part of this decline could be due to inactivity and a reduced level of exercise, though some is undoubtedly due to the long-term metabolic changes associated with ageing. Such changes do not appear to relate to reduced levels of adrenalin or noradrenalin in the elderly. Rather is it suggested that there are changes in the sensitivity of the adrenergic receptors, resulting in lower post-synaptic adrenergic activity. This implies a reduced ability of the receiving cell to pass on the stimulus, a fact which has major implications for the basis of nerve transmission in the elderly.

In the UK, a poor response and bodily adjustment to stress, have been linked to higher than average cardiovascular disease levels amongst older executives. This is particularly associated with those who manage staff, as distinct from finance or inanimate 'things' like computer hardware or production lines. In these ageing executives a number of factors were linked with the high incidence of heart disease. They included:

* recognition that further advancement was unlikely;
* impending retirement;
* isolation and a narrowing of interest. This was often caused by the inability of such staff to relate to the younger staff they were supervising.

While such apparent links should be treated with care, because other factors like high smoking levels may intrude, they do imply an added risk for older management staff. Clearly if our bodies adapt less well to stress, then the risks we face become heightened.

The UK study also supports the idea that psychological stressors may be far more damaging biochemically than those caused by physical pressures. Certainly amongst the elderly staff, most of the pressures were largely emotional or psychological. They may also have appeared endless and inescapable. This relates again to the concept of learned helplessness, so damaging in animals. In one oft-quoted series of animal experiments using monkeys, painful external stimuli in the form of a brief electric shock were used to evoke a response. Of the group of animals half were able to avoid the shock if they pulled a lever, whilst the other half could do nothing, receiving a shock unless the lever was pulled by an animal in the other group. In physical terms the stress was identical, but biochemically it was far more damaging in the group which could do nothing about it.

Although many may not approve of such experiments, this one does at least serve a purpose. It suggests, if nothing else, that we should avoid situations where we cannot influence our circumstances. This may be particularly important as we get older. An extension of this is the idea that we should stop worrying about those things we can do nothing about, and concentrate on those where our actions can have an influence. To some the world may appear a terrible place, but at a global level we can do very little about it. If we continually fret and worry, then all we do is build up a level of frustration and helplessness which as we have seen can be extremely damaging.

Despite the apparent scale of the problem, it is clear that a great deal can be done to reduce the incidence of cardiovascular disease – and particularly coronary heart disease. This has already been shown in the US where preventive programmes, many of them introduced in the 1940s, have succeeded in significantly reducing the level of heart disease. Unfortunately, such a trend has no parallel in Europe where clinicians have emphasised improvements in clinical cardiology, rather than seeking a better understanding of the environmental, behavioural, genetic and biological basis of these diseases. As a result, when WHO reported in 1981 on coronary heart disease trends in Western Europe, it found only three countries [Belgium, Finland and Norway] where the level was declining. In the remaining countries it was either static or showing a worrying move upwards.

The US success in reducing the level of coronary heart disease is not merely based on a better understanding by the clinicians. This has been more than matched by the population's willingness to take part in preventive programmes. These include an increase in exercise, not least with jogging, plus major changes in diet and life style. By far the most important change in diet is a significant reduction in animal fats, which leads to a drop in serum cholesterol levels, and in salt – important in controlling high blood pressure. Those groups interested in maintaining their health are also regulating their use of alcohol. While alcohol *abuse* remains a serious and growing problem in much of the US, there is no doubt that some cardiac conditions benefit from a sensible use of alcohol. Alcohol serves, amongst other things, to dilate peripheral blood vessels and enhance blood flow in the tissues. A lower use of tobacco is another highly effective element in the reduction of coronary disease levels in the US.

Quite why this US pattern has not been followed in Europe is unclear. With its heavy emphasis on individual participation and low costs, such a programme should be attractive to European health authorities. Unfortunately in much of Europe, preventive health programmes are too poorly developed to benefit even from such clear cut results. At an individual level, most Europeans are also far less health-conscious than their American cousins. Fewer health advice magazines are published in Europe, and there often seems to be a general lack of interest in diet and exercise. This, coupled with an affluent and often pressurised life style, is clearly disastrous. Whatever the US experience shows, it is evident that without widespread public support and involvement any health prevention programme directed at the cardiovascular area must be of limited effect.

Although limiting the effects of stress may play a role in reducing heart disease, it is clear that there are many other causes. Stress may be merely the concluding factor, the final straw which tips the balance between good health and disease. This would seem to be confirmed by a UK study which showed that widowers over fifty-five had a 40 per cent increase in death rate in the six months following bereavement. In this group arteriosclerotic and degenerative heart disease showed a massive 67 per cent rise above normal levels. Although such a trend is clearly irreversible for those who suffer major problems, like a stroke or heart attack, the same study offered hope for those who survived beyond six months. Here death and disease rates returned to normal over the next eight years. Whether this implies a reversal of the damage caused by stress, or that bereavement wipes out primarily the weakest with an already existing predisposition to disease, is not clear.

The extent to which stress induced damage is reversible is clearly important, but is an area about which we know relatively little. While we know the incidence of coronary artery disease is higher in urban areas, and increases steadily as an area is urbanised, little research appears to have been done to see if the reverse is true. We do not know if the effects of a lifetime of city stress can be reversed by moving to the peace of the country. What we do know appears hopeful, although this is obviously a very personal matter. If we seek the quiet of the country but desperately miss the hustle and bustle of the city, then we are more likely to do harm than good. When Byron identified Napoleon's unrest as stemming from the fact that 'quiet to quick bosoms is a hell', he could have been describing the effect the move away from the city has for many of us.

Uncertain too, is whether extreme Type A personalities can modify their behaviour to become less damaging both to themselves and those around them. This looks unlikely. Few things are more damaging in terms of stress than repression. If a Type A personality goes through life suppressing his natural emotions, this will almost certainly be damaging. All we can do is recognise that heart disease has a number of causes, and seek to limit the influence of those over which we have some control. Thus a Type A personality who is overweight, smokes, drinks to excess and has a stressful job is far more at risk than someone who is just a Type A personality.

At the beginning of this chapter we said that a great deal was known about the link between stress and cardiovascular disease. Much more still remains to be isolated. Similarly, although epidemiological studies may show strong links between heart disease and stress factors, these links are often poorly understood in biochemical terms. Thus we may understand the implications of certain biochemical changes, but tracing these through and quantifying them in terms of disease may be more difficult. In Europe, the steady rise in cardiovascular disease continues unabated. It is a major waste of health, and indeed life, amongst the comparatively young that cardiovascular disorders are appearing at a steadily earlier age. Clearly it is essential that we halt, or better still, reverse this unhappy trend.

In current research on stress and heart disease, there are

three main areas in which developments are vital. These are:

* what is the interaction between the individual and proven heart disease factors, and is it possible to assign a weighting to the individual factors?
* what physical and psychological mechanisms are implicated in linking stress and cardiovascular disease?
* what are the personal and individual factors which determine why one person gets one disease, whilst another subjected to similar stress escapes entirely or suffers an unrelated condition?

On the answers to these questions may depend how we treat, and more importantly prevent, both cardiovascular disease and other stress related disorders. Such answers are also crucial because our stretched health services cannot cope with the current massive explosion in degenerative cardiovascular disease.

—7—

Stress and mental disorder

We have now examined the link between stress and physical disease. Even where such a link is widely accepted, the manner in which stress causes and exacerbates disease is often far from clear. With psychiatric disease this is even harder to define. Few now challenge the link between stress and mental disorder, though it is extremely hard both to isolate and quantify. Thus a psychiatric condition may have its origins in some adverse experience in childhood, but its occurrence may be manifested by a disturbance in the metabolism maintaining the equilibrium of the brain neurochemicals. As the neurochemicals mediate the nerve actions responsible for perception, muscular [motor] activity and behaviour, it is hardly surprising that their disruption is implicated in psychiatric illness. The fact that some neurotransmitters, like serotonin, have an effect on all the areas mentioned shows how widespread and fundamental any disruption is likely to prove.

As we have already shown stress affects the equilibrium of the neurochemicals in the brain. With the exception of pain or injury, such changes are typically short-lived, and the body reverts quickly to a steady and balanced state. If an existing abnormality or imbalance is already present, however, then the effects of any disruption caused by stress are far less predictable. In such conditions, stress can act as a very dangerous trigger. It can precipitate the symptoms associated with episodic psychiatric disease, and certainly change a controlled situation into one which is far more difficult to handle. The examination of the link between stress and mental disease presents particular problems. Though recent years have seen a massive increase in our understanding of the brain and its chemistry, there are still a great many gaps. In many ways our understanding of brain biochemistry can be regarded as a jigsaw in which some of the pieces are in place, some are waiting to be placed, and some are not even available. Similarly, although much of our knowledge of the brain comes from a close study of its diseases and malfunctions, we have at best a poor understanding of the links between the structure, chemistry and disorders of the brain. If, from this unsatisfactory base we seek to study the effects of stress, we are faced with even more problems. Our biochemical response to stress is not framed in the action of any one substance – be it a neurotransmitter, hormone or neuromodulator. These operate essentially in balance with stress, serving temporarily to disrupt that balance. It is virtually impossible to examine one neurotranmitter in isolation, as depleting one will almost certainly have complementary effects on the others. Neither here does the fundamental process of homeostasis help: the body will always strive to revert to a balanced state.

Neurotransmitters are simple substances or proteins, although their release may govern a range of complex functions. In some cases these varying functions may confuse or conceal the role a transmitter has in inducing mental or behavioural change. Thus if a transmitter has sensory, motor and behavioural functions, we must isolate each before we can assign the role the transmitter is playing in any disease or disorder. Neither, it must be clear, is our understanding of brain neurochemistry complete. More neurotransmitters are being discovered all the time, and it will be many years before we approach a full understanding of brain biochemistry. It is already evident, however, that many neurotransmitters closely linked with our response to stress also perform other functions. Both ACTH and noradrenalin are closely associated with learning, alertness and concentration and, though vital, their involvement in our response to stress may be regarded as secondary. It is not surprising that where the level or balance of such substances is disrupted, behavioural change may be exaggerated.

The mode of action of neurotransmitters and neuromodulators also presents problems for researchers. These may act on more than one receptor and significantly overlap in activity. In such a case, we must decide if a particular substance is implicated in a disorder, or something very closely associated with it. The problem may also lie not with the substance itself, but with the receptor on which it is designed to act. GABA is the commonest inhibitor in the human brain. It has been linked with a number of mental disorders though as with any inhibitory substance, we have a classic chicken and egg situation. In any study of GABA, we have to determine whether it is the GABA itself which is at fault, the receptor on which it is designed to act, or the neurotransmitter whose action it is moderating. Such a series of complex and interactive problems are not uncommon in the study of brain biochemistry.

Neurotransmitters are also present in the brain in minute quantities. This presents its own difficulties, because although fluctuations in neurotransmitters may manifest themselves in major changes in the body's hormone balance, the variations in neurotransmitter levels themselves may be minute. Neurotransmitter substances are also very short lived, and far shorter lived than the hormones which their release may induce. All this, coupled with the body's natural ability to adjust its balance via a series of complex failsafe mechanisms, adds up to major problems for the research scientist. Despite this a great many mental disorders have

been justifiably closely associated with stress. As our understanding of the brain and its pathways grows, it seems that
many more will be shown either to have their origins in our
response to stress, or at least to be made much worse by its
presence.

For most people, the mental disease most readily associated with stress is depression or, as it was once called
melancholia, a disorder characterised by severe bouts of
unrelieved gloom and despair, often apparently unrelated
to any external event. This is a far more common condition
than many realise, statistics suggesting that around 8 per
cent of women and 4 per cent of men suffer depression at
some point in their lives. In most cases, up to 75 per cent,
the disease is mild and largely self-limiting. Only in the
remaining 25% of cases, still a massive patient group, is
there any need for medical intervention.

In clinical practice, it is common to divide depression into
an endogenous and exogenous form. Endogenous depression
is generally defined as an illness with no clearly identifiable
external cause. It is also sometimes referred to as biochemical
depression, which merely serves to confuse the issue, as all
forms of depression appear essentially biochemical in origin.
In contrast, exogenous depression is usually closely associated with a particular event, a bereavement, divorce, job
loss, etc. In either case, let us be clear from the start, all
forms of depression have a close association with stress.

The division into exogenous and endogenous forms of
depression has come increasingly under challenge of late,
with many practitioners claiming it does not really exist.
Certainly it is often complex to enforce, not least because
many depression symptoms may appear remote in time from
the events which caused them, for example in the case of
many women who cope well with the terminal illness and
death of a close relative but suffer depression, not immediately after bereavement, but six or twelve months later.

While the distinction between endogenous and exogenous depression may have implications for therapy, and indeed the patient's long-term recovery, for this book it is of relatively little significance.

It is now widely accepted that depression is caused by the malfunction of one or more of the neurotransmitters in the limbic portion of the brain. Many possible candidates have been put forward, with most modern attention concentrating on noradrenalin and serotonin. As we have already said, these substances are linked with mood, drive and motivation, and have been shown to be severely disrupted in depressed patients. The exact connection between these neurotransmitters and depression is far from clear. Many researchers believe that other neurotransmitters may also be involved. In part this new approach comes from the fact that recent research has challenged the whole role of noradrenalin in the brain. Until now it has been considered as a largely inhibitory neurotransmitter, operating in subcortical regions of the brain like the hippocampus – which is primarily concerned with reasoning. If, as many suspect, noradrenalin has a much wider function, then it could well have major implications for our understanding of depression.

Depression is also associated with high levels of cortisol and free fatty acids in the blood. Both these substances are closely linked with the release of ACTH and the body's response to stress. Whether cortisol plays a wider role in depression, or is just there as part of the body's natural response to stress, is not clear. Cortisol is well down the chain of events which frames our response to stress, and could be present merely because of changes higher in the sequence. Certainly most modern depression research appears to be concentrating on the role of noradrenalin and serotonin, any study of cortisol being largely incidental.

Whatever the precise nature of the serotonin and noradrenalin dysfunction in depression, a great deal of our current therapy is based upon the assumption that one or other of these neurotransmitters is deficient. Where this is noradrenalin, as shown by low levels of its breakdown products in the urine, treatment involves giving the patient imipramine or desipramine, which mimic the action of noradrenalin. Similarly where serotonin deficiency is considered to be the cause of depression, treatment involves the administration of amitripytline, which follows the same biochemical pathways as serotonin. In fact for most depressives such an exact division is not necessary, as in around 70 per cent of clinical cases patients respond equally well to either treatment. This suggests that the neurochemical profile on which such therapy is based is not as clear cut as our theoretical understanding of the condition might suggest.

It is not merely the level of serotonin and noradrenalin which is important, but also the sensitivity of the receptor sites upon which they act. It is indicative of the complex nature of the brain pathways that receptors which are both under-sensitive and over-sensitive have been linked to depression. For most patients both conditions can be normalised fairly readily during therapy. One feature of both the neuroendocrine and the psychological aspects of depression is the inability of physiological systems to cope with external changes and pressures. This clearly establishes a very strong link with stress, suggesting that even if stress is not the primary cause of depression, it will serve to make the condition worse. For this reason most therapy, whether it involves counselling or drug treatments, shows a heavy emphasis on returning these central transmitter functions to normal.

One classic problem associated with the drug therapies used in treating depression is the time lag before they begin to take effect. This varies from patient to patient but is typically around two weeks. With a condition like depression such a delay is important. Patients are accustomed to experiencing an immediate response to treatment and if this is not forthcoming may discontinue therapy. In the case of depression this can be serious – with earlier treatment typically bringing far faster results. Many causes have been put forward for this delay, although none appear entirely satisfactory. The initial reason suggested was that the drug needed time to reach a steady state concentration in the limbic regions of the brain. Although this may be true, it is not a sufficient explanation, and a number of other factors have been put forward, including:

* the chronic nature of the illness. In general terms the longer the patient has suffered from depression, then the longer it will take for the condition to respond to treatment;
* personality traits may influence the patient's response to therapy. This particularly applies if a patient is delusional, hysterical, neurotic – or a hypochondriac. All these conditions typically slow a patient's response to therapy;
* pharmogenetic factors, the patient's biochemical response to the drug itself. This may result in the metabolic breakdown or excretion of too much or too little antidepressant, resulting in the need for the clinician to adjust the dosage level.

While the results of these differences can be demonstrated statistically, their biochemical basis is poorly understood.

In many ways our understanding of depression is still limited. We know little about what triggers the condition, or why one individual will respond in this way, while another does not. Depression has been linked to excessive anxiety, although anxiety itself is certainly not a cause of depression.

This is shown by the fact that the benzodiazepine drugs have little effect in treating depression, and may actually make it worse. These drugs form the tranquilliser group which includes Valium [diazepam], and in function mimic the action of GABA by competing for the same receptor sites.

Certain forms of stress have become closely associated with depression, particularly endogenous depression. These include physical stress such as viral infections, pre-menstrual tension and crash dieting, as well as what might be termed pharmacological causes, such as the ingestion of depressive substances including alcohol (a surprise perhaps to some), oral contraceptives, barbiturates and some anti-hypertensive agents like reserpine. To this we must clearly add the psychological or emotional stressors, for example bereavement, changing job, moving house and unemployment.

Recent research has suggested that the brain may contain an 'anxiety peptide' which is linked with our response both to anxiety and depression. Much of this thinking appears to stem from a closer examination of the role of GABA – the brain's commonest inhibitory substance. GABA, when present, has a tranquillising effect not unlike the tranquillising drugs used in modern therapy. The link between GABA and drugs like Valium is emphasised by the fact that both operate on the same receptors, and GABA can be substituted or displaced by many modern tranquillisers. GABA receptors have also been shown to decrease in times of stress, suggesting a link with both depression and anxiety. The anxiety peptide for which many researchers are now searching is a GABA antagonist which acts like the drug beta-carboline. Secretion of this substance, it is postulated, would serve to limit GABA's tranquillising effect. The precise role of any naturally occurring equivalent substance to beta-carboline is not yet clear, and its isolation could be several years away. If it is a peptide closely associated with anxiety, and thus indirectly with depression, then it will be another link in the chain which surrounds our understanding of this complex disorder.

Many of the core symptoms of depression are all too familiar. Although depression takes many forms, the typical depressive sleeps badly, wakes early and suffers a deep morning gloom which lifts only slowly as the day progresses. Also affected, almost certainly, will be the patient's drive, appetite, weight and libido, while many depressives also suffer from vague, ill-defined conditions like dizziness and palpitations. Modern therapy claims to help over 90 per cent of sufferers, although many clinicians believe that depression is always likely to recur. This is an important fact for those deploying staff. Changing job and moving house are often strongly implicated as a cause of depression: this might well be taken into consideration in transferring or promoting those with a history of depressive illness.

Classic anti-depression therapy is heavily based upon a group of drugs called the tricyclics. Some of these, like imipramine and desipramine, have already been mentioned. They have a long history of use, and are generally very effective in the treatment of the condition. Their main problems lie in a series of side-effects, typically more pronounced in the elderly, including dry mouth, tremors, sweating and constipation. More serious, though far rarer, are jaundice (and a general reduction in liver function), hypomania (a mild form of manic excitement), convulsions and hypotension (low blood pressure). Tricyclics are not believed to be addictive in the strict sense of inducing either psychological or physical dependence. The manufacturers do acknowledge, however, that withdrawal symptoms may be experienced by those who discontinue treatment.

Much of the drive to create new anti-depressant drugs is due to concern over these side-effects. Because of the nature of the condition, many patients can expect to be on anti-depressant therapy for a long time, and therefore even the less severe side-effects can seriously affect their quality of life. Although we now have a large number of new anti-depressant drugs, there is little evidence that these are significantly better at treating depression than many of the longer standing chemical agents. Where they do offer advantages, these tend to lie in their very low level of serious side-effects.

The breakdown of the newer anti-depressant drugs shows how intrinsically linked to treatment is our understanding of brain neurochemistry. In simplified terms, some of these new anti-depressants show a breakdown into three main categories:

1. Drugs facilitating the noradrenergic system:
   [a] by inhibiting the re-uptake of noradrenalin at the synapse so indirectly enhancing the effect of nor-adrenalin;
   [b] by facilitating noradrenalin release;
   [c] monoamine oxidase inhibitors;
2. Drugs facilitating the serotoninergic system:
   [a] by inhibiting serotonin re-uptake at the synapse;
   [b] by acting as a partial serotonin argonist;
3. Drugs which act by blocking dopaminergic receptors.

Many of these drugs clearly seek a high degree of neuro-transmitter specificity. As we progress to a greater under-standing of the biochemical base of depression, this quest for drugs exercising a highly specific action will undoubtedly continue.

Depression can be a devastating disorder, with major effects on performance and attitude at work, and even greater impact on home life and relationships. This means the depressed person can become a major source of stress for others, at home and in the work-place. This is unfortunate because above everything he needs both the support of colleagues and a stable home life. Depression is associated with other disorders, and it is estimated that at least 25 per cent of cancer sufferers experience depression serious enough to merit psychiatric intervention. This is an important link. When we suffer stress, and ACTH levels are high, we are more susceptible to pain and may require higher doses of drugs like morphine. Depression and pain, itself a powerful stressor, are often very closely associated. This makes the depressed patient more difficult to treat for pain relief, an important factor in much cancer therapy.

In addition to depression, the presence of stress is associated with a wide range of psychoneurotic and psychotic illness. Severe stress often precedes such conditions, and may serve to precipitate disorders which are largely quiescent. Many clinicians believe that stress may also render some individuals more susceptible to psychiatric disease, and aggravate and perpetuate conditions which are already present. In broad terms we know a good deal about the psychiatric patient's response to stress. We know that, in general, the greater a person's hereditary predisposition to psychiatric illness, the lower the stress level needed to precipitate problems. While we can identify some of the psychological factors which lead to mental disorder, we are still unable to rank them in any order of importance. We are also unaware of the extent to which such factors act singly, or combine to cause illness. This is almost certainly an intensely individual matter and far more research is needed. Unfortunately the preoccupation, both in the US and Europe, with discharging the sick and inadequate from our mental institutions will not help progress. Modern brain research offers real hope for the better diagnosis and treatment of psychiatric illness; it would be a pity if false economic priorities limited our ability to treat some of the saddest diseases in our society.

The link between psychiatric illness and the rising stress levels in our society may lie behind the increased suicide rates in the West. In one recent study in the UK, suicide rates were shown to have risen 21 per cent in males and 12 per cent in females between 1975 and 1980. The highest rise of all, a massive 36 per cent, was seen in men between the ages of thirty-five and forty-four. As this is the age group concerned with, for example, adolescent children, plateauing career patterns and a general mid-life depression, such figures may well be connected with stress. Evidence suggests that the UK pattern is mirrored by similarly increased suicide rates in most Western societies. In the UK this survey pre-dates the current high levels of unemployment, which could bring a further significant rise to what has already been described as a problem of epidemic proportions.

One of the most tragic of mental disorders associated with stress has been touched upon in an earlier chapter. Anorexia nervosa, a disease which attacks primarily the young, is far more common in Western society than many first thought. Unfortunately many parents are still unaware of how common anorexia is, and so fail to identify early changes in eating patterns in their offspring. The precise origins of anorexia are still far from clear. The disease appears to be caused by some dysfunction of the endocrine system, particularly in the hypothalamus. What is certain is that anorexia has a strong psychological link, and is exacerbated by stress. Much modern anorexia therapy involves the use of anti-depressant drugs linked with psychiatric support and nutritional rehabilitation.

Stress is also linked as a trigger in schizophrenia. This disease is characterised by disruption of the patient's thinking and behavioural processes, and in severe conditions may involve a progressive withdrawal from the real world leading to delusions and fantasies. Schizophrenia, in its milder form, is fairly common probably affecting about 1 per cent of the population. Its precise cause is unknown, but has been linked to hyperactivity in the dopamine system of the brain. This typically only affects one side of the brain, with the occurrence of dopamine receptors being more than 70 per cent higher in the left side of the brain of schizophrenics. Our modern understanding of brain chemistry has largely revolutionised thinking on schizophrenia over the last ten years. Once regarded as a disease of the mind, schizophrenia is now known to be a condition with a definite – even if poorly understood – organic base.

Although dopamine malfunction is clearly implicated in schizophrenia, other neurotransmitters also appear to play a role. One of these is noradrenalin, which is involved in discriminating signals in a part of the brain called the locus caerulus. Noradrenalin receptors are often far-reaching in action, with noradrenalin serving to mediate the outcome of other brain neurotransmitters. Clearly if noradrenalin fails to perform this function in the presence of excessive dopamine release, then it is indirectly implicated in any disorder which stems from high dopamine levels. The noradrenalin response to stress may also indicate why schizophrenia is adversely influenced by the presence of stress. In mild stress noradrenalin levels rise, but the substance is quickly depleted and disappears if the stress is sustained.

Recent research has also linked schizophrenia with gamma-endorphin, a metabolic product of beta-endorphin. Quite what role this may play is not established, although some researchers believe that the endorphins may help in limiting the effect of excess dopamine. Other researchers claim that brain peptides like somatostatin and cholecysto-kinin also play a part in schizophrenia. Most modern schizophrenia treatment is based upon drugs which block the dopamine receptors. These are effective, although a better understanding of the neurochemical base of schizophrenia may enable us to design drugs which are even more specific in their action.

Stress is associated with a number of specific psychiatric conditions, and with behavioural changes which can be linked with other mental conditions such as dominant behaviour and aggression. In animal studies high levels of serotonin have been linked with dominant behaviour, and it appears that a similar pattern exists in man. This dominant behaviour can easily translate into aggression, with some animals showing their most fiercely aggressive behaviour in the presence of high levels of serotonin. Although the evidence is somewhat ambiguous, most researchers now believe that serotonin levels rise significantly when we are stressed. If this is so, it could establish a biochemical link between stress and much of the aggression and violence which exists in our society. Whether or not such views are valid, a more cautious conclusion suggests that stress would certainly trigger aggression in an individual with an existing condition which gives a predisposition to violence.

Malfunction of serotonin transmission in the pineal can also give rise to other problems. Acetyl transferase is the enzyme which controls the translation of serotonin into melatonin. If this is disrupted, as it can be by severe emotional stress, then the individual is denied sleep. Even more important is the fact that melatonin has a secondary tranquillising effect which can be crucial in a patient who is disturbed. We are close here to a self-perpetuating cycle, in which serotonin is also involved in stimulating the release of ACTH. This would not only deny the disturbed patient sleep and tranquillity, but could also result in bouts of extreme hyperactivity – and even violence.

Also implicated in much psychiatric disorder is the relative concentration of certain bulk and trace elements including calcium, magnesium, zinc and copper – all of which have been shown to be abnormal in certain psychiatric conditions.

Post mortem analysis of the brains of schizophrenics shows abnormally high copper levels but significantly low levels of zinc. The implications of this are not clear, although some clinics report good success rates when treating schizophrenics with a range of minerals and vitamins. One suggestion is that zinc is responsible for the storage of certain neurotransmitters, a function which clearly cannot be realised when zinc levels are low. If this is so, then zinc and other mineral deficiencies could lie behind many psychiatric disorders. This is an area where more research is urgently needed.

As we strive to understand better the biochemical base of mental disorder, and so frame better support and therapy, the costs to society and the individual are clear. Psychiatric disease attacks one in six in industrialised Western societies. Even if we ignore the personal costs and suffering, then the cost to our overworked health services is massive, and becoming close to unbearable. If we are concerned about the level of crime, then we should be aware that a great deal is committed by the mentally ill and the inadequate. Many of those in prison are more sick than villainous, a fact readily acknowledged by those running penal institutions. Whilst modern technology has done much to improve the diagnosis and treatment of psychiatric illness, it has done little to help us frame preventive programmes. If stress is at the base of much mental disease, either as a cause or a catalyst, then stress prevention and control programmes could be vital.

Although mental disorder is common, it is not well understood by the public. Many people have a stereotyped image of the mentally sick which is far from the truth. The close, and usually incorrect, link between psychiatric illness and violence in the mind of the public is in part to blame. Although the cinema, books and magazines might suggest otherwise, the average mentally ill patient is not at all like the poor unfortunate played by Anthony Perkins in *Psycho*.

It is strange that as public interest in health grows, this does not generally extend to mental disorder. This remains a taboo area, allowing film producers and others freedom to create the bizarre and the exaggerated.

At a different level, we also make demands on people without necessarily recognising the fragility of their psychiatric condition. We often hear surprise expressed that it is the most calm and stable amongst us who suffer breakdowns. What we have failed to see is that outer calm is a shell, purchased by suppressing the emotions. For many – if not all – this type of repression is acutely damaging. In statistical surveys, Latin races show a lower incidence of stress-related psychiatric disease. It is hard not to relate this to their volatile emotions, and to their willingness to give them free rein. The fact that such behaviour is accepted by Latin societies as normal is also important, allowing an outlet for stress which is both effective and unremarkable.

While some of the problems which face the mentally ill are caused by ignorance and thoughtlessness, still more are caused by outright hypocrisy. While society may adopt a sympathetic attitude to the physically ill, this often does not extend to those with psychiatric conditions. This applies even in those societies, like the US, where psychiatric illness is best recognised and treated. The US has a host of medical practitioners specialising in the treatment of mental disease – including some 30,000 plus psychiatrists alone. This gives the highest per capita density in the world. Indeed, for many US citizens, having their own psychoanalyst has become a status symbol. This should have helped temper public attitudes, but this is clearly not the case. In recent years, at least one Presidential candidate's running mate has had to stand down once a history of minor psychiatric disorder was disclosed.

Such discrimination is based on the idea that once a person has suffered some form of psychiatric disorder, there is always the chance of a recurrence. If an employee has a major physical breakdown, like a coronary, then most companies will make allowances. If this involves a reduced regimen to avoid a recurrence, then this is accepted and understood, but often the same degree of consideration is not found for those who suffer nervous breakdowns. This is particularly unfortunate given the close link between stress and mental disease, and the need of such patients for support and understanding. By denying them the chance of rehabilitation, we are affecting not only their life and employment, but also their chance of a full recovery.

As research into brain biochemistry progresses, it is becoming evident that the link between stress and psychiatric disorder is far more important and fundamental than many researchers had anticipated. Many of the hormones and transmitters most closely associated with our response to stress are also implicated in some of the severest mental disorders. It is hardly surprising then that stress can both cause psychiatric disease and make it worse. Furthermore, because of the intermittent and episodic nature of stress, it can also make the condition far harder to treat.

Later we will consider some of the drugs used in treating both mental disorder and other stress-related conditions. Suffice it to say here that we are too prepared to resort to drugs to cushion us from some of the emotional problems we face. For some – if not many – this causes its own mental difficulties. The body is designed to cope with both physical and mental stress, and though we may need support in times of crisis, like bereavement or job loss, we should not use chemical agents all the time. The widespread use and abuse of tranquillisers is to be deplored: we have no God-given right to tranquillity, and this remote and fragile dream is least likely to be found at the bottom of a pill bottle.

—8—

Stress and substance abuse

The next three chapters deal with the undoubted link between stress and substance abuse. If the inclusion of alcohol and tobacco with other drugs is uncomfortable for some, we make no apologies. All these 'drugs of solace' are similar in action, if not in the minds of their users. That some substances have gained social, and more importantly economic, acceptance is largely irrelevant to our review. All are chemical props which provide a short-term solution for which we must ultimately pay. We may temporarily defer payment, by constantly topping up with our chosen poison, but eventually the body demands payment either in the agony of withdrawal, or in the more sinister intrusion of disease or death.

In considering substance abuse, we have opted to start with drugs. This choice requires some explanation; in North America and Europe drugs cause less death and disease than either tobacco or alcohol. Nevertheless, drug abuse is far more feared by the public. Familiarity and ignorance are in part to blame, but so is the level of social acceptance which, until recently, surrounded tobacco and alcohol.

The media help to frame our image of the typical addict. In the case of tobacco the images have tended to be positive, tobacco being associated (falsely) with masculinity and independence as in the Marlborough series of advertisements. The stereotype of the drunk is based on the idea that heavy drinking is in some way amusing, though few things are less funny and more offensive than an out of control alcoholic. Such a light-hearted image says nothing of the link between alcohol and violence, and the carnage caused on our roads by drivers who drink to excess. Contrast this with the media's dark image of the drug user, willing to commit any crime to support a growing habit. Though there is a proven link between drug abuse and crime, as the crime statistics of most US and – more recently – European cities show, this is often less clear than many suggest. Such crimes are committed typically to raise funds to support a habit, not because the individual is out of control as a result of any substance taken. Many drug addicts, both male and female, resort to nothing more criminal than prostitution to raise money – a crime in which they themselves are really the only victim. The link between prostitution and drug abuse is undesirable for many social, moral and health reasons; at the health level it is linked with the spread of serious disorders including both hepatitis B and AIDS.

Drug abuse is better researched and understood than are alcohol and tobacco abuse. Although considerable research is now directed at the use of tobacco, much of this concentrates on the problems stemming from tobacco's link with heart, lung and general disorders. The brain biochemistry of addiction to tobacco, and indeed the reasons why we smoke, have been given a far lower priority. The fact that all illicit drugs, including the amphetamines, heroin and cocaine, also have – or had – clinical applications also helps our understanding, as these drugs have often been closely researched in connection with their legitimate therapeutic use.

In considering drug abuse we need a definition of abuse. Elsewhere in this book we have been critical of the medical profession's heavy reliance on drug-based therapies. Although much of this might be termed misuse, it can hardly be classified as abuse. In our context abuse is defined as the use of drugs usually self-prescribed and administered, for non-medical reasons – and typically without medical supervision. This excludes the careless prescribing which leaves as much as 10-15 per cent of the population in some Western countries largely dependent on mild tranquillisers. Into the category of drugs abused come a wide range of narcotics, anti-anxiety and anti-depression agents, analgesics – and many more. Where alcohol is alcohol, whether taken in the form of gin, whisky, beer or brandy, there are dozens of drugs which our society finds the desire to misuse. It is also probably fair to say that drug abuse in isolation is relatively rare: most drug users also abuse other products including nicotine, alcohol and solvents. In an actuarial study of heroin deaths in the US State of Columbia between 1979 and 1982, 74 per cent of fatalities were also associated with alcohol misuse – a pattern most believe to be fairly typical.

Although we have separate chapters on drug, alcohol and tobacco abuse, the interaction of all these products with our response to stress is very similar. Even where the modes of action of the substances abused are not identical, the aims of the abuser are typically the same. Abusers fall into two main categories, those who want stimulating and take such products as amphetamines, and those who want tranquillising – isolating from the ills and stresses of society. What quickly results is that the body's own natural rhythms are replaced by an artificial chemical rhythm, which may be highly resistant to stress but induces major and chronic problems of its own. The ability of drugs to produce such effects has its origins in the biogenic amine neurotransmitters which were reviewed in Chapter 3. Indeed, with drugs, alcohol and tobacco all having a marked effect on major neurotransmitters like noradrenalin, serotonin and dopamine, it is hardly surprising that stress and substance abuse are closely associated. One particular region of the brain, the locus coeruleus, is closely involved with our response to stress. The same region also appears to be implicated in addiction, and many of the problems associated with both dependence and withdrawal.

Within the brain's locus coeruleus, the level of noradrenalin activity is associated with both existing stress and our response to stress. Sustained high noradrenalin levels in this region of the brain result in individuals who are tense, anxious, nervous – and hyperactive. In a balanced situation this condition should quickly be ameliorated by the action of enkephalins – the body's own natural opiates. These have a soothing effect and induce a state of calm and reassurance. Problems occur in those whose noradrenalin levels do not revert to normal, or who are continually subjecting their body to mental, emotional and physical stress. Here the temptation is for clinicians, or the individual, to find an alternative to the brain's own enkephalin. Opiate narcotics, like heroin, mimic the effect of the enkephalin, binding to the same synaptic receptors. One effect of this intrusion of an outside substance is that the neurons themselves, reacting to a feedback mechanism, produce less enkephalin. This leaves the body largely and increasingly dependent on the synthetic opiate. Such a pattern leads to a dangerous spiral: in which increasing levels of opiate are needed not merely to counter the initial problems, but to cope with the body's own reduced level of enkephalin production.

Dependence or addiction are complex and poorly understood. All biochemicals in the body are in a state of constant flux, being broken down, excreted or in some cases recycled. Over all this is the process of homeostasis, outlined in Chapter 3, whereby the body constantly strives to maintain its balance and equilibrium. This means that, although naturally occurring enkephalin, or a synthetic opiate equivalent, will counter the effects of increased noradrenalin in the short term, this improvement will be far from permanent. The opiate or enkephalin will be rapidly removed by the body's natural processes, allowing noradrenalin levels to rise. This leads to further opiate being required, the interval between doses typically becoming shorter and the level of the dose tending to rise steadily. Such a pattern clearly produces problems when the drug is withdrawn. Here noradrenalin levels rise unchecked in the locus coeruleus, a problem compounded by the body's own reduced production of enkephalin. In analysing this response we should be clear that it is not the high levels of noradrenalin which are the problem, but that these become sustained. The brain in fact has come to rely on the presence of the synthetic opiate to counter its natural or distorted response to stress. The result is the exaggerated stress-like symptoms seen in the withdrawal of drugs, alcohol or nicotine. Fortunately these symptoms of physical dependence can be helped, typically by the administration of appropriate drugs which lower the level of noradrenalin active in the brain.

The literature of drug addiction frequently identifies two basic forms of dependence: physical and psychological. In physical dependence the basis of addiction stems from the reliance on drugs outlined above. It has a clear biochemical base, which gives hope for successful treatment. The basis is far less clear in psychological dependence where the addiction, it is claimed, comes largely from an emotional need for the drug. This distinction is now the subject of some dispute, and we will return to it in a later chapter when we examine dependence on the minor tranquillisers. It is relevant here because it has definite links with the current increased use of cocaine. Historically cocaine has been expensive and largely confined to heroin users augmenting their main addiction. Because tolerances are not clear with cocaine, this has led some to assume that cocaine itself is not physically addictive. Such an assumption seems both unlikely and extremely dangerous. While we may not yet fully understand the basis of cocaine addiction, this is no reason to assume it is safe. Indeed clinical experience in the US would seem to suggest a massive degree of dependence amongst many cocaine users. With crack, the cheap and reconstituted form of cocaine, now becoming widely available both in North America and Europe, a far more detailed understanding of the nature of cocaine addiction is essential.

In fact as far as this book is concerned the distinction between physical and psychological dependence is not of major importance. Both are acutely damaging physically and emotionally. Indeed many clinicians now suggest that psychological dependence on drugs like heroin is far more serious than the effects of physical dependence. This could in part account for the depressingly low success rates of many detoxification programmes. These continue despite the fact that recent discoveries in brain neurochemistry have brought a far better understanding of much of the basis of physical dependence. We are still, however, a long way from curing the craving associated with drug and substance addiction generally, although research into agents which can manipulate and modify the stress-response neurotransmitters gives more hope for the future.

Most clinicians still recognise that drug addiction requires a holistic approach, which considers not just the nature of the patient's addiction, but also the circumstances which brought it about. In few other medical conditions is the patient's social and economic background as relevant as in drug addiction. Indeed, many clinicians now believe it is virtually useless to treat an addict and then push him back into the same environment which helped cause the addiction. This again indicates a reason for the failure of many detoxification programmes, not least those which are linked to prison communities. Brain biochemistry research may point the way forward, but it is of limited benefit if society does not begin to recognise that substance abuse is a complex social, medical and economic problem, whose solution does not lie with the medical professions alone.

For the researcher all forms of substance abuse present problems. Medical research generally is heavily dependent on data culled from animal experiments and models. These are often of limited benefit in the field of addiction where it has proved almost impossible to develop animal experiments providing results of significance to the human condition. Although the pharmacological effects of drugs may be similar, most animals do not become addicted in the strict sense of the term. The reasons for this are not clear, but it may be partly because it has proved almost impossible to replicate in animals the complex mix of chemical effect, environmental stress and metabolic imbalance which lies behind human addiction. Add to this the complexity of the psychological components involved in the 'craving' process, and some of the difficulties faced by researchers will be clear.

While research in biochemistry still struggles to understand craving and addiction, major steps are being made in social and psychiatric research, helping to tear down some of the long accepted misconceptions about drug addiction. Much of this research has concentrated on the pattern of drug use, which has changed significantly over the last fifty years. In the 1920s drug use, both in the USA and Europe, was largely confined to outsider groups such as musicians and ethnic minorities. Indeed, research suggests that where drug use in a major city is a minor problem, it is still likely to be confined largely to groups which are outside the normal social framework. In cities where drug abuse becomes a major problem however, in numeric and social terms, then it shows an alarming readiness to spread to all sectors of society. Here it is also likely to be very closely linked to powerful stressors, particularly boredom and anxiety. One careful US study on Vietnam veterans showed that social class was largely irrelevant in addiction, although growing up in an inner city area, being black or entering the service at an earlier age were significant and associated with higher rates of addiction.

Social research is also changing our thinking on how people are introduced to drug taking. The sinister image of the drug pusher haunting school playgrounds is less important than many might expect. US research shows that most drug users are introduced to drugs by a friend, the typical first dose being a gift not a purchase. Although the 'legalise marijuana' lobby might find it uncomfortable, there is also a definite link between marijuana use and the move to harder drugs. Something like 50 per cent of marijuana users are estimated to move on to hard drugs, a fact which deserves consideration both by those contemplating using the drug, and by those advocating changes in legislation surrounding its use.

One factor causing concern both in North America and Western Europe is the increasing use of drugs by young people, although with the spread of drugs to all sectors of society, it is becoming increasingly difficult to recognise and isolate any group which is particularly vulnerable. US studies show that some 60 per cent of school seniors have experimented with illicit drugs, though most still reject their long-term use. One comprehensive study and follow-up of US high school students showed that drug use is not confined to the subnormal drop-outs so popular in our media's image of the drug addict. The typical profile of a potential drug experimenter – and hence addict – contains many factors which should give rise for alarm. According to this US study it includes:

* a narrow age range for the first experimentation, typically between thirteen and twenty-five;
* an IQ superior to the average;
* under-achievement despite a good level of intelligence;
* lack of motivation and a sense of purpose;
* more depressive symptoms than the average, although there is little evidence in this survey that users turned to drugs to escape major problems;
* far from being socially maladjusted, users in this survey were more sociable than the average;
* sexually active at an earlier than average age;
* given to challenging authority via minor breaches of discipline;
* non-religious and not attached to home or family;
* tolerant of deviant and aberrant behaviour in others;
* unemployed or drifting from one non-career job to another;
* for college and university students, much more likely to be studying arts and humanities than the hard sciences and mathematics.

Such a breakdown is particularly worrying, not least because the people described could be expected to become among the more innovative and challenging members of our society. It is not sufficient to assume that today's young are secure within a strongly welfare-based society. Material provision alone is not enough. Boredom we know is a powerful stressor, and each generation devises its own priorities, pressures and stress. For many young people, unemployment is a powerful cause of stress which hangs over both their late academic and early working lives. Add to this the indifference and impersonality of much of modern life, and we perhaps begin to understand why some of the brightest of them reject what modern society offers.

In considering drug abuse and its relationship with stress,

we are immediately faced with difficulties stemming from the range of drug products available. Drug users and addicts, a distinction we must draw, show an alarming willingness to experiment both with single drugs and drug mixtures – or cocktails. These can include narcotics, minor tranquillisers and anti-depressants, some of which they may be taking legitimately. As a general rule all drugs are more dangerous in cocktails, not least because it makes treatment in the case of an overdose far more hazardous and uncertain. Neither, as already indicated, do most drug users necessarily confine their activity to drug abuse. The use of drugs in association with alcohol is common, and can be acutely damaging. The action of many drugs, particularly the barbiturates, is altered or enhanced by the presence of alcohol, a fact which can often prove fatal.

The drugs which are most commonly associated by the public with addiction are the opiates. These include heroin – useful in clinical applications – but feared by many with a limited understanding of drug misuse. Opiates can be swallowed, dissolved, sniffed or smoked, though injection into the bloodstream gives the most striking effect and is commonly linked with addiction. This is an unfortunate route for the addict, because injecting substances, particularly in non-sterile conditions, is associated with several serious problems including hepatitis, gangrene, abscesses and – more recently – AIDS. The effects of opiates are well documented and include a feeling of drowsiness, well-being and content, the direct opposite of our reactions to stress. At low levels opiates cause little interference with sensation, motor skills or intellect, although at medium or higher doses sedatory effects take over. With cocaine in particular the feeling of contentment, coupled with a sensation of heightened intellectual capacity, has led some users (not to mention the pushers) to claim that cocaine is a drug with virtually no adverse effects. This is not correct. No matter how a person feels, intellectual capability and performance are not as effective as they were before the drug was taken. Drugs like cocaine can also amplify mood, making a person even more depressed, anxious or aggressive than before the drug was taken.

In some ways public concern over the opiates, and heroin in particular, is unfortunate: it hides some of the major risks associated with other drugs and substances. Although recent publicity programmes in Europe and North America have concentrated on the fact that heroin damages the mind and body, many clinicians believe that the long-term risks of the drug are overstated. This does not mean that the authors of this book advocate heroin misuse. It does mean, however, that we believe the problem can be better tackled by a *real* awareness of the facts – not official scaremongering. It is certainly true that some heroin users move in and out of abusing the drug over an extended period with little apparent damage. Where death results from heroin use this typically comes from an accidental overdose, sometimes stemming from a change in tolerance to the drug, or from some adulteration in black market drugs.

Adulteration is a major problem in illegal drug supplies: black market heroin purchased in the US is typically only 5 per cent pure. Although in Europe the figure is higher, and can reach as high as 40 per cent, most of what is purchased is – or should be – an inactive and harmless base. As a result in all cases the user, and most particularly the user mainlining [injecting], is totally dependent on the pusher both for the quality of the initial drug and the nature of its base. Much death, and some appalling long-term suffering, stems from adulteration. It is strange that while few people would buy a car from a known criminal, many addicts will inject into their veins or suck into their bodies products supplied by some of the most undesirable members of our society. A lack of judgement, as well as the absence of any conscience or will, characterises most – if not all – addicts in the latter stages of their addiction. Deaths from opiate abuse are not common in the UK: in the fifteen years between 1967 and 1981, 1,499 people died from problems related to drug abuse – mostly with the opiates. Compare this with a conservative estimate of 1.5 million who died in the same period from tobacco-related conditions.

Many clinicians are now deeply concerned about the spread of cocaine use in Western society, and not just among the young, the deprived and the poor. Cocaine use appears to be growing fastest in business and middle-class communities, where it is becoming accepted and considered trendy. In its effects, cocaine differs somewhat from heroin inducing a feeling of well-being coupled with an indifference to pain and fatigue. As mentioned, it also gives a false sensation of strength and mental capacity, making its use particularly undesirable among senior executives needing to make major decisions. Larger or serial doses of cocaine lead to agitation, anxiety, paranoia and in some cases hallucinations. Whatever its transient effects, cocaine is not a safe drug, and it should not be seen as socially acceptable.

The conventional administration method for cocaine is by sniffing, or less commonly freebasing [smoking]. Sniffing brings its own problems as cocaine destroys both the membranes lining the nasal passages and the septum dividing the nostrils. These can only be repaired to a limited extent. As already stated, the nature of any physical dependence to cocaine is not clear: this stems more from our ignorance than from the fact that the drug itself is not addictive. Certainly cocaine can induce a massive degree of pyschological dependence, as can be seen in many US users. Similarly there seems nothing in the literature or our experience to suggest that cocaine is a problem-free drug, the 'Soma' of Huxley's *Brave New World*. Though the pushers would like us to believe differently, cocaine is in no way special. That it is abused in the leafy suburbs, not just the back-street ghettos, does not excuse its misuse. Public attitudes do influence the cocaine user: if we accept cocaine passively then its use can only become more widespread,

The abuse of cocaine, as with heroin and other drugs, shows close links with our response to stress. We know that boredom is a powerful stressor, and ennui lies at the heart of many middle-class users' cocaine habit. While the ghetto heroin user may turn to drugs to escape from the stress brought on by poverty, unemployment and despair, many who use stimulants like cocaine and the amphetamines do so because they are almost *too* secure. This is particularly true of those who are young or in early middle age, where some form of outside challenge should be an essential part of life. It is also true that many wealthy and middle-class people feel that their wealth cushions them from the real effects of drug abuse, that they can handle drugs better than the poor, the deprived and the inadequate. This is highly dangerous: drugs are egalitarian – they will kill anyone.

It is impossible here to examine all the drugs which show a high level of abuse. Indeed man's ingenuity in abusing the products designed for his welfare seems at times boundless. In addition to the opiates, abuse of the amphetamines and other stimulants gives major cause for concern. These arouse and activate the user, acting rather like adrenaline to increase respiration and heart rate. Although amphetamines are not associated with physical dependence, they do induce considerable psychological dependence. This can result in habituation and tolerance leading to the need for steadily increasing doses. Among the early uses – or misuses – of amphetamines was their supply to soldiers in the trenches during the First World War. The aim was to keep the troops awake for long periods, though the practice was quickly discontinued as side-effects like irrationality, lack of appetite and paranoia came to the fore. Stress compounds any adverse side-effects induced by the amphetamines – and few situations can have been more stressful than the trenches of the First World War.

One problem quickly faced by those using amphetamines is the need to take steadily increasing doses to postpone the onset of fatigue. This can damage the heart and major blood vessels, particularly in those with existing coronary conditions. Regular amphetamine use can also lead to feelings of persecution, paranoia, delirium, panic and hallucinations – which can all too easily lead to violence. Not surprisingly amphetamines are also associated with severe antisocial behaviour: indeed, the implications of their misuse are often severely underestimated.

Also underestimated by many is the significance of marijuana. In much of the USA, marijuana use is now treated with the same indifference as the alcohol prohibition laws in force during the 1920s and 1930s. A similar casual pattern exists in a large part of Europe, with some governments tacitly condoning use – if not traffic – of the drug. Marijuana has in many countries become the acceptable face of drug use, with some now actually lobbying for its sale and use to be made legal. Until recently, most opposition to marijuana legalisation has been because of its apparent link in the chain which leads to hard drug addiction. This in itself is probably not enough, although many researchers doubt that marijuana is the safe, recreational drug that some claim. Certainly THC [tetrahydrocannibol], its active ingredient, is potentially addictive and has been shown to accumulate in the body where high dosage levels are used. Marijuana also acts as a stimulant and can – like cocaine – falsely boost confidence. The early use of hashish [marijuana] by the guild of assassins involved exactly this artificial boost to confidence, a boost which became so important to them that the assassins took their name from hashish. Although many still believe it is virtually impossible to overdose with mari-

143

juana, and that the drug is not addictive, such views remain unproven scientifically.

Whether addictive or not, marijuana quickly impairs mental and dexterity skills, having an intoxicating effect not unlike alcohol. If nothing else, this makes those taking the drug a menace to others when driving or operating machinery. In some ways, marijuana is more dangerous than alcohol: the dosage level is more difficult to control, and users may not recognise the full extent of its effects. Many who are stressed or under pressure take marijuana to help them to relax, a use which may help solve immediate problems but can offer no long-term benefit. Side-effects with marijuana appear relatively rare, although in some cases it can give rise to short-term psychoses, with a clinical picture not disimilar to LSD.

Those lobbying for marijuana sale to be made legal frequently claim it is less harmful than either alcohol or tobacco, a view graphically expressed by Paul McCartney with his comparison of marijuana and rum punch. While McCartney's views may be technically correct given our current state of knowledge, they do appear to avoid some of the main issues. If we were starting from scratch, no-one could advocate the introduction of tobacco into our society. Its link with disease and premature death is too strongly proven. That it remains on sale at all is because of complex economic reasons, and our determination to maintain the right to choose our own route to hell. In comparing tobacco and marijuana, those seeking to legalise the drug do not do their cause any favours. It could well be that some relaxation of the laws surrounding marijuana may be possible: we do not yet know enough about the drug or its effects to frame an answer. The latest research does not look hopeful, however, suggesting that marijuana is more harmful than many had originally anticipated.

Drug abuse shows patterns and fashions. For many the

only thing which remains constant is the underlying reason why they turn to drugs – the stress and pressures they face. During the 1960s and early 1970s, there was a heavy emphasis on LSD and the barbiturates. This has changed, these drugs now being largely displaced by heroin and more recently cocaine. Such a switch has many reasons but is in part due to cost and availability, heroin in particular being cheap and easily available in North America and much of Western Europe. Also implicated in changing patterns of drug use could be adverse publicity. LSD received considerable media attention in the late 1960s over bad trips leading to unpleasant hallucinations and psychedelic experiences. It was also linked with a number of deaths among people who felt that they could fly, in fact an uncommon aberration. Similarly, publicity over the problems of barbiturate overdoses, certainly when linked with alcohol, should have deterred all but the foolhardy or suicidal.

Outside those drugs already mentioned a range of psychoactive drugs and other drug products are also widely abused. These include drugs used to treat anxiety, depression and psychoses. Included in this category are the minor tranquillisers, like the benzodiazepines, which mimic the effect of GABA and suffer the problems of being both abused and misused, and the major tranquillisers (the neuroleptics), which are used therapeutically to treat patients whose anxiety conditions have reached psychotic proportions. Many of the drugs in this category, like largactyl, work as antagonists for the noradrenalin receptors, so inhibit one of the major neurotransmitters involved in the stress response. Also widely abused are analgesics, the painkillers which are now so widely available in non-prescription form in all Western countries. Apart from the damage these drugs can cause to the gut and the kidneys, they can also produce a surprising degree of tolerance and physical dependence. This means again the use of steadily higher doses to gain the same effect. As a result, in many countries government agencies now require drug companies to produce dependence and tolerance data on all analgesics, a requirement which is typically filled by the use of Rhesus monkeys who self-administer the drugs involved.

Practitioners of all disciplines now recognise the importance of stress in the addictive process, whatever the substance abused. We strive constantly to achieve self-imposed goals in areas such as territory, resources, social relationships and sex, but success in everything is impossible. This implies a degree of frustration, a most potent form of stress. As a result, we spend our lives with a nagging stress response or, if we like, constantly nagging noradrenalin levels in the locus coeruleus. The wide availability of drugs makes it all too easy to eliminate this malaise by the introduction of outside agents. Unfortunately these agents can quickly become a problem in their own right, and a source of both dependence and addiction.

Advances in our understanding of brain neurochemistry raise hopes for the future. Much of this research concentrates on the complex problem of tolerance, and its link with withdrawal symptoms. Unpleasant withdrawal symptoms, and the continuation of the craving process, are fundamental in the failure of many rehabilitation programmes. Some researchers have even postulated the possibility of a unique protein involved in tolerance. This could be an enzyme, or even some change in a known neurotransmitter substance or receptor. What is known is that if we deplete the levels of noradrenalin, dopamine and serotonin then it inhibits the development of tolerance. This is important because in the presence of tryptophan, a natural food constituent used in concentrated form to treat insomnia and depression, tolerance develops faster.

Whatever the results of research on brain biochemistry

and addiction, this area alone will not provide all the solutions to the problems of substance abuse: there are also political, economic and social considerations. Unfortunately, in our cost-conscious societies, self-inflicted disorders like those posed by substance abuse are given a steadily lower level of priority. As a result, in many countries, people developing dependence – of any form – fail to receive the help they require. The desire to abandon an addiction is an essential part of any addict's rehabilitation. Sadly, even where this is present, guidance and support are often lacking from the community at large. In many countries, particularly in Western Europe, there is an inherent hypocrisy in government attitudes to drug abuse in particular. In times of high unemployment, the use of alcohol and tobacco has been shown to decline (a fact which seems largely cost related), while drug abuse tends to rise. By concentrating on the drug pushers and users, many politicians perhaps feel they can deflect attention from their failure to tackle the root cause of much addiction.

While several European governments struggle to frame balanced approaches to the problem of drug abuse, it would be unfair not to acknowledge the scale and complexity of the problem. It is certainly true that so far no developed country has managed to formulate an effective response to the problems of drug traffic and misuse. Those tried have ranged from punishment and prohibition, including imprisoning or defining as mentally ill the addicted, to outright maintenance. A controversial issue, maintenance involves providing a closely controlled supply of the addict's drug, or something less damaging like methadone. Those that support maintenance claim it decriminalises drug abuse, and reduces both the level of drug related crime and the number of addicts dying as a result of adulterated supplies. This may be true but maintenance can cause problems of its own, as demonstrated by Holland, which is fast becoming the drug centre of Europe – if not the world – as a result of its very liberal drug maintenance programmes.

This book is primarily about stress and its effects in the business environment. Although recognising the link between stress and drug abuse may be important, it does not necessarily help in framing solutions. It does not help the manager who finds staff turning to drugs at times of difficulty. Perhaps a more balanced and open approach to drug related problems is required. Many have benefited from the openness of discussions relating to alcohol and tobacco abuse, but this has no real parallel in the drugs area – a fact unquestionably linked to the criminal aspects of drug abuse and supply. For far too many – not least parents – drug abuse is the new taboo, fringed by ignorance and a lack of understanding of the true implications of abuse. We fear what we do not understand, and that fear is at the base of many of the misconceptions which still surround drugs and their misuse.

For the would-be user, and indeed the executive employing staff who use drugs at times of crisis, a few facts should be made clear. There are no safe drugs: every addict started his addiction with the phrase 'I can handle it'. All drugs, no matter what is claimed – or indeed felt, impair mental and ultimately physical performance. There is a clear and proven link between drug misuse and crime, both crimes of violence and of theft. People abusing drugs are a menace to themselves, their employers and those around them. Above all, for every biochemical lift a debt must ultimately be paid. For some this will be paid in disease and death, for many more it will be paid in ruined careers, marriages or personal relationships. At the end of the day, the answer will always lie in the hands of the individual, though a balanced and honest view on substance abuse from society at large could certainly play a major part.

—9—

Stress and addiction: alcohol abuse

While little good can be said about drug misuse, the position with alcohol is not quite so clear-cut. Evidence suggests that at low levels alcohol may actually be beneficial to health, though this benefit quickly disappears if the amount taken is too high, or the pattern of drinking too regular. The first doctor to recognise and attempt to quantify the benefits of alcohol to health was a nineteenth-century physician called Anstie, and the Anstie limits for using alcohol in a safe and controlled manner are still largely valid. These suggest an average of no more than one or two measures of alcohol a day, with a broken pattern including some days of total abstinence. At this level the drinker is the master of the situation, though still enjoying any benefit alcohol may provide. These claimed benefits, which are still in many cases questionable, include the relief of stress – which looks particularly doubtful, the stimulation of digestion and an improvement in blood circulation. They also apply only at very low levels of alcohol intake, and are quickly displaced by more negative effects as alcohol plasma levels begin to rise.

Also questionable is the long accepted claim that moderate alcohol users live longer than the completely temperate. Many studies have been done on this subject and the results of most are at best equivocal. Longevity is anyway a topic of massive complexity, and one into which a host of variables

149

intrude. The inability to isolate alcohol from the mass of genetic, social and environmental factors which determine life span make such studies useless to all but the alcohol lobby. It is also perhaps time that we stopped looking at the mere length of life, and paid more attention to its quality. Excessive long life is of little use if we end our days as shambling mental inadequates. Thus, where alcohol may be a source of pleasure and support for some, it is a major cause of disease and death for others. Some measure of the scale of this problem can be seen from recent studies in the US which suggest that, as a health risk, alcoholism now comes third behind heart disease and cancer. In the UK, not a European country associated with major alcohol problems, recent official figures suggest that more than 5 per cent of the population have serious problems stemming from alcohol misuse. This is a cause not just of disease and death, but also of job loss, violence, broken marriages – the whole spectrum of human misery.

Why do so many turn to drink? Why also do some, often under great pressure, manage to control their drinking at a social level, with little apparent harm or damage to themselves or those around them? The answers are complex, although they appear closely associated with our response to stress. The link between alcohol and the stress hormones and neurotransmitters certainly explains why alcohol can give a short-term lift, which appears at least temporarily to remove or obliterate our feelings of stress. Unfortunately this lift *is* short-term and alcohol can quickly take over to become a problem in its own right. As we said in the chapter on drug abuse, the body's natural responses will quickly remove any natural or artificial substance which blocks or mimics the effect of a neurotransmitter. This applies equally to alcohol, leading to the need for regular and steadily increasing doses to maintain the same effect. This clearly explains both the route and the mechanism for alcohol addiction.

The initial effects of alcohol on the body's metabolism are very similar to the effects of stress itself. Alcohol appears to stimulate the hypothalamus, and certainly causes the output of ACTH to increase. As we saw in Chapter 3, the release of ACTH is at the core of our body's response to stress. As a result of its release, adrenalin levels rise, and so indirectly does the level of serum cortisol. While cortisol levels rise in normal alcohol use, this rise is not sustained in the alcoholic, a fact which suggests that alcohol's ability to help with our response to stress is strictly limited to low and intermittent use. Outside this rise in cortisol levels, alcohol also induces an increase in the output of adrenalin. This hormone increases heart rate and the metabolism generally, and its action is potentiated by the presence of alcohol. This accounts in part for the feeling of strength and rejuvenation even low levels of alcohol can provide when we are tired. Outside these basic effects, which also include a rise in noradrenalin activity, alcohol induces a host of biochemical changes in the body. These include absorptional and nutritional changes, some or all of which may be pertinent to the body's response to stress.

In terms of body biochemistry, alcohol is a unique substance. It is endogenous [naturally occurring] and, unlike with many drugs, there is a dedicated enzyme system in all body cells designed for its oxidation [breakdown]. This enzyme, called alcohol dehydrogenase, recognises alcohol as a potent, energy producing foodstuff rich in calories. Alcohol dehydrogenase is fast and highly efficient, and is theoretically capable of oxidising some two quarts of whisky per day in a healthy adult. That this theoretical capacity can never be met stems from the toxic nature of the reduction products of dehydrogenase activity. These quickly disrupt the equilibrium of the cell, and prevent its other metabolic activities. In this respect, there is a strictly limited rate-dependent level of alcohol dehydrogenase activity well below its full theoretical capacity.

Where alcohol levels are present in excess of those which can be tackled by alcohol dehydrogenase, a back up system comes into play. This is known as MEOS – the microsomal ethanol [alcohol] oxidising system. This involves the activity of enzymes within the cellular microsomes – microsomes being minute cellular elements which are usually involved in protein synthesis. During alcohol elimination, the relevance of the microsomes lies in their ability to remove xenobiotics [foreign substances] from the cell. Where dehydrogenase is specifically designed for the elimination of alcohol, the microsome system acts more generally, to treat and remove alcohol as if it were merely another foreign substance. The involvement of the microsome system is important because it has the ability to increase its capacity in line with the amount of alcohol taken. This gives a basis for tolerance which, as we know, develops quickly in alcohol use.

In the abuse of any substance tolerance is an important factor on the route to addiction. We should perhaps digress to point out that not all alcohol abusers become addicted, and neither is it necessary to be addicted to be physically, emotionally and socially damaged by alcohol. With alcohol, tolerance means that as the MEOS system becomes steadily more efficient in removing alcohol, so must the user increase the volume of alcohol taken to achieve the same effect. At least superficially such a pattern might not look particularly dangerous, and some might even suggest it is merely a well-designed biological system expanding to cope with an increased demand. In fact the reverse is true, because the presence of alcohol has a very wide-reaching effect, and not just on the cell and the MEOS system.

What we have described here is the beginning of tolerance,

not physical dependence or addiction. Although tolerance is linked with both dependence and ultimately alcoholism, this area is a complex and tortuous one, in which brain mechanisms – not least those surrounding our natural response to stress – are intimately involved. Neither does the involvement of the MEOS system have implications for alcohol alone. As stated earlier, this system can adapt and become involved in the elimination of all xenobiotics. Where its activity is dedicated to the removal of alcohol, then not surprisingly this affects its ability to metabolise other substances, including drugs. In the presence of smaller quantities of alcohol the speed of drug metabolism may be enhanced, and hence the effect and utilisation of drugs made more immediate. At higher quantities, of either drugs or alcohol, the action of the MEOS system may be impaired, so enhancing the effects of the drug – or making it more toxic. In all cases, the link between drugs and alcohol is an unhappy one.

The overall effect of alcohol metabolism, and really at quite low levels, is to shift the oxidation equilibrium of the cell. This equilibrium has an important influence on metabolism and is known as the redox potential. While alcohol's effect on the redox potential is probably more complex than we need to go into here its overall effect is of vital significance. This is to push the cell towards the reduced, or hydrogen-containing, state. This change has massive implications not least on some of the sex hormones. It sees a change in the sex steroids from an oxidised [keto] configuration to a reduced [or aldol] state. This probably accounts for the deficiency in the level of testosterone, the male sex hormone, seen in many male alcoholics. This combined with the prolonged life of oestrogen, a female sex hormone naturally present in small quantities in men, accounts for the feminisation seen in some male alcoholics. It also accounts for the loss of virility associated with alcohol

abuse. This in itself may be stressful, and that stress is likely
to be compounded and largely self-perpetuating in those
who use alcohol to reduce sexual anxiety.

Although alcohol's effect at a cellular level is crucial, not
least in the nature of the diseases it causes, much of its link
with stress comes through its impact on brain neurochemistry. At high levels, alcohol is known to slow conduction in
nerve fibres by as much as 4 per cent, a significant figure.
More importantly, alcohol can also reduce the speed at
which a nerve impulse traverses a synapse, probably by
interfering with the release of the neurotransmitters. This
effect is of interest because it has been demonstrated at very
low levels, and probably accounts for the immediate effect
alcohol has on walking and talking. Alcohol exerts a considerable effect on the brain's neurochemistry, with particular effects on the hormone ACTH and neurotransmitters
like serotonin. This means that the effects of alcohol are
often closely linked to our diurnal rhythms. Thus drinking
at lunchtime may prove more potent than drinking in the
evening, a phenomenon which is largely missing in the
alcoholic, whose diurnal rhythms are in any case suppressed
or obliterated. Such a pattern also means that regular drinking, even at low levels, can be dangerous with the body's
rhythms quickly coming to expect a regular shot of alcohol.

While alcohol's interaction with many of the stress neurotransmitters and hormones is unquestioned, this still remains a very complex area. In many well documented cases,
stress has been shown to reverse completely the intoxicating
effects of alcohol. Thus sudden 'shock' can certainly reverse
the physical effects of alcohol, if not immediately, then far
faster than the body's natural elimination processes would
seem to make possible. What appears to happen is that the
sudden, violent shock reverses the effect alcohol has on the
brain's inhibitory neurochemicals, giving the brain in effect
a massive – if seldom used – override capability. This

restores both mental and physical acuity at an astonishing rate, though such a mechanism is used only in exceptional circumstances and is of little use to the alcoholic.

The more common link between stress and alcohol is the use of drink as a prop in times of difficulty or crisis. If alcohol offers any help here, it must at best be limited and short-term. Anyone who uses alcohol regularly to counter stress will rapidly develop the problems of tolerance, requiring steadily higher doses. The effect of alcohol on our anxiety state appears to be very personal: in many cases alcohol only makes the downcast and anxious even more depressed. Though its transient effects hide the fact, alcohol is itself a depressant, whose regular use can do little to solve the effects of stress. For the heavy user, intoxication may obliterate the world for a few hours: it has no longer term benefits. Alcohol also serves to depress the brain's inhibitory pathways, including those involving noradrenalin and GABA, which accounts both for alcohol's overall excitory effect and the manner in which it removes behavioural inhibitions. This suggests that some people drink essentially to escape the effects of the body's own inhibitory neurotransmitters. In all cases the amount of alcohol which can be utilised is limited by the body's own metabolic processes, and beyond that limit damage and disease can quickly occur.

The damage caused by alcohol is extreme, can occur at surprisingly low levels of use, and unlike most drug damage can often prove permanent. Alcohol can, and does, adversely affect virtually every organ in the body. Among the earliest signs of alcohol abuse are those seen in the liver. Even in those not regularly using alcohol to excess, one severe bout of drinking can be followed by a definite enlargement of the liver. This quickly subsides providing the user gives the organ time to recover, and is not using alcohol continually to excess. More important to the liver is the link between alcohol misuse and changes in fat metabolism. Sustained immoderate alcohol consumption induces changes in most – if not all – the mechanisms involved in fat metabolism. These include the increased mobilisation of fat from other tissue stores, a decreased oxidation of fatty acids, plus the preferential deposition of fat in the liver. Most of these effects relate to high levels of acetate [an alcohol by-product] in the blood, and the changes in the redox potential mentioned earlier. The overall effect is to promote fat synthesis, block its use and encourage its deposition in the liver.

Even before permanent damage like cirrhosis steps in, any disruption to the liver – one of the body's most versatile and remarkable organs – is highly undesirable. High doses of alcohol affect the function of the liver enzymes, and this can [again] interfere with the action and effect of many drugs. The presence of high levels of alcohol also reduces the ability of the liver to produce plasma proteins like prothrombin and fibrinogen. This results in a variety of disorders which include jaundice and excessive bleeding. Such a pattern can only serve to reduce the body's immune resistance, so compounding still further the risks posed by high levels of cortisol in the blood.

In the public mind, alcohol misuse is closely associated with cirrhosis of the liver. That we do not fear this damaging and often fatal disease as much as we should is probably due to its long period of development. This can take over twenty years, though at all stages the damage linked with cirrhosis is irreversible. That the disease takes so long to manifest itself stems entirely from the remarkable nature of the liver, which as an organ continues to function long after large sections of it are destroyed. What cirrhosis implies is the steady replacement of healthy liver cells with fibrous, dead tissue. This results in a steady loss of liver function, with major implications for health. Cirrhosis deaths in most Western countries are rising significantly, with one recent

US study showing that alcohol abuse was a causative factor in more than 90 per cent of all fatalities. Most alarming is the rise of cirrhosis in women, which has direct parallels with the increased use of alcohol by women generally. For complex biochemical reasons, the use of alcohol by women is particularly damaging. Cirrhosis is induced in women by lower alcohol levels, and develops faster. This suggests that the rise in cirrhosis deaths in women will continue, as many pay for taking their place as equals in our drink-conscious society. We should not overlook the effect alcohol has on the brain. This can come in the form of physical damage or of severe mental psychoses. Hallucinations and delirium tremens are well recognised extreme effects of alcohol, but they lie at the end of a whole range of mental and psychological problems associated with alcohol misuse. Most Western countries now report a massive increase in the number of patients entering mental institutions with drink-related disorders, and indeed treating alcoholics is a major growth area of modern psychiatry. Heavily implicated in much alcohol-related brain damage is acetaldehyde – the first oxidation product of alcohol. Like alcohol itself, acetaldehyde has its own enzyme system [acetaldehyde dehydrogenase] designed for its degradation. Unfortunately this system is slower acting than alcohol dehydrogenase, a fact many believe has its link with the damage caused by high levels of acetaldehyde in the brain.

Recent research has also shown that alcohol misuse, particularly in bouts of very heavy drinking, is associated with many instances of cerebrovascular occlusions [strokes]. This is particularly true in younger patients. In one US study, 43 per cent of stroke patients under forty had been intoxicated in the 24 hours prior to their stroke. More cautiously, the same study concluded its belief that around 20 per cent of all stroke cases under the age of forty were alcohol related. This seems to confirm a belief long held by many, that alcohol abuse is implicated in many cardiac and circulatory disorders. If this is true in the generally healthy patient, then alcohol abuse is even more dangerous in those with an existing cardiovascular condition.

One link between alcohol and cardiovascular disease is hypertension, which is closely linked with stress. Since the early 1960s, it has been known that there is also a link between alcohol use, more particularly abuse, and hypertension. As mentioned earlier, hypertension is a precursor to a wide range of cardiac and other disorders. One problem here is that low levels of alcohol – and we mean Anstie low – have been shown to reduce the risk of some heart disease. This appears to be associated with the stimulation of lipoproteins which protect against heart disease. Unfortunately, such a pattern has a very narrow clinical spectrum and at higher alcohol levels lipoproteins may be produced which are actually harmful to the heart. Many clinicians now believe there is a group of cardiac disorders which are specifically alcohol-related. These are characterised by serious ECG abnormalities, enlarged heart and biventricular heart failure. Clearly such patients must abstain from alcohol use entirely.

Alcohol misuse can also have extreme effects on the blood itself. Some of these relate to folic acid deficiency, which can lead to anaemia, particularly in those patients with gastrointestinal bleeding – common in alcoholics. High levels of alcohol use can also inhibit bone marrow proliferation and can cause a special form of anaemia known as sideroblastic anaemia. Platelet counts may be disrupted in alcoholics, and abnormalities of the platelets including potentially serious ones like aggregation, are also common. Above all these effects, alcohol is toxic to white blood cells and this has implications for the immune system in alcoholics.

Although some still believe the findings to be ambiguous,

alcohol misuse also appears linked with an increased incidence of certain forms of cancer, including tumours of the mouth, throat and liver. Less disputed are the widespread effects alcohol has on the gastrointestinal tract. Prolonged use can cause ulceration of the gastric mucosa ranging in severity from gastritis to outright haemorrhaging. Again, this has implications for those who drink because they are stressed. As we have already seen, stress alone has implications for the gut which can only be compounded in those who also abuse alcohol. Many who abuse alcohol also misuse aspirin, particularly to relieve a hangover. This combination can be devastating for the lining of the gut. Certainly in those who must drink to excess, aspirin is to be avoided in the treatment of any after effects. Other alcohol-induced difficulties in the gastrointestinal tract include problems in the duodenum – including ulceration, diarrhoea, hyperperistalsis and a range of changes in the gut's absorption ability which can lead to malnutrition.

The link between malnutrition and alcohol use may seem strange given that alcohol is rich in calories. In all, 600 ml of 86 per cent proof alcohol contains some 1,500 calories – up to 75 per cent of the required daily intake of a healthy adult. Unfortunately, alcohol is lacking in all other nutrients. Alcoholics are typically deficient in vitamins and most noticeably thiamin [B1] and pyridoxine [B6]. Alcohol also disrupts [neurochemically] the appetite, and makes fundamental changes in the body's ability to digest food. The result is a situation where an individual may be significantly overweight, due to excessive fat deposition, but still chronically undernourished. Alcohol also suppresses the effect of the anti-diuretic hormone, resulting in the excretion of solute free water: this can lead to a water deficit and aberrations in the mineral balance of the body.

As already touched upon, alcohol has a fundamental effect on sexual activity and the sex organs themselves. In men,

the changes associated with alcohol misuse are widespread
and include:

* hypogonadism [the secretion of inadequate sex hor-
  mones];
* testicular atrophy leading to sterility;
* feminisation, including loss of the male pattern of secondary hair, gynocomastia [breast formation], etc;
* impotence.

As well as reducing testicular weight, alcohol misuse also
serves to reduce the diameter of the seminiferous tubules,
the amount of germinal epithelium present in the testes and
the nature of spermatogenesis itself. All these changes are
disastrous in terms of sexual potency.

Probably the most embarrassing and humiliating of male
sexual disorders associated with alcohol misuse is erectile
impotence, an all too well recognised condition which has
many evocative names, the politest of which is probably
'brewer's droop'. This form of impotence can happen at
very low levels of alcohol use, and should provide an early
warning to those on the path to alcohol addiction. It is
strange that the media and advertising industries like to link
sex and alcohol. We are told that to drink is sociable,
companionable, macho and above all a sign of self assurance.
If we drink, we are led to believe, we are sexually attractive,
and the models of the drink advertisements will flood to our
sides – and more importantly our beds. Were the advertisers
to indicate the true effects of alcohol on our sexual prowess,
alcohol sales would slump overnight.

Alcohol also has a severe effect on the sex organs of
women, a fact which was long overlooked because most
studies on alcoholism concentrate on men. In women, alcohol misuse can cause menstrual abnormalities, including the
cessation of periods, oestrogen deprivation in the uterus and

fallopian tubes and malfunction of the placenta. Alcohol use is particularly damaging in women who are pregnant, and a foetal alcohol syndrome leading to abnormalities in the newborn is now a recognised condition. Unfortunately in pregnancy most damage from alcohol abuse appears to be done in the first trimester, when many women may not even know they are pregnant. The link between alcohol abuse and foetal abnormality deserves far more consideration, not least because a good deal of current alcohol advertising is directed unashamedly at women. Women also ingest large amount of sweet and mixed drinks in which the alcohol content may be hidden or largely unidentified.

The effects of drinking in pregnancy are serious and complex. They are also long term and are certainly not confined to the newborn. One recent US study showed that even adolescent children of alcoholics performed less well at school, a fact related more to neuropsychological criteria than the problems of living in a disrupted household and an emotionally labile environment. The same US study showed that the children of alcoholics were more disruptive at school, and more likely to be involved in incidents of delinquency.

This superficial review of the devastating effects of alcohol should deter all but the foolhardy. One major problem associated with alcohol is that physical damage occurs at a surprisingly low level of use. This can be as low as 15 centilitres of pure alcohol per day, a figure which sits uncomfortably with annual average alcohol consumption rates of 9 litres [the UK], 12 litres [the US], 18 litres [Italy] and 27 litres [France]. If we allow for the temperate and the moderate drinkers, such figures imply a massive level of alcohol abuse in all the countries mentioned. That these figures relate to official sales, and do not include home brewing or distilling, should also be a matter for concern. Our study has concentrated on the use of ethanol. Anyone who chooses to imbibe home distilled spirits, with their mix of alcohols, can expect those problems already mentioned plus a whole new round of disorders specifically associated with illegal distillation. These can all too easily include insanity, blindness and an extremely unpleasant death.

While historically temperance movements have been regarded with scorn, recent years have seen several new bodies set up to combat the effects of alcohol. Many of these, like the US organisation MADD [Mothers Against Drunk Driving], concentrate on the massive hazards to others from those who abuse alcohol. Alcohol even at low levels reduces motor skills, co-ordination, vision and reactions. This applies to a varying extent to every drinker, and makes anyone driving or operating machinery after drinking a source of danger both to themselves and others. In the UK, Action on Alcohol Abuse [an anti-alcohol lobby group] showed that 45 per cent of road accident deaths involving young people were alcohol related. The same group also showed that 33 per cent of all domestic accidents, 30 per cent of traffic fatalities and 30 per cent of drownings had a link with alcohol. Perhaps even more worrying was the fact that, in more than 50 per cent of UK murder convictions, the person committing the crime was drunk at the time. Another recent review of alcohol misuse published by the *Chicago Tribune* linked alcohol with 64 per cent of US murders, 41 per cent of assaults, 34 per cent of rapes, 30 per cent of suicides, 56 per cent of fights in the home – and as much as 60 per cent of all child abuse. Furthermore 50 per cent of US drivers involved in serious traffic accidents have been drinking.

One problem with recognising alcohol abuse is that its onset is insidious. In the early stages those suffering – or at risk – may be the last to perceive the fact. Alcohol use, and even abuse, is hedged round by social factors. We accept social drinking – and even the use of alcohol to counter stress – and this extends into the acceptance of low levels of drunkenness. Our image of the alcoholic as a shambling, pathetic figure with shaking hands is far from the truth. This is the terminal picture of someone suffering from chronic alcohol poisoning. The real image of the drunk is more likely to be the smart business executive, desperately trying to hide his need and habit behind slightly slurred speech and initially minor changes in motor co-ordination.

Although this chapter concentrates primarily on the deleterious effects of alcohol, we cannot separate these from the reason why many people drink. This is undoubtedly closely associated with stress, and the inability to cope with the pressure and tensions of modern society. Such individuals typically begin by using alcohol at a low level to overcome the effects of fatigue, pressure and anxiety – though this can quickly progress to a different and more sinister use, where alcohol is used to obliterate the world and its troubles for a few short hours. Although stress undoubtedly lies at the heart of most serious drinking problems, other factors also play a part, and one of these is availability. One recent UK study showed that cirrhosis was twenty-two times more prevalent among company directors than among manual workers: this deserves consideration by those comtemplating yet another luncheon invitation, and appears to confirm the long held belief that ease of access is an important factor on the route to addiction.

For industry at large alcohol abuse is a major problem, and not just among the executive community. It also shows few signs of diminishing. At work alcohol has been shown to lower efficiency, increase absenteeism, mar personal relationships, impair judgement and cause accidents. In the UK, alcohol related problems have been estimated to cost industry more than £1,000 million a year – a figure which is almost certainly too low. In the US, where more than 5 per cent of the work-force are estimated to have alcohol related problems, the cost is even higher at more than US $10,000 million per year.

One result of this cost to industry, particularly in the US, has been the development of some highly effective industry-based alcohol rehabilitation courses. Many of these operate in close parallel with company stress programmes. We said earlier that the success of drug treatments was depressingly low: happily the same cannot be said of alcohol programmes. Some of those used by US industry show success rates as high as 70 per cent, which often means they pay for themselves in terms of improved output and industrial relations. The reason for such a difference in success rates is not clear. Like drugs, alcohol induces a high degree of tolerance and addiction, and the early symptoms of withdrawal are typically unpleasant – and can be life-threatening. One factor may be that the alcoholic, certainly in the early stages, remains within society so is provided with a greater degree of support than the drug user. Another may be a higher degree of motivation in the alcohol user. Whatever the reasons, they could have major implications for the way we treat substance abuse generally.

In understanding and treating alcohol addiction a number of other factors seem to be significant. These include genetic factors: certainly tolerance appears to be closely linked with genetic criteria. Alcohol metabolism also varies widely, and can take place up to three times faster in some individuals than others. Again this appears to be a genetic accident and cannot, for those looking to reap the benefits, come about as a result of conditioning or frequent alcohol misuse. Speed of intake, nutritional state and [possibly] physical condition all appear to modify our response to alcohol – which is certainly far from static. For researchers alcohol offers much the same problem as drugs. Most animals reject alcohol automatically so in any experiment will only accept its administration in abnormal conditions. For stress-linked studies in particular this is clearly unsatisfactory. Similarly in human volunteers the link between alcohol and stress presents major problems, not least where attempts to create an artificially stressful environment are concerned. Clearly stress only exists where the subject believes the risk is genuine, a fact all too well understood by most volunteers presenting for any form of stress experimentation.

Despite the difficulties of isolating results, there is evidence that low levels of alcohol do reduce tension – and so can help in handling stress. This is very much in line with most alcoholics' given reason for drinking, which is to reduce anxiety. Unfortunately in many individuals tolerance and addiction quickly move in to displace any beneficial effect of alcohol. The fact that most alcoholics quickly come to hide their addiction also has an important link with their main reason for drinking, especially as solitary drinking has been shown to have less effect on anxiety than social drinking. Above all the link between stress and alcohol brings its own strange results. Research suggests that those who cope well with stress will also handle well their use of alcohol. They will not see it as a prop, but rather as a part of social intercourse which they can take or leave as circumstance demands. This in fact appears the perfect profile for sensible, safe alcohol use. It therefore seems that nature has been less than kind to those who struggle to handle stress, as many are also denied access to the controlled use of alcohol.

In our review of alcohol use and stress, we inevitably come back to the role of governments in both its supply and control. Elsewhere in this book we have indicated our belief that there is a fundamental hypocrisy in governments who decry the use of alcohol and tobacco, but are nevertheless content to accept a massive income from the taxing of these commodities. This is not the full extent of many administrations' hypocrisy. Recent years have seen massive strides forward in our understanding of the link between alcohol and disease. Despite this in many countries the powerful alcohol lobby has ensured that alcohol price rises are kept to the minimum, while a relaxation in licensing laws sees alcohol made available through an ever increasing range of outlets. Above all, advertising encourages all, including the weak, the inadequate and the young, to drink for the most spurious of reasons.

Only in one area, traffic accidents, has public pressure forced most governments to act. This has led to the introduction of blood alcohol limits on those who drive, although these are often assigned in the most arbitrary and unscientific manner. The BAC [blood alcohol concentration] limits now widely used are measured in the volume of alcohol contained in 100 mls of blood. This is set at zero in the USSR and most Eastern European countries, 80 in much of Western Europe, 125 in Eire and 150 in some US states. Given the varying effects of alcohol from one individual to another even the West European levels look too high, while those given for Eire and the US states are positively ridiculous.

One area where most governments should be doing more is in publicising the risks of alcohol misuse. These programmes should be directed at the young who are in many ways at greatest risk. Pre-pubescent drinking is particularly damaging and can delay the onset of puberty and damage later sexual activity. Most countries report a higher than average incidence of young people involved in drunken driving – both as culprits and victims. Also of concern is the rise in drinking among women, a problem which is compounded by the fact that alcohol's damaging effects are enhanced in women. In the past the number of women alcoholics was low: less than 20 per cent of the total. This is changing, with the UK's Alcoholics Anonymous reporting that women now form 35 per cent of its membership, a figure which roughly bears out the known ratio of men and women alcoholics in the UK.

Throughout this book we have emphasised the role of the individual in combating stress-related problems. This remains true where alcohol is concerned although here more help and support should be provided. Too few in industry accept the proven link between stress and alcohol misuse. It is for many easier to dismiss or discipline staff who have major problems – and so evade the issue. Once the stress/alcohol link is accepted, then there is a good basis for company stress management and alcohol abuse programmes. If people understand why they turn to drink when they face stress, then research suggests they are less likely to do so: no-one likes to be seen to be dependent on outside props.

For the authors of this book the link between stress and alcohol causes particular problems: both drink – and neither advocates the temperance movement. At low levels of use, alcohol does relieve tension and anxiety. Estimates suggest that in North America and Western Europe around 60 per cent of all adults drink, most in moderation with little damage to their health. This clearly rules out the nightmare of another Volstead Act. If we do not, or realistically cannot, ban alcohol then we must accept a massive re-education programme directed at all sectors of society – including the business communities who provide many of the worst cases of abuse. The alternative is to accept a massive rise in both the physical and psychiatric diseases associated with alcohol abuse. Most clinicians now believe that each individual has a unique alcohol profile: this is the level at which they can handle alcohol and reap its benefits at minimum risk to their health. We must all recognise our own personal alcohol profile and from it discover whether alcohol is likely to remain a support or become a serious problem.

—10—

Stress and addiction: tobacco abuse

Although for some tobacco may have a transient effect in relieving stress, there is no safe level of tobacco use. Although the tobacco lobby may claim otherwise, even at low usage levels tobacco can have a devastating effect on health, despite a switch to low-tar brands. Tobacco use is associated with a range of lung, cardiovascular and other serious disorders, and is undoubtedly a major cause of premature death in all Western societies. That the risks of tobacco are not even more clearly stated is because most diseases have a number of contributing factors. With tobacco being only one factor, we may argue over its significance but there is no doubt about its integral link with a number of serious conditions. One recent actuarial study in the UK suggested that of every 1000 young men who smoke, one will be murdered, six will die in traffic accidents – and a further 250 will die prematurely from smoking related disease. Less scientific but perhaps more graphic is the idea that every cigarette taken shortens our life span by 5 minutes – a figure which quickly cumulates.

Given the level of publicity, few can now doubt the link between tobacco and disease. Why do people continue to smoke, and more importantly why do they take up the habit? The answers are again closely linked with our response to stress. The main active ingredient of tobacco is nicotine, a substance with a most complex biochemical profile which enables it to exercise a mix of stimulating and calming effects. While such a dual action might initially benefit those under stress, tobacco smoke also contains numerous other substances, many of which are acutely damaging to health. The result is that we pay for the limited benefit tobacco offers in handling stress with a massive risk to our general health. This is itself a cause of stress, with many smokers worrying about the effects on their health and secretly or openly wishing to stop. As society increasingly rejects smoking (smokers are now in the minority in most Western societies), those continuing the habit are also faced with feelings of isolation and rejection. As we know, rejection by a peer group is also acutely stressful, whether or not it is recognised and acknowledged by the outsider group itself.

What we see then in the average smoker is a complex profile in which any apparent benefit from nicotine use is limited by health worries and a sense of isolation and rejection. Despite this pattern, many continue to smoke, and clearly gain relief from the use of nicotine. Physically nicotine's effects are very far-reaching. They include an increase in heart rate, a lowering of skin temperature, and an increase in the activity of central neurotransmitters like serotonin, noradrenalin and adrenalin. In its link with stress, nicotine's most far-reaching action is probably achieved by raising cortisol levels. As seen in early chapters, cortisol is closely associated both with our general response to stress and in determining how well we cope with stress. The manner in which nicotine raises plasma cortisol levels is not fully understood. It certainly stimulates CRF release which in turn controls the release of ACTH – a stress hormone with wide reaching effects on learning and alertness. Such a pattern is important in our understanding of the craving associated with nicotine addiction. When CRF is administered to smokers they lose their craving, suggesting the need for a cigarette could be triggered by a drop in cortisol levels, and certainly one of the earliest effects of nicotine is to stimulate an immediate rise in the plasma cortisol level.

In fact such a pattern is almost certainly too simple. It is uncertain how nicotine stimulates CRF release, although receptors which accept and bind to nicotine are very widely distributed throughout the brain. These receptors also show a significant increase in heavy smokers, and this is linked to the type of tolerance and dependence tobacco induces. In addition to its action in the brain, it also seems likely that nicotine raises blood cortisol levels by acting directly on the adrenal glands. Such supplementary action, which would not involve ACTH, looks likely though so far it has not been clearly demonstrated. A dual mode of action of this type would also perhaps help us understand the complex effects tobacco exercises on the user. The release of ACTH would certainly account for the immediate lift linked with tobacco use. ACTH is associated with learning, memory and concentration, and we know that many smokers use nicotine to gain or enhance these. The release of ACTH is also involved in determining our basic diurnal rhythms: this may be related to the smoking rituals with which many users surround their waking and sleep patterns.

While the release of ACTH helps explain the lift produced by tobacco, we must also find a base for its soothing and calming action. This probably comes from the 'reward' effect associated with high levels of cortisol. It is certainly linked with the release of beta-endorphin, which we have seen is associated with a sense of well-being and even euphoria. The link between nicotine and the release of beta-endorphin is important, partly because it gives a further basis for both dependence and addiction. As we have seen with other drugs [and nicotine is a drug], the body quickly adapts to the presence of substances which stimulate or mimic the effects of the endorphins or enkephalins. The result is the beginnings of dependence or addiction, with the body demanding a regular intake, and producing adverse and unpleasant effects if that intake is not maintained.

Nicotine addiction is very difficult to treat, and many find major problems in withdrawing from tobacco use. Although personal motivation is still a factor in determining success, tobacco programmes often have lower success rates than those directed at alcohol users. One problem is that heavy or chain smoking in particular quickly becomes linked with our pattern of life and work. In such circumstances the smoker may find it difficult to go even short periods without a cigarette, and may have difficulties starting the day without this artificial boost to ACTH levels. High ACTH levels in the morning are closely associated with alertness and waking up, and for many smokers it is virtually impossible to start the day without at least one cigarette. For those addicted – or close to it – the withdrawal symptoms associated with nicotine deprivation are not life-threatening, although they can be extremely unpleasant. They also closely mimic our natural response to stress. A tobacco user who stops will be faced by an immediate rise in noradrenalin activity in the locus coeruleus. This will not be countered by an attendant rise in beta-endorphin or enkephalin activity, as these substances will have been suppressed by the regular use of nicotine. The overall effect is a sustained feeling of anxiety, depression, malaise and pressure which leads to the behavioural and temper changes associated with trying to give up smoking.

Recent research has improved our understanding of nicotine addiction, and has also brought hope of new treatments to counter the effects of withdrawal. We now know that there is a positive relationship between smoking patterns and the nature of nicotine addiction. It comes as no surprise that heavy smokers are far more nicotine dependent than light smokers. More surprising perhaps are some other factors linked to tobacco use. These include:

* men typically are more successful in giving up smoking than women;
* in those giving up, there is a definite correlation between success and education. This shows as a higher success rate in those who have gone through some form of higher education;
* the extrovert is generally more successful in giving up than the introvert. In all forms of addiction a powerful, independent personality can be a useful support in overcoming the inevitable problems of withdrawal. Man is, however, a complex animal and where such personality factors are linked with stubbornness, they can also reduce the hope for success, whatever the degree of criticism and opposition the individual faces;
* there is a link both between the level of consumption, and the time the individual has been a user. In general heavy smokers with a long term of use have the greatest difficulties;
* not surprisingly non-inhalers find it far easier to stop;
* there appears to be a link between high levels of alcohol and coffee use and difficulties in stopping smoking. Such a pattern should probably be viewed with particular care as it could relate more to the social nature of tobacco use than any great craving in the individual.

It should be stressed again that all these are statistical generalities, and should not be used to deter anyone who is considering stopping or reducing their use of tobacco. Much current research is concentrating on minimising the effects of tobacco withdrawal. Clearly, where these are extreme, and similar to the stress response itself, there is continued pressure on the user to return to his addiction. If we can provide support to counter the initial effects of withdrawal, then the hope for long-term success is far greater. One exciting development, discovered it seems almost by accident, surrounds the use of the drug clonidine. This is an anti-hypertensive agent whose use has also been shown to diminish the activity of noradrenalin in the locus coeruleus region of the brain. The effect of this reduced noradrenalin activity is to eliminate much of the anxiety, irritability and restlessness associated with stopping smoking. Certainly clonidine, and a range of other substances and treatments which act on our stress response, give great hope for the future.

Many people have already been successful in their determination to quit smoking. This is significant, because statistical surveys suggest that the body quickly recovers from the adverse effects of smoking. This means an almost immediately reduced risk of most disease, a fact which deserves consideration by those who defer giving up because they think the damage will already have been done. In the UK alone, there are now estimated to be more than 10 million ex-smokers, many of whom provide the most vitriolic elements in the anti-smoking lobby. This is not surprising: many smokers who quit the habit continue to miss the social and psychological – if not the physical – aspects of tobacco. They fear that seeing others smoke will increase their own risk of returning to their addiction. Unfortunately such a fear is not entirely groundless: some smokers do return to their habit long after they have apparently stopped, often because of acute or sustained stress.

In most Western countries tobacco use is declining, and tobacco users are now in the minority, a fact readily emphasised by those looking for changes in the law surrounding tobacco use. In the UK, the number of adult males who smoke dropped from 62 per cent to 42 per cent of the population between 1960 and 1984. At the same time, the number of adult females who smoke dropped from 44 per cent to 32 per cent. Also changing is the pattern of tobacco use. This remains highest among the lower socio-economic groups, particularly manual workers. In this group, UK statistics suggest that around 50 per cent still smoke, compared with only some 16 per cent for the professional classes. In part education is to blame, although it is not enough to account totally for such startling differences. The whole basis of health education is better understood by the professional and managerial classes, who also benefit from the availability of better medical advice and support. Cigarettes, despite frequent price rises, remain the poor man's source of comfort, whereas alcohol addiction is more common among the business and executive communities. This pattern, which is common to most Western societies, presents further difficulties. Many of the diseases associated with smoking benefit (to some extent) from an early diagnosis and treatment, but the lower socio-economic groups have poor health education and support programmes, and are largely ignorant of the basic aspects of health and diet.

Whatever the tobacco lobby may claim, the link between tobacco and disease is now clear and established. That we cannot indicate how many cigarettes a day will definitely cause lung cancer relates more to the complexity of the disease and to personal variability than to the safety of cigarettes. What we can say is that 10 per cent of those who smoke heavily will die of lung cancer, a disease whose incidence is negligible in those with no environmental cause. In the UK, the Royal College of Surgeons estimates that there are at least 100,000 deaths annually directly attributable to smoking. Of these, around 70,000 are lung disorders, either cancers, emphysema, bronchitis or obstructive lung disease. In the US, smoking is linked with more than 120,000 deaths from cancer alone. These statistics are a damning indictment but do not reflect the full scale of the problem.

As well as lung disorders, smoking is heavily implicated in a range of other clinical conditions. Indeed as a general rule smoking serves to make most disorders worse, and can certainly have implications for therapy. Recent years have seen a significant increase in our understanding of the link between smoking and cardiovascular conditions. This link is now known to be far more serious than some had anticipated. Furthermore, if smoking does not actually cause a particular heart condition, it will certainly make it more difficult to treat. In many cardiac cases, whether the patient smokes, or can stop, may determine the final outcome of the disease. Certainly, to smoke with a known heart condition is dangerous and will limit the benefit of therapy.

Smoking is linked with a number of other forms of cancer apart from lung cancer. These include lip and mouth tumours, which may arise in part because of the thermal trauma associated with smoking. Smoking has also been linked with pre-malignant changes in the oesophagus (throat) and is certainly implicated as a cause of throat cancer. Less clear is the link smoking may have with stomach cancer and other cancers of the gastrointestinal tract. Very heavy smokers do show a higher incidence of stomach cancer, although this may be connected with the fact that many smokers also abuse alcohol. Alcohol is known to damage the gut, and whether higher than average rates of stomach cancer in alcohol/tobacco abusers are due to drink, tobacco or both is not clear. Also confused is the link between smoking and peptic ulcers. It is not clear if the same stress that makes the patient smoke also causes the ulcer, or if there is a more direct link. What is certain is that heavy smoking makes ulcer treatment far more difficult. Many anti-ulcer drugs appear less effective when used by heavy smokers, including Smith, Kline and French's cimetidine, the major ulcer treatment breakthrough of the 1970s.

Several recent well publicised studies have shown that subliminal smoking, that is breathing the tobacco smoke of others, is also acutely damaging. Non-smokers who live or work with smokers have a significantly higher rate of many smoking-related diseases, including lung cancer. Tobacco smoke in its fully oxidised form is particularly damaging to health and this, coupled with personal variation in susceptibility, makes it entirely possible for a non-smoker to die while their smoking partner remains virtually unscathed. Even where subliminal smoking does not cause life threatening conditions, it can worsen both minor and serious lung conditions. This is of particular relevance to children whose parents smoke. Certainly any disorder like asthma can only become more difficult to treat if the patient is continually subjected to a smoke filled environment. Not surprisingly, recognition of the damage caused by subliminal smoking has brought increased pressure from the anti-smoking lobbies, and this seems likely to grow as non-users demand the right to choose whether or not they breathe tobacco-polluted air.

Changing public attitudes to smoking are putting increasing pressure on those who still choose to smoke. Many office and work-places now ban smoking in all but designated areas. Theatres, cinemas and restaurants are all under pressure either to ban smoking, or make special non-smoking areas available. In air and rail travel the space allocated to smokers appears to get smaller and smaller, while the attitude to those who light up in non-smoking areas gets more vigorous and violent. Harsh public attitudes may harden the approach of some smokers, but others are embarrassed by finding themselves virtually pariahs. We are moving towards the banning of smoking in most public places, confining it to consenting adults in the privacy of their own homes. Such a trend could be important: breaking the link between smoking and social activity would reduce still further the number of tobacco users.

Despite the overall trend, each year sees a new generation of smokers come on-stream, and smoking among the young is a particular cause of concern. Starting the habit seems to be linked with the type of deliberate risk-taking we discussed elsewhere, with the need for a challenge in our secure society. For the more sensible this comes in the form of dangerous hobbies like hang-gliding, parachuting and mountaineering, but for others it takes the form of substance abuse. Tackling smoking amongst the young is difficult: they are unconcerned about the long-term risks to their health. This makes re-education and the control of tobacco advertising of crucial importance. Virtually all countries in the West exercise controls over tobacco advertising, and this has resulted in many tobacco companies switching their main marketing drive to the Third World. In the past, most tobacco advertising concentrated on the social and sexual aspects of smoking, and its link with the great outdoors, attempting to convince us that tobacco made us more vigorous and attractive to the opposite sex. Public awareness has largely discredited this form of advertising, though some still seek to emphasise the average smoker's distaste for fresh air by showing them lighting up while riding horses or herding cattle. One particularly insidious form of advertising, now adopted in the West, is sports sponsorship. This seems a strange combination given the effect of tobacco on health and sporting performance. It is, however, an effective and important form of advertising for the tobacco companies, and it seems particularly directed at the young. If tobacco companies sponsor a sport, then many young people will link that brand of tobacco with the names of their sporting heroes. Tobacco companies claim that sports sponsorship is aimed entirely at changing brand loyalty. Such an argument looks at best disingenuous.

Too many young people are still turning to tobacco. In part this stems from the example set at home, and there is a direct link between young people smoking and tobacco use by their parents. Legal age and restrictions on purchasing

177

appear to have little effect. One recent US survey showed that, amongst children who smoke, 95 per cent have a favourite brand long before the legal age at which smoking is theoretically permitted. Rebellion, and the stimulus and challenge it provides, is partly to blame but is not enough to account for the still quite significant number of young people who take up smoking. Another reason is clearly stress levels among the young. Though the welfare state may remove one form of stress, it imposes others which more than compensate. For the young, a sense of personal identity and individuality is essential, and this is often lacking in our impersonalised society. Add to this the spectre of unemployment and it is hardly surprising that many people grow up with a sense of frustration and despair. Whatever the cause, our lack of success in curbing smoking among the young is depressing. Though we can concentrate on helping existing users stop smoking, our real hope for the future must be in deterring others from starting. Health education may play a part, but further major restrictions on tobacco use, pricing and advertising seem necessary.

Advertising, and the media in general, frame an important part of the link between stress and tobacco use. As we have seen, the media help shape our attitudes, and not always in the most positive manner. In many ways the media drive us towards the use of potent substances like nicotine and alcohol to deal with day-to-day stress. By demonstrating that the use of outside chemical props to combat stress is not unusual or adverse, the media condone and encourage such use. Then begins the stressful spiral of worry over a very damaging habit. For those who attempt to give up, stress immediately rises to far greater levels than those faced when the habit was started. At this point massive willpower, or outside support, is needed if the addict is not to return to the habit from which he is trying to free himself.

One problem in advocating increased restrictions on

tobacco use and advertising is the ambivalent approach of most governments. Throughout the West, tobacco taxation has become an important source of national revenue. In the UK, the government takes more than £50 million a day in tobacco taxes, a figure which has parallels in all Western countries. To lose such a source of direct revenue is clearly unacceptable – at least in political terms, requiring a massive restructuring of the taxation base of most Western countries. Furthermore, by accelerating death in the middle-aged and elderly, the tobacco industry provides massive savings on pensions, social security, hospitals and all social benefits. Smokers are not the drain on our health services they might appear. Many – if not most – more than pay for the limited help modern health technology can provide to counter their years of abuse. Tobacco has become intrinsically linked with the economic fabric of most developed nations, and to make significant changes involves not just the medical professions but also the consensus of the population and the agreement of all political factions.

One group who will doubtlessly oppose change is the tobacco lobby, which over recent years has grown in strength and influence in most Western countries. Its influence has often countered the price rises which might deter tobacco use, and has certainly stopped many of the changes in advertising designed to reduce smoking in the young. In the UK, at least one junior health minister was transferred for supporting changes in the legislation surrounding sports sponsorship by tobacco companies. This is unfortunate because such changes are necessary. The tobacco lobby in most countries is very active in contributing money to political party funds, thus deterring that party from making significant changes once in office. The tobacco companies spend millions, while most of the anti-smoking groups operate on a shoestring. The lobby system is part of the democratic process of all Western countries, and many pay the ultimate price for the highly professional manner in which the tobacco companies are able to manipulate and exploit the system.

The hypocrisy of the tobacco lobby is hardly surprising: vested interest will always move to secure its position. More important perhaps are some of the misconceptions which surround smoking, which is still associated with masculinity, independence and worldliness. This could not be further from the truth: smoking is a massive sign of personal insecurity. By lighting up, the smoker is saying to the world that he cannot cope without some outside prop. Nicotine is a drug. By using it continually we quickly reach the point of dependence, and what better definition of personal inadequacy do we need than that we cannot last even a few hours without the need to artificially suppress our stress response.

Stress and smoking are now inextricably linked, not least in the minds of those who continue to smoke. Certain stressful jobs are linked with a higher incidence of tobacco use. One recent survey of the nursing professions showed that psychiatric nurses had the highest level of tobacco use. This is hardly surprising given the nature of their job and the pressure under which many work. Tobacco use is also closely linked with boredom, and has been shown to be more common in people whose jobs involve long periods of inactivity: soldiers, sailors, taxi drivers and, perhaps more surprisingly, prostitutes. The understanding of such patterns is important. If we can analyse the manner in which people use tobacco, and why they use it, then we can take steps to replace it with something far less noxious.

At present tobacco use remains one of the West's most serious and intractable health problems. Its use is diminishing but not at the rate those concerned with health would like to see. Some insurance companies now offer significant discounts to those who do not smoke: such decisions being made, not on emotional or political grounds, but on the basis of actuarial facts. Nevertheless, many continue to smoke, and will inevitably finally pay the price.

That tobacco is one of the hardest forms of addiction to tackle is demonstrated by the high failure rates of many tobacco addiction programmes. Successes often stand at no more than 20 per cent, a figure which remains depressingly constant. Substitutes like nicotine chewing gum may help in the short term, but they should not be considered as a long-term replacement for smoking. Although many of the problems associated with tobacco come from smoke, tar and impurities rather than nicotine, there are other reasons why we should not artificially seek to maintain high nicotine levels. Nicotine is a powerful substance with far reaching effects outside the transient changes we seek when we use it as an aid to combat stress. Aids like nicotine chewing gum should be used with care and then only under medical supervision to overcome the immediate effects of tobacco withdrawal. Early studies suggest that nicotine gum may itself be addictive. There is no easy route to combat tobacco addiction. We can limit some of the worst side-effects of withdrawal but not remove them entirely. It is up to us instead to handle stress by a change in life-style rather than by turning to artificial aids like tobacco.

—11—

Life style and stress

In the final part of this book we will examine some of the techniques which can help us manage our response to stress. There is little sign that the stress in our society is declining. We already face a virtual pandemic of the wear and tear disorders linked with stress. As our understanding of the cause of disease expands, it looks certain that stress will be linked with many more diseases, either as a direct cause or as a contributory factor making the underlying condition worse – and far harder to treat. The authors of this book feel that much of our ability to handle stress depends on our own approach, attitude and life-style. Though the medical and psychiatric professions have a place, much of the early responsibility for combating stress must lie with the individual. Health is not acquired by treating disease. Vitality, stamina, drive – and indeed a high level of tolerance to stress – come from physical fitness coupled with a balanced and sensible life-style.

Central to any consideration of life style is diet. Over recent years this has become a contentious area, with its own cottage industry of writers and publishers all seeking to influence what we eat – and how we eat. While much of this comment is valid and some excellent, some is spurious, seeking merely to emphasise one extreme viewpoint. In the terms of this book diet has a twofold significance. At one level what we eat clearly affects our general health and so has an indirect influence on how well we cope with stress. Of more direct significance is the fact that certain foods, known graphically as 'trigger foods', can bring about an almost immediate and extreme stress-like response. This is of importance in many conditions including stress-related disorders like migraine and asthma. We hear a great deal at present about food allergies, an area of considerable and growing research. We already know that, for some, avoidance of certain foods can reduce the occurrence or severity of a range of disabling conditions. As our understanding in this area grows, it looks certain that many of the brain neurotransmitters we have already examined, or possibly their precursors, will be shown to be involved in food allergy.

A typical Western diet is far from ideal. In general we eat far too much animal protein and fat, typified by meat, cheese, butter and eggs, too much refined sugar and flour, and too few complex carbohydrates like whole grains, roots, vegetables and fruit. The move towards frozen and pre-processed foods also produces problems, resulting in a diet which is high in calories and over-rich in cholesterol, but bland, low in bulk and fibre and often deficient in some vitamins and minerals. If all this sounds familiar, it is not the intention of this book to become another health food manual. What we are urging is balance in what we eat; we are less concerned over dictating what foods must be avoided. If our life-style – or business environment – dictates periods when we must eat rubbish, then these should always be countered by periods when we pay greater attention to the quality of what we eat.

One major problem of the Western diet, which some nutritionists also call the 'diet of affluence', is that we gain too high a percentage of our calories from animal fats. These are rich in cholesterol which, as we have seen, can be acutely damaging to the cardiovascular system. In all, a typical Western diet gains some 40 per cent of its calories from the ingestion of animal fats. This is too high, with most nutritionists recommending a figure of 35 per cent – or lower. We are not advocating a meat free diet: we can easily get down to within the 35% figure by switching *some* of our interest from red meat to poultry and fish, and by reducing sensibly our intake of such products as butter, cheese and eggs. The preparation of food is also important: we should choose lean cuts, pare excess fat and grill meat in preference to frying it in animal fat. The idea that to be healthy we must live on nuts, pulses, fruit and cereals is a fallacy.

The typical Western diet is low in fibre, and much of the fibre we take in bread, pasta and pastries is too refined. Twenty years – and more – ago, nutritionists decided (mistakenly) that fibre was of little nutritional value. The result is that many of our modern food processing methods concentrate on removing it. On average, the typical Western diet contains less than 20 grams of fibre a day, significantly less than 30 grams considered necessary for good health. Fibre is known to improve gastric motility generally, and play a particularly important role in fecal elimination. Recent years have seen a rise in fibre-based diets directed at the obese, and while these appear to have worked for many, such an extreme emphasis is probably unnecessary. We can increase our fibre intake easily by the use of more fruit, fresh vegetables and cereals – plus a switch away from the purchase of bread and cakes made with refined flour.

One problem of low fibre diets is that they provide insufficient bulk to help with the process of elimination. This is compounded by the heavy use of sugar – particularly in much processed food. In the US, the average consumption of sugar is 125 pounds [57.5 kg] a year – a massive figure which has close parallels in Western Europe. By far the bulk of this sugar is taken indirectly in the form of processed foods, soft drinks and pastries, rather than as sweets or in tea and coffee. For most of us this sugar is a dietary non-necessity which is high in calories but low in bulk and other dietary requirements. Excess sugar leads to obesity, and the attendant health risks mentioned earlier, plus other disorders including diabetes and tooth decay. The characteristic pattern of stress over-eating often includes a heavy emphasis on sweets, pastries and chocolate, so adding obesity to the problems the individual may already face.

High calorie diets, based on low bulk and processed foods, tend to be a feature of Western society. If we also add alcohol, we see a pattern of food intake which is very high in calories, but low in other dietary elements – and certainly low in residue. The result is we put on excess weight while our bowel attempts to maintain the process of elimination. Processed food also contains too much salt: a Western diet is estimated to provide seven times more than the body requires. This can disrupt other mineral balances particularly potassium. High salt levels are also linked with, and certainly exacerbate, hypertension. We should cut back on salt-rich processed foods and avoid the use of salt as a food supplement: a natural balanced diet contains more than enough salt to meet a healthy person's requirements.

Pre-processed and frozen foods can be low in essential vitamins and minerals. Frozen vegetables are often deficient in zinc, a trace element which we have seen is depleted when we are stressed. Also destroyed by pre-processing – or poor preparation – are many of the vitamins whose presence is linked with our ability to cope with stress. Thus the B vitamins are linked with nerve function, B1 with sleep and B6 with nerve growth. Vitamins C and E can easily be removed during processing, but both function during exercise in preventing the oxidation of the tissues, and may also have a more far-reaching role in the brain. Like all vitamins, Vitamin C is present in the body in only limited amounts – in an adult human about 2 grams. This is especially important for smokers, because smoking depletes the level of vitamin C in the body.

The changes in diet which are necessary to improve health are not as massive as some might suggest. They can be summarised as:

* a reduced level of animal fat intake – including a moderate switch away from red meat to fish and poultry;
* a reduced cholesterol intake achieved largely by the replacement of animal [saturated] fats by vegetable [unsaturated] fats;
* a reduced intake of sugar and salt;
* an increase in dietary fibre – fruit, fresh vegetables, whole grains:
* above all a balance between intake of calories and calorie expenditure.

Any review of diet and stress must consider the importance of the 'trigger foods'. Among the most common are cheese, with its high concentration of tyramine, red wine [histadine] and other foods like chocolate, yeast and beef extract. The one thing all 'trigger foods' have in common is that they contain high concentrations of the precursors of biogenic amines like serotonin, noradrenalin and dopamine. In the case of red wine, this can give rise to high levels of histamine in the brain, resulting in an extreme reaction, most typically in the form of a severe, migrainous headache. Whatever the nature of their action all those foods mentioned can induce a severe stress-like response in those who are susceptible. The same can also be caused by caffeine which exerts a definite and often undesirable effect on brain sugar metabolism. Also implicated are foods containing seasoning salts, particularly monosodium glutamate. In its natural form [glutamic acid], glutamate is itself a neurotransmitter. It may not be as central as the classic neurotransmitters dopamine, noradrenalin and serotonin but, taken in excess, it can create an undesirable effect.

The use – and indeed misuse – of food additives is more common than many realise. One recent survey of a standard shopping basket showed that the food purchased contained no fewer than 150 chemical additives. This is hardly surprising given that one staple commodity like bread can have up to twenty additives. The main uses of additives are as colourings, flavourings, stabilisers and antioxidants. Such chemicals are now an intrinsic part of a modern multi-billion dollar food industry, where food is mass produced but sold through outlets where shelf turnover is often poorly controlled. While this accounts for the emphasis on stabilisers and antioxidants, it does not explain colourings and flavourings. Here the food industry claims to be merely reflecting public taste, while clearly leading the public – children in particular – to demand the extravagantly flavoured and the luridly coloured.

In terms of our health, the food additive industry has a poor record. Although all chemicals added to food are subjected to rigorous testing for toxicity and carcinogenic or teratogenic properties, there have been a number of notorious examples where food additives have been hastily withdrawn. Food additives may also have psychoactive qualities – like glutamate – which it is difficult to isolate in animal experiments. Such substances may not be toxic in the chemical sense, but they may exert an effect on the excitory or inhibitory neurotransmitters of the brain. This again may produce the extreme and violent stress response seen in food allergies. Many of the people expressing concern over food additives cite problems like eczema, asthma, headaches, gastric irritation, hyperactivity, fits, diarrhoea – and many more. All of these can have close links with our response to stress. Tartrazine, which is widely used to provide the yellow colour in a host of products from fizzy drinks to fish fingers, has been linked to hyperkinetic behaviour and learning problems in children – yet it remains in very wide use. The authors of this book recommend the avoidance of additive-rich foods. With additives now being listed on labels we can at least attempt to avoid some of those which present the greatest problems. This could include the new sweeteners, which are amino-acid based and could act as 'trigger foods'. As yet no-one knows enough about food allergies and the psychoactive effects of food additives – more research is urgently needed.

Caution is also needed in other areas of food processing and preparation, such as the increasing use of irradiation sterilisation. This may fundamentally alter the nature of the food, not least by destroying some of the vitamins it contains. It is now possible for an individual to fail to have a balanced diet, not because the food is wrongly chosen, but because processing has changed the nature of that food. The wide use of microwave ovens in both professional and domestic kitchens has major implications. Irradiating food destroys its B vitamins, which we know have a major role in helping determine our response – and indeed our resistance – to stress.

So far we have concentrated on what we eat. Where stress is concerned it is also essential to examine how and when we eat. Eating is, or should be, closely linked with our biorhythms. If we eat regularly, then our body adjusts to that pattern, and our blood glucose level remains regular and balanced. If we are stressed and snatch at our food in a few stolen moments, then it is not surprising that we have problems with our digestion. We have seen that when we are stressed the motility of the gut is depressed. It will therefore function less effectively when a few badly masticated mouthfuls of hamburger are thrust upon it. The answer is to set aside regular times for eating and then to eat slowly. We in the West could learn a great deal from the Chinese tea ceremony, a procedure perfectly designed to slow down and ritualise the process of taking food. This may seem impossible within a busy executive schedule, but the alternative is an afternoon of discomfort, and a digestive system which could be on the downward path to something more serious than indigestion.

Among business executives one frequent cause of dietary disruption is jet lag, and the effect jet travel has on our biorhythms is due partly to eating at a time when the digestive system is largely shut down. This pattern is not helped by the frequency with which airlines thrust food and drink at their helpless passengers, and the lavish nature of much of the food provided in first and upper class cabins. There is no simple answer to jet lag though we can do much to limit its worst effects by eating less and drinking more non-alcoholic beverages. President Reagan has worked out his own regime to limit the effects of jet lag. This includes:

* no alcohol, but plenty of other liquids – up to 5 pints a day;
* eat easily digested carbohydrates in the morning, last through the afternoon on plenty of tea and coffee, and take protein only in the evening;
* sleep as much as possible;
* break journeys with 24 hour stops wherever possible.

We have mentioned briefly the need to balance food intake and energy utilisation. Without this we begin the drift towards obesity with its physical, mechanical and psychological problems. Much of Western society not only eats too much high calorie food but also has a sedentary pattern of life and work in which any surplus energy has little chance of being utilised. The result is the deposition of fat in our bodies – and more importantly in our arteries. In Table 2 we have listed some common activities, together with their average level of calorie utilisation. The figures show that many of us have a life style which is concentrated far too much at the top of the table.

Table 2. Activity table: calories per hour.

Activity	Women	Men
Sleeping	60	80
Resting	65	85
Standing	85	110
Writing	90	120
Driving	120	150
Walking	180	240
Making love	150–300	180–420
Gardening	200	250
Dancing	200–350	250–420
Swimming	400	600
Running	500	650
Squash	650	800

Source: Cannon and Walker.

Over recent years a great deal of questionable material has been written over the value of exercise in the control of stress. Much of this comes from the recognition that beta-endorphin can be released when we take vigorous exercise. Early thinking seemed to suggest that those who were taking exercise were in some way motivated by a desire to gain the calming, pain-killing or euphoric effect of beta-endorphin – in much the same way as those who overeat. In fact such a pattern looks unlikely: much exercise is too gentle for significant levels of beta-endorphin to be released. Though this release may be important – or vital – for the trained athlete or professional sportsman, it looks less significant for those who take exercise merely to help with stress. Where beta-endorphin is released its main benefit may be that it restricts the action of stress hormones like cortisol. This puts an end to the depressed, defeated feeling so common in those who are stressed: an end in fact to the feeling of learned helplessness. Much of the benefit of exercise comes from the manner in which it 'burns off' the by-products of our stress response. As we have seen, when we are stressed adrenalin is released, which in turn induces the release of energy pre-cursors like fatty acids and sugar into the blood. These form an important part of the fight or flight response. With much of the stress of modern life lacking any physical dimension, these energy elements have 'nowhere to go' and run the risk of being deposited within the blood vessels. Even surprisingly low levels of exercise can prevent this happening, a fact of vital significance to all who have a sedentary life-style coupled with high levels of sustained stress.

In considering exercise we need to distinguish between competitive games and the more gentle exercise taken to maintain fitness – and help combat stress. If we get involved in seriously competitive activity then this will impose a stress all of its own. Such competition need not involve others. Many who take up running become obsessed both with the activity itself and with running against the clock. While this may be harmless for some, for others it will serve to replace one stress with another. What we are concerned with here is more gentle exercise programmes designed to help tackle the effects of a sedentary and often over-indulgent life style. The whole area of competitive and indeed professional sport deserves separate consideration: it has a pattern and profile of stress which is distinctive and often unique.

When advocating exercise we must recognise that many readers will start from a position of considerable unfitness. This makes general recommendations difficult. Certainly violent games, and indeed violent exercise, are totally unsuit-able for flabby, middle-aged people who have taken no

exercise for ten or twenty years. In such cases a new programme involving a degree of violent effort will not only be
unhelpful – it could be positively dangerous. Not only can
such a drastic change impose a strain on the heart, it can
also damage muscles and joints. The answer is again balance,
with new exercise programmes beginning slowly, and gradu-
ally building up to a level where we can make more serious
demands on our bodies.

The range of keep fit books – and videos – now available
to those who decide to get fit is too great to review in depth
here. For the unfit, such activities as walking, jogging,
swimming and controlled gym exercises are best recommended. Golf is a popular choice for many business
executives, though this may be of limited benefit if we play
with business associates and merely transfer our problems
to an outside venue. Golf is also for many a very frustrating
and infuriating game. Even so, like all other sports and
exercise, it is an effective way to release the products of
stress. In many ways sport brings us closer to our animal
origins in the way it provides a physical outlet for the
by-products of stress. Though the immediate effect of sport
may, and indeed should, be to induce tensions of its own,
these are quickly eliminated taking with them many of the
problems posed by our high pressure society.

For those who find difficulty in motivating themselves,
company health programmes can often be surprisingly effective. In those who are less than totally committed, the
pressure and support of a peer group can make giving up
more difficult. A great deal has been written about the
success of Japanese company exercise programmes, while in
Europe the Swedish car manufacturer Volvo probably leads
the way. Here exercise is mandatory, everyone from the
Managing Director downwards being required to take at
least 30 minutes exercise a week.

The success of these initiatives shows that exercise patterns need not be comprehensive or time consuming to be effective. As little as three sessions of 20 minutes per week can produce surprising results. In the UK, the telecommunications company STC introduced just such a limited programme for its headquarters staff during 1983. Although the scheme was optional, some 180 out of 210 chose to take part. The scheme involved an initial health check followed by the design of a personal fitness programme in line with the individual's own aims and objectives. The programmes involved warm-up exercises, stretches, joint mobility exercises, cardiovascular training, muscle strength and endurance training plus dietary advice and relaxation training. A typical exercise pattern was designed to last 20–25 minutes, the aim being that the individual should exercise three times a week. After 12 months the programme was assessed in some detail. Those who had continued with their exercise pattern had shown significant improvements in lung function and had lost considerable unnecessary weight, while seven mild hypertensives now had their condition under control without the need for drug therapy. STC also reported a significant improvement, of nearly 25 per cent, on an already low figure for sickness absence. Most surprising of all (for some) was that the pattern of exercise did not prove a fad, and after 12 months more than half of those who had embarked on the programme were still active.

Exercise also offers psychological benefits, providing a diversion into something totally different, a distraction from our day-to-day worries. For many sport also gives an opportunity for self expression which is often lacking in our work, and provides a good outlet for aggression which would be damaging or unacceptable if released elsewhere. We may laugh at the Japanese practice of supplying a model of the managing director for junior staff to assault, but it does allow a healthy physical outlet for anger, frustration and stress.

Another way to forget our worries is through a hobby. Hobbies can give the body a chance to recover from the worst effects of stress, and also produce the sense of meaning, identity and purpose often lacking in much of modern life. The choice of hobby is a very personal matter, and in terms of relieving stress the only requirement is that our involvement be total and uninhibited. In our hobbies at least we should say 'To hell with what others think' and indulge ourselves to the full. Many eminent people have had hobbies they have pursued almost to the point of fanaticism. Henry Hoover, one-time US President, claimed there were only two occasions when he could fully relax – when in prayer, and when fishing. Not surprising then the Assyrian proverb 'Gods do not subtract from the allotted span of men's lives the time spent fishing'.

In using hobbies or outside interests to combat stress, one cautionary note is perhaps necessary: it is vital that we select one which is not in itself stressful. Any over-stressed businessman who thinks he can relax by diving into the maelstrom of local politics is likely to find he has replaced one form of stress with an even more voracious one. The new vogue for home computer games is not without risk. A study at the UK's Birmingham University has indicated that adults playing computer games are at risk from a very high and unrelieved stress response. The stress in playing competitive, sedentary – and above all – frustrating computer games is not dissimilar to that we encounter when driving.

As well as relieving stress, an interest in sports and hobbies broadens our range of interests in life. The idea that to be successful we must devote ourselves exclusively to work is a fallacy. If we find time to relax then we turn again to work with our vigour and interest renewed. We are in fact far more effective. There is no-one more limited and uninteresting than a person whose life and conversation revolve around their work. Where such people take their work and its problems home with them, it is hardly surprising that their personal relationships are vulnerable and more likely to break down. It is not enough to be successful at work: to be happy and fulfilled we must also be successful in our private lives and in our personal relationships. We hear a great deal now about workaholics, with the media suggesting such a trait is somehow desirable. Those most at risk appear to be the creative and the self-employed, though all can reach a point where their work takes over to become the sole point in their lives. What we are advocating is not idleness, or a negative attitude to our employment and employers, but again a form of balance in which work takes on a central role which is neither destructive nor total. To achieve this a few ground rules are necessary:

* do not socialise exclusively with work colleagues. Where this becomes necessary avoid the topic of work;
* where possible avoid irritating personal relationships both at home and at work;
* take proper breaks and holidays;
* if you are compensating for a lack of interest in life by working too hard and too long then do something about it;
* where possible confine contentious and difficult issues to the early part of the day. Try and spend the last part of the working day winding down;
* at home agree a limited period – say half an hour – during which work issues can be discussed. Outside this avoid the topic of work – and particularly its problems.

Diet, exercise, hobbies and relaxation should all play a part in our improved life style. So too should rest and sleep, though for many this remains a difficult area. To some extent an improved life style should help us sleep, though for many this may not be enough. In the US, an estimated 50 million people have sleeping problems, which come behind only headaches and the common cold as a reason for seeking medical help. In 1981, the US issued a massive 29.9 million prescriptions for sedative-hypnotic drugs to aid sleeping, a distinct improvement on earlier still higher figures. More recently at Stanford University, researchers have proved successful in helping wean long-term insomniacs away from drugs — some after periods of use as long as twenty years. Much of the Stanford programme concentrates on relaxation exercises and developing good sleep habits, though considerable attention is also paid to reducing the incidence of daytime stress. Indeed Stanford appear to have found a direct link between daytime stress and sleeplessness. In many cases this stress in insomniacs is compounded by a general poor adaptation to stress, and more negative self-images than are found among healthy sleepers.

Insomnia remains a major problem. As we have stated elsewhere, sleep plays an important part in our response to stress, with many of the early adverse effects of stress being reversed by sleep. Sleeplessness has many causes, including psychiatric disorders like depression, chronic drug misuse, excessive efforts to fall asleep and such conditions as myoclonus (an infection) and sleep apnea. It is also clear that for some the bedroom becomes associated with sleepnessness, rather than rest and relaxation. This means that sleeplessness becomes an almost self-perpetuating condition. There are no simple answers to insomnia, but the following tips are preferable to diving into the pill bottle:

* adopt fixed eating and retirement patterns. These firmly establish the biorhythms and give the body a chance to wind down and relax in a normal manner;

* avoid working late at night and up to the point of retirement;
* do not stay in bed if you cannot sleep. Get up for a while, do something undemanding, and then try again;
* avoid caffeine, alcohol and, particularly, tobacco late at night;
* find out if for you sex is relaxing or arousing, and adjust your pattern of life accordingly.

When considering life style and stress, we must also consider the nature of the stress involved. This book is really about chronic and persistent stress: acute and extreme stress is another topic. In the US particularly, PTSD [post traumatic stress disorder] is now recognised as a clinical condition. Much of the work in this area has been done on Vietnam combat veterans, with an estimated 500,000 of those involved in the Vietnam War returning in need of psychological and emotional support. One aspect of PTSD faced by Vietnam veterans is the condition known as Alexithymia – a blindness to emotions. This can result from psychic trauma in early life, and is a particular feature among those Vietnam veterans who were captured and suffered torture and abuse. Alexithymia is characterised by permanent demonstrable damage to the hippocampal cells of the brain, probably brought about by excessively high and sustained levels of the adrenal cortical hormones. It is difficult to treat and appears permanent. Alexithymia is also linked with other disorders including the type of coronary prone behaviour (Type A) mentioned earlier.

One problem in relating stress to specific diseases is that we cannot readily develop empirical models that link specific levels of stress to a particular clinical condition. At the University of California's Los Angeles Psychiatric Unit, efforts are now being made to establish a scale of combat exposure which can be directly related to the level of PTSD diagnosis. Such a development could be important, in enabling psychiatrists to predict future problems. One difficulty already encountered by the study is that in combat stress builds cumulatively when the individual is subjected to a series of horrific events. It also suggests that such an experience increases significantly the probability of later stress-related conditions.

PTSD research and applications have now been extended to cover other stressful situations including pathological grief, industrial accidents, rape and disaster. PTSD is characterised by a number of factors laid down by the American Psychiatric Association, which may or may not be present. These should be recognised as natural responses to sudden and extreme stress. They include:

* a tendency to re-experience the event, whether in the form of dreams, memories or even re-enactment;
* a tendency to a reduced involvement in the outside world, together with the numbing of response;
* hyperalertness – or exaggerated startle response;
* feelings of detachment or estrangement;
* sleep disturbances;
* guilt, both about surviving and the behaviour required to achieve survival;
* memory impairment and/or loss of concentration;
* avoidance of actions which bring back memories of the trauma;
* an intensification of symptoms when in contact with events or people who bring back memories of the trauma.

Several psychologically based defence mechanisms have been identified as significant in extreme trauma-based stress. These will be discussed in a later chapter but include repression, rationalisation, denial and projection, which are largely unconscious. Here it is sufficient to point out that PTSD research is playing an important part in our ability to understand all acute stress-related conditions.

This chapter has covered some of the ways in which an improved life-style can help us cope with stress. Our approach has been to seek realistic, rather than extreme, solutions which seem appropriate for the hard-pushed businessman. If we recommended strenuous regimes of exercise coupled with stringent calorie controlled diets, then these would not be followed. Nor, in many cases, are such extremes necessary. The hysteria of many dietary manuals – particularly those which recommend diets free from animal products – is to be deplored: they induce in many people an unnecessary level of concern over their diet. The fundamental need in diet is for balance, within which we can *occasionally* cheat a little, provided we are prepared to rectify this later. The problems come when we cheat too often. The aim is become fitter and more resistant to stress, not run in the next New York or London Marathon.

In the fight against stress, it is important that we adopt a positive not a passive approach. This idea is not new: as early as 1913 two German clinicians, Mosse and Tugenreich, wrote: 'The state of health of each person is the effect of the environment and the reactions of the body. This reaction is determined by a sum of factors which are normally described as constitution. This constitution is not innate – but is the result of both innate and acquired characteristics.' What they had recognised is not merely the manner in which our bodies react to outside situations, but the ways in which we can help and pre-condition them to cope better. In this chapter we have sought to identify some of the ways in which such pre-conditioning and resistance become possible: not just from diet, fitness and a healthy sex life, but from a positive and pushing mental attitude. As we have seen, if we sit back and accept what stress has to offer, then its effects are compounded by our own passive approach. If we fight, and do not undermine our body's ability to fight, then we may still suffer stress, but we will have much less to fear from it.

—12—

The role of chemotherapy in stress-related disorders

We have seen that stress is established as a fundamental cause of many diseases, and makes other conditions worse and far harder to treat. The pervasive nature of stress makes it difficult to write about the link between chemotherapy and stress. Clearly disorders like ulcers, heart disease or cancer have an appropriate drug regime whether or not the condition is caused or exacerbated by stress. To review the chemotherapy of stress-related conditions would be to review largely unnecessarily a substantial part of modern clinical practice. For this reason we have concentrated on those drugs and treatments which seek to gain their effect by some influence on brain neurochemistry: tranquillisers, neuroleptics, anti-depressives, etc. These have been for years the most widely used and prescribed drugs in most Western societies, and seem likely to remain so despite modest attempts to curb their use in many countries.

Allopathic [conventional] medicine has three main options when treating stress-related conditions: drug therapy, counselling and support, and – in extreme cases – ECT [electroconvulsive therapy]. As we have stated earlier, Western medicine is typically heavily based on pathology correction, that is the diagnosis, treatment and correction of the symptoms of disease. This also means that therapy is very heavily drug based. In terms of stress conditions this is unfortunate because correcting symptoms does little or nothing to identify and relieve the underlying cause of the disorder. A great deal more could often be achieved through psychotherapy and counselling, but these are often lacking within our time and cost conscious health services. Indeed, in much of the West a pattern is emerging where those who can afford them enjoy psychotherapy and support, while those lacking resources embark on courses of drug therapy which are – at best – purely palliative.

Throughout this book we have tried to emphasise simple and practical solutions to the problems of stress. We have emphasised changes in life-style and attitude which have been shown to help counter the worst effects of stress. Above all we are seeking to strengthen our resistance to stress by means which are gentle, utilise our natural chemical rhythms and are not damaging in themselves. Although drug therapy has a place, our belief is that many embark on courses of drug treatment when simpler and more effective alternatives are available. Much of the responsibility for this lies not with the doctor but with the patient. We have grown up to expect that any interview with a clinician is terminated by a prescription. We are ill-prepared to accept that advice alone may be just as beneficial, and indeed many are resistant to accepting such advice if it does not comply with the life-style they enjoy and prefer. Knowing much of their advice will be ignored, doctors are faced with a dilemma. Do they provide drugs they may believe to be second best, or do they leave a patient to suffer the consequences of an extreme stress response?

Most clinicians work under massive time pressure and, as we have seen, stress-related conditions are notoriously difficult to isolate and diagnose. In most cases the hardest thing for a doctor to diagnose is that a patient is perfectly healthy and normal. This is made more difficult by the assumption that something must be remiss, or the patient would not have come in the first place. The onus is then on the doctor to provide a diagnosis and treatment, if only to reassure the patient that his condition is under control. Many patients have a hazy and confused understanding of medical science, despite the recent upsurge of interest in medical matters by the media. One recent study of patients visiting US general practitioners showed that although 80 per cent felt their health would be better if they reduced their stress levels, most of them did not know where to begin, and felt the advice they received from television, newspapers, books and magazines was more confusing than helpful. We have criticised elsewhere books on health, diet and fitness which are not objective but merely emphasise one narrow viewpoint. By creating doubt and uncertainty such books do more harm than good.

One area where the authors find it difficult to be objective is the use of ECT for the treatment of violent psychoses, schizophrenia and depression, which in many cases are directly related to stress. ECT comprises the application of high energy, in all some 100 volts, across the skull of the disturbed patient. ECT differs significantly from electro-acupuncture, where *minute* electrical impulses are used to stimulate the release of the endogenous opiates. The technique of electroacupuncture, and its implications in stress and addiction therapy, will be reviewed in a later chapter. Its essential difference from ECT lies in the level of electro-stimulation used, and the accurate and specific siting of the electrodes. This results in the close control of both the process and any side effects involved. By contrast, ECT appears both crude and random. The process, which typically lasts about one second, is repeated until the patient experiences a severe convulsion. The procedure is usually repeated at two to three day intervals. After this the patients are, it is hoped, calmer, with their core symptoms, whether related to depression, schizophrenia or some other disorder, considerably reduced.

One objection to ECT is that we do not really understand how it works. This would probably not matter were the treatment not so extreme and violent. Given the delicate nature and balance of brain biochemistry, it is evident that any massive electrical shock [and in terms of brain electrochemistry it is massive] must induce far reaching physiological changes. That some of these appear to benefit the mentally disturbed patient is not surprising. One effect ECT has is to stimulate the release of met-enkephalin in the hypothalamus and the limbic regions of the brain. As met-enkephalin is one of the endogenous opiates, it has a calming effect and a major influence on our behaviour. This will help quieten severely disturbed patients, and make them more medically manageable, but it is questionable whether it helps cure their underlying condition. It is surely inappropriate to use such an extreme and potentially damaging treatment merely to create a patient who is more amenable.

The side effects and damage caused by ECT are well documented. Among the worst is a significant loss of memory function. This amnesia varies in severity according to the type of ECT used. Lowest levels appear to result from high energy, sinusoidal [the electrical waveform used] ECT, although even here memory impairment is significant. Memory loss also increases with the frequency of ECT treatment, though whether this is due to the increased energy levels needed to induce later convulsions, or from more far reaching physiological changes, is not clear. Patients experiencing ECT are certainly more tranquil, although this tranquillity is achieved at the expense of amnesia and disorientation. For many within the medical professions ECT is now a controversial issue, and its use does appear to be declining.

Some claim the practice is close to barbaric, performed largely in ignorance and unjustified in even the most extreme of cases. It is therefore impossible to conceive the situation where the authors of this book would advocate the use of ECT.

In considering drugs, and the range of psychoactive drugs now used in stress therapy, a few facts require explanation. Too many people still assume that pharmacology is an exact, almost mathematical, science in which a specific dose will produce a precise effect. This is not the case. Pharmacology may be exact in the dose and quality given, but patients are far from exact in the way they respond. The biological variation in our response to drugs is considerable, as can be seen from the placebo effect. In clinical practice, a placebo may be defined as a substance given to please – rather than benefit – a patient. Placebos form an important part of the reassuring, psychological relationship between a doctor and patient. Placebo therapy is not rare, used only occasionally to placate the difficult or nervous patient: a recent UK study showed that some 20 per cent of drugs prescribed had no discernible pharmacological action. Placebo therapy has a significant place in the history of medical science.

Given the psychosomatic base of much stress related disease we should not be too critical of placebos. They often produce an effect, both in emotional and somatic [physical] disorders, which is not demonstrable in animal experiments. One problem is the wide variation patients show in placebo therapy, and the fact that such variation is unpredictable. In one US study, placebo results varied by as much as 300 per cent, being mainly influenced by the patient's personality and social attitude. Clinicians recognise that even highly specific drugs may be influenced by emotional, relational or social factors, but 300 per cent is extreme and well outside normal clinical variation.

We will now review briefly some of the major drug categories which are used to help us cope with stress. In all cases when reviewing side-effects and withdrawal symptoms we must recognise the importance of individual variation: a side effect which is acutely distressing to one patient may be absent in another. This is just as well. The UK Committee on the Safety of Medicines showed that the three most widely used monoamine oxidase inhibitors [a group of anti-depressants] had some 180 recorded side effects. Above all we must recognise that our state of mind and physical condition may influence the way in which we respond to a particular drug – and how effective it proves. Even our relationship with our physician can be important: Jonathan Swift recognised this when he wrote; 'No man values the best medicine if it is adminstered by a physician he hates or despises.' Clearly a good relationship between a doctor and patient is significant, as is a positive attitude to any drug therapy undertaken.

The drug group most closely associated with stress is probably the tranquillisers because of their widespread use and because of the attention they have received from the media – attention that is not always fair or balanced. Tranquillisers are usually used to treat anxiety, although the range of conditions for which people turn to them is considerable and includes insomnia, depression, pre-menstrual tension, marriage problems, panic and worry. The commonest tranquilliser group is the benzodiazepines, which include diazepam [Valium], chlordiazepoxide [Librium] and flurazepam [Dalmane]. Diazepam and chlordiazepoxide are the commonest drugs prescribed in most Western societies, and have a long clinical history of use which is often outstanding. The problems with the benzodiazepines relate not so much to the drugs themselves, but to the manner in which they are used and prescribed. The benzodiazepines are highly effective in treating crippling anxiety, and provide outstanding muscle-relaxing qualities, but we now know they are not the safe, dependence-free drugs which they were once considered.

The benzodiazepines have been in use for some twenty years, and have largely displaced other drugs like the amphetamines, barbiturates and propanediol in the treatment of anxiety. One attraction of the benzodiazepine group is that they are not toxic, and are in overdose among the safest drugs in common use. These tranquillisers gain their effect indirectly because they mimic the action of GABA – the brain's commonest inhibitory neurotransmitter. By occupying the receptor sites of GABA, the benzodiazepines allow the action of the three major biogenic amines – serotonin, noradrenalin and dopamine, to become potentiated. This is important because low levels of these three substances are linked with the presence of unnatural levels of anxiety or depressive illness. One important feature of the benzodiazepine tranquilliser group is that their action is not specific to one neurotransmitter substance. By acting on GABA, or more accurately the GABA sites, the benzodiazepines affect the action of all the major biogenic amines. This is useful in many clinical conditions although, as we will see, more recent psychoactive drugs which are neurotransmitter specific are also beginning to play an important part in the treatment of depression.

Tranquillisers have now become an important part of therapy in all Western countries. Although estimates vary, the number of people taking drugs in the benzodiazepine group is massive. In the US, some 15 per cent of the adult population are prescribed minor tranquillisers in any one year – although only some 6 per cent of this group take the drugs for more than one month. In the UK, some 3.5 million adults [14 per cent of the population] use benzodiazepine drugs, with the most worrying figure of all being that some 250,000 people have been taking them continuously for more than twelve months. This is despite the fact that such long-term use is against the manufacturers' advice, which suggests that the benzodiazepine drugs should not be used for long periods, and indeed questions their effectiveness in treating anxiety for periods of longer than four months. Whatever the effectiveness of the drugs, long term use is clearly linked with the important question of dependence, now known to be far more serious with the benzodiazepines than was at first thought, and all the more worrying because it can occur at quite low, and certainly clinical, dose levels.

Dependence on the benzodiazepines has exactly the same base as the dependence we reviewed in the chapter on substance abuse. In any given situation the body will seek to achieve a biochemical balance. If we provide a benzodiazepine substitute for GABA, then the body will react with a reduced production of GABA. This is fine until the GABA substitute is withdrawn, at which point the brain is short of its commonest inhibitory substance, and the action of the biogenic amines is not merely potentiated – it runs riot. The result is the acute and unpleasant withdrawal symptoms many – if not most – experience when withdrawing from even short-term benzodiazepine use.

As the benzodiazepines are (comparatively) safe, with a long clinical history, some question the need to withdraw long-term users. Apart from the moral question of continuing to prescribe or take a drug which is doing little good, there are other considerations. The benzodiazepines have been linked with memory loss and learning difficulties in animals, even at low doses. The drugs can make patients listless and remote, especially elderly, long term users. Above all in many applications the drugs are purely palliative, enabling patients to evade though not solve their problems. If we use tranquillisers to treat someone whose anxiety stems from poor housing or overcrowding, we merely chemically isolate the patient from the problem; we do nothing to solve it, or to make the patient more able to face reality. It is not hard to see how we reached the present situation of tranquilliser misuse. The early literature on the benzodiazepines claimed they were safe and dependence free, with outstanding results in treating severe anxiety and its attendant conditions. Faced with a mass of stress-related disorders, many showing unclear psychosomatic symptoms, doctors were tempted to use tranquillisers knowing that if they did no good, they would certainly do no harm.

A greater awareness of the dependency risks posed by the benzodiazepines has seen their use curtailed both in the US and Western Europe. Despite this, many governments still fail to adequately fund tranquilliser rehabilitation programmes. In the UK alone, 3.5 million are considered to be at risk from tranquilliser dependence, yet this area has less than 5 per cent of the funds allocated to heroin abuse – with an at risk group of some 50,000. What is needed is far more awareness of the risks associated with widespread tranquilliser use, coupled with prescribing policies which utilise the drugs' positive attributes but limit the length of time patients are likely to be involved in their use.

In the UK, minor tranquilliser prescriptions are only declining at a rate of around 3 per cent a year. More attention is being paid to withdrawal problems, but here progress is not helped by the fact that most minor tranquilliser manufacturers give little or no guidance on the question of dependence and withdrawal. We now know that benzodiazepine dependence, like tobacco, is among the hardest to conquer: Professor Lader of the UK's Institute of Psychiatry recently stated that the minor tranquillisers could produce withdrawal symptoms which are far worse than heroin. These symptoms are extremely varied and far reaching. In the UK, the National Tranquilliser Advisory Centre [TRANX] lists more than three pages of withdrawal symptoms, although these are seldom given in full to patients because they can prove extremely discouraging. TRANX lists them under four main headings:

1. *Changes in sensation.* These include feelings of unreality, tinnitus, nightmares, hypersensitivity, numbness, blurred vision, unsteadiness, illusions, balance difficulties.
2. *Mood changes.* These include apprehension, paranoia, labile emotions, apprehension, anxiety, restlessness, sadness, lack of confidence.
3. *Bodily symptoms.* These include appetite loss, hyperventilation, nausea and vomiting, palpitations, tremor, diarrhoea, changed menstrual patterns, changes in libido – most typically reduced.
4. *Mental functions.* These include poor concentration and memory, lack of drive and initiative, lack of decisiveness.

There is no established therapy for withdrawing from tranquilliser use. Some advise an immediate cessation, although TRANX produces a series of data sheets which advise a more controlled withdrawal in which the dose is reduced over a two to three-week period. With tranquillisers, initial withdrawal symptoms can appear within hours, or be delayed by as much as eight to ten days. TRANX suggests that, for longer term users, the peak of the withdrawal comes six to eight weeks after the last pill is taken, although the symptoms may continue for several more months. One recent study claims that there is a direct relationship between the persistence of the withdrawal symptoms and the length of time the tranquilliser has been taken. As a rough guide the study suggests thirty-five days for each year the drug has been taken, though whether this is based on biochemical data or the experience of the physicians concerned is not clear. For patients the major problem of tranquilliser withdrawal is that the pattern of symptoms shows a series of diminishing peaks: patients who feel they are over the worst are suddenly faced by a fresh bout of extreme and unpleasant symptoms, and at this point many regress, finding that even the lowest dose of benzodiazepine will immediately relieve the unpleasant effects.

The changing patterns of tranquilliser prescription, now particularly seen in the US, suggest that in the future we will be faced with far fewer cases of long-term tranquilliser dependence. Many clinicians now also report a change in public attitude, with patients being less prepared to accept the minor tranquillisers. This attitude contrasts considerably with that seen ten or fifteen years ago, when many seemed to want nothing more than a fresh round of what became known as their favourite 'sod it all' tablets, and the Rolling Stones sang of 'mother's little helpers'. Many studies have been done on tranquilliser use, but there seems no clear group who needs them or benefits from their provision. Much current attention is directed at why women show a far higher use of anti-anxiety drugs generally. In both the US and Western Europe, women are twice as likely to use tranquillisers as men, with figures approaching 30 per cent of all adult women being not uncommon. A number of reasons have been put forward for this difference, though all are largely speculative. They include:

* women's changing role in society, and the problems of making a career in what remains a male orientated society;
* role conflict, which is often pronounced for working women, and which we know can be extremely stressful;
* women's emotions are (supposedly) more labile;
* isolation, particularly among women tied to a home life

or largely confined by children or the care of sick
relatives;
* men respond to their problems differently and are more
  likely to end up dependent on tobacco or alcohol than
  on tranquillisers;
* women visit their doctor more often, either on their
  own behalf or on that of their children. This means any
  problems are more likely to be recognised.

Cynics might also suggest that many male clinicians handle
women's problems badly, and with a lack of sympathy and
sensitivity which leads to the prescribing of ever greater
levels of tranquillisers.

Although by far the most heavily used, the benzodiazepines are not the only drugs in the treatment of serious anxiety
conditions. Beta blockers, which at higher doses also have
applications in hypertension, are relatively safe even in
moderate overdose. They gain their effect by a more specific
action than tranquillisers, working on the adrenergic receptors. Probably the best known of the beta-blockers used to
treat anxiety are propanolol and practolol. These drugs are
particularly effective when treating patients whose anxiety
includes somatic [physical] symptoms like tremors, palpitations or dizziness.

Less safe even in moderate overdose are some of the other
drugs used to treat depression. This is particularly true of
the tricyclics which in the UK now account for around 10
per cent of all hospital admissions for accidental poisoning.
In many of these cases coma results, with death occurring
in as many as 10 per cent of all overdose patients. The
tricyclics, which include imipramine and amitryptyline,
have a long history of use and are now fairly numerous.
They have found particular applications in the treatment of
endogenous depression. The tricyclics function by raising
the levels of active serotonin and noradrenalin in the brain.

How they achieve this varies, and specific tricylics are now available which differentiate between the two amines. Typically these drugs prevent the re-uptake of the neurotransmitter – or neurotransmitters – by the synaptic vesicle [the holding container in a transmitting axon which lies alongside the synaptic gap]. This does not increase the total neurotransmitter produced, though it does potentiate the action of what is available. As we have seen, low levels of serotonin and noradrenalin are linked with anxiety and depression, so anything which helps prolong the action of these substances is useful in therapy.

Also active in prolonging the action of the neurotransmitters are the monoamine oxidase inhibitors [MOAIs]. As the name implies, these drugs inhibit the action of the monoamine oxidases, the non-specific enzymes which are responsible for both the formation and the degradation of serotonin, noradrenalin and dopamine. Where monoamine oxidase is inhibited, this increases the active concentration of these neurotransmitters within the synaptic cleft. Again in therapy this has implications for the lifting of depression. One feature of both the tricyclics and the MOAIs is that they are typically non-specific in action: they act either directly or indirectly on a range of neurotransmitters. This has led to a search for anti-depressant drugs which are neurotransmitter specific and so have less far-reaching effects.

The development of highly selective anti-depressant drugs is a complex area, and still in an early stage of development. In many cases the drive to such drugs comes not from their clinical performance in treating anxiety and depression, but because they have better toxicity profiles, are less sedating and are certainly safer in overdose. They are possible because of our improved understanding of brain neurochemistry. The complex interaction between the neuropeptides and neurotransmitters has meant that specific drugs which can act on only one system have seldom produced the improvements which might on paper have been expected. Indeed, as no man is an island, no neurotransmitter operates in isolation. This means that while a new drug may fulfil its promise and act on only one neurotransmitter system, its indirect implications for other sectors of brain neurochemistry may cloud its benefits.

Our limited understanding of much brain biochemistry does not help progress. We know that in stressful situations brain dopamine, serotonin and noradrenalin levels should rise naturally. We know, or believe, that rises in noradrenalin are linked with coping – probably because the neurotransmitter fulfils some inhibitory role. What we are less clear about is the interaction between the various neuropeptides and the biogenic amines. We do not really know how neuropeptides like met-enkephalin modulate the action of noradrenalin, nor the exact nature of the apparent link between cholecystokinin and dopamine. Many believe that neurotransmitters like noradrenalin provide an immediate response to stress, while the subsequent release of met-enkephalin serves to modulate or limit that response. This fits with the 'fight or flight' phenomenon where the body quickly overcomes the initial shock of stress to provide a rational and balanced approach to the situation. What we are talking about is the neuropeptides 'fine tuning' our response to stress. How far we can go down this road is not yet clear, although the answer to these – and many more – questions lies at the heart of our understanding of depressive illness, and of our quest for anti-depressive drugs which act specifically and effectively on one neurotransmitter system.

The last major drug group we need mention here is the neuroleptics. These are the major tranquillisers which were briefly mentioned earlier in connection with schizophrenia. The main application of the neuroleptics is in the treatment of functional psychoses, but at lower doses the drugs also have important anti-anxiety qualities. Neuroleptics act to block the dopamine receptors, and thus play a role in the inhibition of dopamine transmission. This is particularly important in the treatment of schizophrenia, a disorder linked with abnormally high levels of dopamine in the brain. The neuroleptics also appear to act indirectly on noradrenalin, which is believed to have a biochemical role in the aetiology of a number of psychotic conditions. In their treatment of anxiety the major tranquillisers seem to offer few advantages over the *controlled* use of the benzo-diazepines, but in longer term use they may be preferable because of their lower tolerance and dependency profiles.

It is the authors' opinion that, while drug therapy does have a place in the treatment of stress, many are too prepared to see drugs as a panacea. Drugs should be regarded as a final solution only to be attempted when other actions have failed. Above all what concerns us is the public's casual attitude to many drugs: we seem to think there is nothing odd in taking drugs which make us alert when we *should* be tired, tranquil when we *should* be sad, and calm when we *should* be agitated. Mood enhancement, be it through drugs, tobacco or alcohol, is the name of the game. It is, however, a very dangerous game because there is no such thing as a totally safe drug, and sooner or later we must pay for every lift we receive as our body seeks biochemically the comfort of equilibrium.

Many books have been written on the adverse side-effects of drugs and they are most welcome, engendering as they do a healthy suspicion in patients over what they thrust into their bodies. Those clinicians who feel such an approach causes apprehension and concern should consider the history of tranquilliser use in the West. Thousands of patients, including some 250,000 in the UK alone, are now dependent on tranquillisers, and they face either the continuation of that dependence or the agony of withdrawal. They were

virtually all led into their difficulties by sincere physicians who did not understand the dependency implications
of the drugs they were prescribing. By all means patients
should take drugs prescribed by their physician, but they
also have the right to know the nature and the implications
of what they are taking, and about any alternative therapy
which is available.

In two areas side-effects are particularly important: when
drugs are taken with alcohol or during pregnancy. As mentioned earlier all drugs have a synergic or antagonistic effect
in association with alcohol, and their action becomes unpredictable – and in some case lethal. Tranquillisers and anti-
depressants taken with alcohol are far more dangerous than
many realise. As a general rule drugs and alcohol should not
be mixed, and neither, except under medical supervision,
should drugs themselves be mixed to excess. One problem
of our pill-conscious society is that clinicians may not know
exactly what their patients are taking, from over-the-counter
[OTC] medicines and analgesics to recreational drugs. Much
of the onus for what is taken in such cases must lie with the
patient, not just the clinician.

Also resting largely with patients is responsibility for
drugs taken during pregnancy. One problem is that drugs
– like alcohol – are most dangerous during the first trimester,
and especially in the first month when many women do not
know they are pregnant. For this reason, women in whom
pregnancy is a possibility are best advised to avoid all
drugs. Certainly no drugs should be taken outside medical
supervision. This is now easier to enforce, though it took
the thalidomide tragedy to bring the risks to public attention. Most of the drugs reviewed in this chapter have not
been shown to have significant teratogenic effects, although
some argument still exists over the benzodiazepines. In many
cases we do not fully understand the risks drugs pose in
pregnancy, and animal experiments and toxicological studies

produce limited results. In such a situation we must clearly err on the side of caution.

As we have seen all the drugs used for treating or ameliorating stress, anxiety and depression gain their effect by some action on the biogenic amines. This action may be direct on the biogenic amine itself, or indirect through action on the amines' receptor sites or the enzymes associated with the amines' creation or degradation. We now have a considerable battery of mood-enhancing drugs available. We need to determine how these drugs will be used, and what place drug therapy has in the whole treatment of stress. We repeat that drug treatments of stress-related conditions like anxiety and depression are purely palliative, and suggest that drugs such as tranquillisers should be used for short-term support in situations like bereavement and marriage breakdown, rather than in long term problems. Above all drugs cannot offer a solution alone, but should be part of an holistic approach to the treatment of stress.

Alternative medicine

This book is concerned with recognising stress, and with identifying the means by which we can control our response to it and limit its more damaging effects. It is less concerned with finding solutions which are based solely on particular types of therapy, whether conventional, psychiatric or fringe (or alternative). Our main concern is to find treatments which are effective for the individual, because we know that our response to stress is highly individual, and which are gentle in their approach. For this reason we have tried to avoid the use of drugs, not because we do not believe in chemotherapy, but because we believe that drugs should come late in any chain of treatment – where other forms of therapy have failed. Such an attitude leads to a consideration of fringe medicine, though this is an area which must be approached with caution. As scientists we expect to draw our findings from a pool of data, carefully conceived and evaluated. With alternative medicine this is seldom possible. Too often we find ourselves among a mass of quasi-scientific claims framed in language bizarre, antique and emotional. This helps nobody, and is particularly unfortunate because many, including the authors, believe fringe medicine has much to offer.

The antipathy between fringe and conventional medicine is not new, and certainly inhibits objective evaluation. In 1986 the BMA [British Medical Association] produced its report on fringe medicine. This report had been initiated at the request of Prince Charles, a known supporter of alternative medicine. He must have been disappointed with the BMA's findings, which proved negative and amounted to little more than a defence of conventional medicine. The BMA's unwillingness to find any real base or need for alternative medicine does not fit with many UK patients' attitudes, nor does it agree with the increasing number of UK doctors, the BMA's own members, who are looking for solutions to their problems in the field of fringe medicine. Alternative medicine in the UK – like many Western countries – is burgeoning, fuelled in part by cutbacks in the conventional health sector, but also by an awareness that alternative medicine is effective for many conditions.

The one factor which continues to isolate alternative medicine, even in the eyes of many of its supporters, is its unwillingness or inability to subject its techniques to objective scientific trials. This fact is already recognised by some areas, like homeopathy, though is still largely ignored by others. Properly conducted scientific trials require certain criteria, including:

* purity of chemicals, as laid down by international standards;
* constant experimental environments;
* controls to check variables;
* adequate samples to allow for valid statistical analyses.

Many of these are lacking in much research conducted in the fringe medical field. In this, fringe medicine is not unlike a commercial enterprise which suddenly decides to conduct its annual accounting procedures in a totally new manner. Not only would this isolate the company in terms of communication with the world at large, it would also bring into question the company's credibility and whole style of management. Many in the fringe medicine field claim that what little research they do is ignored because it does not appear in major medical abstracting journals like *Index Medicus* and *Excerpta Medica*. This is true, though the fault probably lies more with the nature of the research than with the priorities of the journals involved.

It is difficult, though, to apply such generalities to a field as diverse as fringe medicine. Many of the techniques used are unrelated, their only common base being that they are outside the sphere of what we regard as conventional medicine. Many fringe medicine techniques have their origins obscured by the mists of time, while others like homeopathy and hypnosis are of more recent origin. Some of the fringe medicine disciplines, particularly the relaxation and meditation techniques, are often closely linked with religious or philosophical beliefs. This causes problems, because it is often impossible to accept one without the other. It may well be that the reader wishes to find a new religion or philosophy of life: this we know *can* offer exactly the comfort and support so important in stress management. The detailed examination of the philosophical base of such techniques is, however, outside the terms of this book, and so we have concentrated on the therapeutic benefits involved.

In a book of this size, it is difficult to cover the whole spectrum of alternative medicine. We have sought to divide it into three main areas, although these are not mutually exclusive, nor are patients necessarily confined to seeking help from only one discipline. The three areas comprise techniques which involve taking [or applying] something, those – like osteopathy and faith healing – which involve the laying on of hands, and those which involve the teaching of relaxation and meditation. In all cases we have tended to defer to those techniques which appear to have particular relevance to the treatment and management of stress. This is not difficult. Fringe medicine has always been closely linked with the vague, imprecisely defined psychosomatic conditions we now know are frequently caused by our body's response to stress. Alternative medicine has in fact been treating for centuries the results of stress, though perhaps without knowing or being able to quantify the basis of that treatment. In this it is not so different from conventional medicine which still, in many areas, obtains an improvement or hopeful outcome without really understanding the scientific base of that result.

Among the earliest of the fringe medical disciplines is herbalism. It is not hard to imagine the earliest cave dwellers seeking therapeutic help from the pharmacological properties of plants. Many of the witches, so feared and respected in the Middle Ages, were clearly little more than solitary, elderly women with a good understanding and experience of the medicinal qualities of plants. Many also sought to surround their abilities with dark, mystical and spiritual capabilities, and so they were often persecuted and punished. This attitude still plagues much of fringe medicine. Many plants *do* have definite pharmacological properties, but practitioners must avoid making false and unsubstantiated claims which tend to deflect away both would-be patients and those involved in conventional medicine.

In the West, the heavy technical base of the pharmaceuticals industry tends to mean we have lost sight of the pharmacological properties of plants. Though the herbals of the Middle Ages ran to hundreds – if not thousands – of pages, herbalism in the West is an art now practised by relatively few. Indeed, with the casual use of pesticides indiscriminately devastating our natural flora, many herbalists must struggle to find the basic ingredients of their potions. There has been little contact between herbalism and the West's conventional pharmaceuticals industry, which is surprising given the costs of researching modern drugs and of bringing them to the marketplace. Such an approach does not exist in the Far East, as shown by the recent decision in China to undertake a detailed evaluation of the herbal remedies long used in folk medicine.

The crude, pharmacological properties of plants are massive. Early poultices used by folk medicine to treat wounds have been shown to have antibiotic properties, while the tonic qualities of plants have a long history of use. One 1969 US study of 158 folk remedies showed they contained a total of 116 plants of known tonic qualities, typically used in multiples of between two and seven plants per potion. This heavy emphasis on tonic effects is important, not least if we consider the link between herbal medicine and stress. As we know, any substance which has a tonic or stimulating effect can help sustain our response to stress, provided that is we can overcome the risks associated with regular use and dependence.

It is impossible to review here the whole range of plants used in herbal medicine. Among the best known are *Atropa belladonna* [deadly nightshade] which contains in natural form the drug atropine. In conventional medicine, atropine is used in the treatment of heart conditions. In herbal medicine it is also used for the treatment of nervous conditions, stemming in many cases from the patient's inability to cope with stress. Also receiving much recent attention is the 'drug' Iscador, which is derived from the northern mistletoe *[Viscum album]*. This has been used in Europe from the time of the druids to treat everything from cancer to nervous conditions. Mistletoe is the classic example of a beneficial plant whose undoubted qualities are framed round and largely hidden by the mystique attached to it. An epiphyte with an unusual growing pattern, mistletoe appears to have puzzled and interested our primitive ancestors. That this still has echoes in today's herbal medicine is less forgivable. As it is, Iscador does seem to have very definite pharmacological properties, many of which relate to nervous conditions, and many to the treatment of stress-related disorders.

In the eyes of the public the one herbal substance undoubtedly linked with the treatment of stress is ginseng *[Panax ginseng]*. This has been used, particularly in the Far East, for thousands of years. It has a mass of claimed effects ranging from tonic to aphrodisiac. Much of the research on ginseng has been published in Russian, Chinese and Korean medical journals, and is not widely accepted in the West. The plant does have interesting qualities, although whether these are as extreme as is often claimed looks unlikely. Ginseng does act as a stimulant and has properties which could help support our response to stress. It is claimed that its anti-fatigue properties only come into play when an individual is stressed or faces a challenge. In this it appears to act indirectly on the adrenal cortex and have a carbohydrate sparing effect. If such an unlikely deferred effect is possible in ginseng use, then it deserves more detailed examination. Its active ingredients could provide exactly the type of prophylactic treatment for stress which conventional medicine so desperately requires: provided we could create from them a product which is both safe and dependence free.

Closely linked with traditional herbalism is the technique known as naturopathy. This seeks to allow man's natural healing powers to come to the fore by removing some of the obvious and less obvious barriers to good health. Naturopathy has much to offer, and its underlying philosophy is not so far removed from that of this book. Unfortunately the techniques are often associated with extreme views on vegetarianism and temperance which confuse unnecessarily the basic issues involved. Naturopathy also struggles to overcome the stigma of the infamous 'monkey gland' treatments of the earlier part of this century. These seem to have done little good to either the reputation of fringe medicine or the patients involved.

Another technique of naturopathy involves the application of vitamins, either specific vitamins or more general treatments involving several. We know that certain vitamins are linked with our ability to handle stress. B1 is associated with sleep, while B2 and B6 are involved with nerve growth and function. Also involved in our ability to handle stress are the trace metals. At one US centre, Pfeiffer's Brain Biocenter, interesting results are now being obtained in treating schizophrenia with trace metals. In this study, solutions high in zinc, magnesium and vitamin B6 have largely replaced drug therapy. This follows recognition that many schizophrenic patients who commit suicide have low zinc and magnesium levels in the brain but high levels of copper. Once again this appears to be an instance where a closer understanding of brain neurochemistry has the potential to revolutionise therapy in a serious and frequently stress-related condition.

One of the hardest alternative discipline to evaluate is homeopathy, developed in the nineteenth century by a Dr Hahnemann, and based on the principle that like cures like. It involves a detailed examination, followed by the provision of low doses of the animal, mineral or vegetable substance which the doctor believes to be at the root of the patient's condition. The problem is that homeopathy has no apparent scientific base, so many conventional clinicians who are receptive to techniques like herbalism and naturopathy are deeply sceptical of its benefits. Indeed homeopathy, probably more than any other alternative therapy, separates the fringe from the conventional. Most evaluations of homeopathy have proved equivocal, save perhaps one on rheumatoid arthritis. Even this study is not totally satisfactory, because rheumatoid arthritis is a notoriously difficult condition in which to evaluate therapy, with the patient's state fluctuating naturally throughout the day.

Arthritis provides a good example of the principles in-

volved in homeopathic therapy. The condition is characterised by high levels of copper in the tissues. In homeopathic
treatment, still more copper is provided, although this time
in highly dilute form. The copper supplement is normally
diluted in alcohol and considered to be 'potentised'. A great
deal of debate in homeopathic circles now surrounds the
dilution strengths used in arthritis treatments – and other
therapy. Many homeopaths still use Hahnemann's original
dilutions but some prefer other dilution strengths they often
keep secret. The variable nature of homeopathic solutions
is one of the factors most offensive to conventional medicine.

A fundamental law of physical chemistry states that the
minimum number of atoms of an element which can exist
in a solution is 6×10^{23} – Avogadro's number. Homeopaths
using dilution above this level refer to these solutions as
'material doses'. The problems come where homeopaths
claim solutions more dilute than this, down to 10^{-200} – a
physical impossibility as far as conventional scientists are
concerned. Such a dilution would involve solutions containing less than one atom of the substance, again a physical
impossibility. Despite this many homeopaths claim the
ability to create such solutions – *and indeed claim they are
the most potent.* Many homeopathic solutions are also very
crudely made, often using tapwater, which must make a
nonsense of claims to very accurate dilution levels – or indeed
high levels of purity. In many homeopathic treatments the
homeopathic solution is not administered directly to the
patient but to herbal or other remedies he may be taking:
the solution is sprayed over the pills with no guarantee of
how much of the potentised material comes in contact with
the medication. While most homeopathic practitioners are
undoubtedly sincere, such bizarre preparation methods put
them at odds with scientists who are trained in more conventional disciplines.

One theory put forward over the last few years is that

homeopathic medicine may, in some way as yet unknown, affect the neurotransmitters and neuromodulators. Certainly the discipline places a heavy emphasis on homeostasis, claiming that people feel better if their body is functioning in balance. Indeed if one feature characterises the whole of alternative medicine it is the heavy emphasis on restoring the body's balance, from with the Chinese concept of yin-yang, to the most recent developments in fringe therapy.

Homeopathic doctors also take a great deal of care in diagnosis, many spending far more time with their patients than is common in conventional medicine. In stress-related disorders this is important and beneficial. Homeopathic doctors also pay close attention to such factors as their patient's life-style and diet. In a recent development, echoed in conventional medicine, many homeopaths are using constitutional types as an aid to diagnosis. This typing, based on physical and psychological criteria, aims to determine what sort of people are most susceptible to particular diseases.

Despite the fact that few conventional scientists have been able to demonstrate any basis on which homeopathic procedures might work, the discipline goes from strength to strength, with many major cities now having large-scale homeopathic hospitals. Many conventional clinicians are adding homeopathic treatments to their range of skills, so it looks unlikely that the technique has nothing to offer. One factor could be the placebo effect, though homeopaths would be justifiably insulted to have all their therapy attributed to this alone. Placebos are far more important than many recognise, and it is not impossible that homeopathy, with its close link between doctor and patient, has found some way to enhance or systematise the placebo effect. As we have already seen the body has a tremendous innate ability to heal itself. Homeopathy could perhaps have found ways to harness this ability. Certainly increasing numbers of patients, disgruntled with conventional therapy, feel homeopathy has something to offer, especially for rheumatoid, dermatological and allergic conditions.

Although support and counselling play a part in them, herbalism, homeopathy and naturopathy normally involve the patient ingesting something. This means that any effect which is induced comes either from the crude, pharmacological properties of the plants involved or from the placebo effect. In recent years, partly because of the unhappy record of the conventional pharmaceuticals industry, a number of false claims have been made over the safety of herbal remedies. While it is generally assumed – correctly – that these are safer than conventional drugs, because the active ingredients are usually in lower concentrations, any claim that herbal medicines are totally safe must be incorrect. Like any other medicine, herbal remedies gain their effect by ingredients which are active within the body. If we then abuse such remedies, we risk inducing a response outside the desired effect, which may be damaging. While some herbal remedies, like ginseng, appear to be very safe in high dosages this cannot be assumed of everything. If a herbal drug is safe in very high overdose, then we must ask ourselves what effect it is inducing, and why on earth are we taking it in the first place. With herbal remedies, as with conventional drugs, tobacco and alcohol, we should constantly question what we are taking into our bodies – and what its short and long-term effects are likely to be.

The second major division of alternative medicine involves the laying on of hands or some form of physical manipulation. This is probably the most diverse sector of alternative medicine, ranging from faith or psychic healing to acupuncture, massage and osteopathy. Again it is not difficult to see the origins of practices like faith healing. In primitive societies, and indeed in many modern societies, religious advisers hold a special place. It is only a small move to extend their role from a purely spiritual one to one which also involves concern with their flocks' physical well-being. Throughout this book we have emphasised the importance of counselling and support in the treatment of stress-related disorders. Religion gives very effective support, so it is hardly surprising that some believers find it both satisfying spiritually and helpful in overcoming persistent psycho-somatic health problems.

While religion provides comfort, faith [or psychic or spiritual] healing claims that there is energy in the human mind which can be tapped and directed towards another. Typically the transfer of this energy, which is supposed to balance or harmonise the patient's physical state, is conduc-ted by the laying on of hands. Such a technique fits closely with the type of support mechanisms we know can be helpful in medicine. It is interesting as an aside to note that some psychologists are now using touch – though without the spiritual dimension – as a means to relieve stress and ag-gression. Faith healing is not new, it is mentioned in the Old Testament, and is clearly linked with the medieval practice of casting out demons. Modern medicine has tried to find a basis for the technique: we know that when we are depressed our beta-endorphin levels are low, so we are more sensitive to pain. Physical contact, support and encourage-ment help to lift depression and raise both beta-endorphin levels and our pain threshold. Whatever the basis of faith healing, it still finds many converts and has more than 7,000 registered practitioners in the UK alone.

A less complex method of physical therapy is massage. This is widely accepted as beneficial both by conventional and fringe medical practice. Unfortunately massage has become debased in many Western societies as a mere front for prostitution: this also makes it difficult for genuine practitioners to advertise and attract clients. A wide range of massage techniques exist, all basically seeking to stimulate a response from the body by finger pressure. Not surprisingly massage is effective in treating muscular conditions, and has found important applications in rheumatism and arthritis. Perhaps slightly more surprising is its use in other areas. Massage, particularly the shiatsu techniques, has been shown to be effective in the treatment of asthma and migraine – both essentially stress-related disorders. At London's Charing Cross Hospital, patients in the cardiac unit benefit from massage – which has now been shown to lower blood pressure. In general massage offers the sort of simple, contact therapy which we know can be useful in the treatment of stress.

Massage is a fairly gentle technique. The same cannot always be said of related therapies like osteopathy and chiropractic. These both concentrate on the spine complex of nerves, and aim by some quite vigorous manipulation to relieve a range of conditions. Most associate osteopathy and chiropractic with the relief of back pain and related disorders like sciatica or the condition known as frozen shoulder. In the UK, both chiropractic and osteopathy are being examined by conventional medicine, usually in association with orthopaedic surgeons and consultants. Back in the fringe medicine area both techniques continue to find wide applications, including the treatment of many stress and tension-related conditions. Many claim, and appear to experience, considerable benefit from such disorders as asthma, dizziness, migraine and general headaches. The basis of this improvement is not clear, so again we are faced with the problem of a mass of satisfied patients, with no clear scientific explanation for either their treatment or their improvement.

Both osteopaths and chiropractors claim their therapy finds points of restriction in the nerves and bones of the skull and spine, which can be relieved by skilled manipulation. They claim that even the fossas [pits or depressions which house the brain] of the skull can become restricted and blocked. The aim is to release this restriction or blockage by manipulation, after which osteopaths claim they can actually feel the body's fluids begin to flow. Whether or not this is so, both osteopaths and chiropractors pay particular attention to the release of tension, which cannot be bad. One problem is that manipulation, be it done by a masseur, chiropractor or osteopath, can be positively harmful if it is done badly. This is particularly true where serious problems exist, or where the patient has muscular wasting due to a condition like poliomyelitis or arthritis. Happily, certainly in Western Europe, both chiropractors and osteopaths have worked hard to maintain standards and develop professional levels both of treatment and qualification. This in part accounts for the closer link between these techniques and conventional medicine than is seen in other fringe medical areas. Both osteopathy and chiropractic appear to offer benefits for those suffering from some stress related conditions. To be cautious, these techniques are probably best used as an adjunct to orthodox medical treatment. In all cases they should be undertaken by skilled practitioners whose qualifications and experience are recognised by the appropriate professional bodies.

Acupuncture also involves the restoration of bodily flows, although in this case the flow is allegedly energy not bodily fluids. Practitioners of acupuncture believe that energy flows within the body along well-defined pathways or meridians. They also believe that malfunction in this flow lies at the heart of much physical disease. In acupuncture therapy, needles are inserted at very precise points, the aim being to balance and restore the energy flow. Acupuncture in its various forms dates back more than 4,000 years, with most of the techniques practised in Europe and North America having their origins in China some 2,500 years ago. Acupuncture typically uses long needles much finer than those used in hypodermics, although it can also use fine splinters of wood which may be ignited over the acupuncture points in a method known as moxibustion. Some practitioners use a needle-less technique known as acupressure, where the fingers are used to manipulate or rotate the acupuncture points to produce much the same effect.

Although acupuncture was first introduced into Europe and North America during the nineteenth century, it has taken a long time to gain acceptance. In 1963, a US study showed that the acupuncture points were characterised by lower levels of electrical resistance than the surrounding skin, although this discovery in isolation meant little. Only with advances in our understanding of brain biochemistry, and the discovery of the endogenous opiates, has this research taken on a new significance. Acupuncture needles are usually made of steel and have a silver, gold or copper head. When inserted into the body, acupuncture's proponents claim, the needle produces a minute electrical phenomenon, which many believe stimulates the release of beta-endorphin. Use of the conventional acupuncture points has now been extended to electro-acupuncture, where minute levels of current are passed through the needle with the specific intention of stimulating the release of beta-endorphin, and favourably influencing the metabolism of brain neurotransmitters like serotonin. From early results, we know electro-acupuncture works to relieve pain, and may have important applications in countering the worst effects of drug, tobacco or alcohol withdrawal.

In the West, acupuncture has been used mainly in the treatment of pain and pain-related disorders. In the Far East, it is also widely used to produce analgesic or anaesthetic effects prior to surgery. This may be done either independently, or in association with modern painkillers and anaesthetics. The argument here is that acupuncture is natural and does not have the dangerous side-effects and toxicity of modern anaesthetics. If this is true, then acupuncture must also create less interference with physiological processes generally. Anaesthesia therapy is largely confined to China, although many in the West are studying its benefits. In 1980 the World Health Organisation appeared finally to acknowledge the benefits of acupuncture. In a carefully worded report, which emphasised the work in China on acupuncture analgesia, WHO announced that it would ' use all possible resources at its command to promote and develop the practice of acupuncture within the general health system'.

Although WHO has officially endorsed acupuncture, we are still a long way from a full understanding of the mechanisms involved. These appear to go beyond what can currently be explained by the neurotransmitters and endorphins involved. Certainly when a needle is inserted there is a rise in beta-endorphin levels. This has been demonstrated by an analysis of the patient's cerebrospinal fluid. Whilst this could account for some of the pain-resolving qualities of acupuncture, it does not explain the technique's success in treating anxiety, tension and other stress-related conditions. One suggestion is that acupuncture has a far wider effect on brain neurochemistry than just the release of beta-endorphin. Serotonin levels have also been shown to rise during acupuncture treatments and, as we have seen, this powerful central neurotransmitter is involved in our mood and well-being. Another suggestion is that acupuncture is somehow involved with the pain-gate theory. We must find answers if electro-acupuncture is to fulfil its potential and become the important treatment for pain, withdrawal and stress which looks entirely possible.

When first introduced into Europe and North America acupuncture received a very hostile reception. The same could be said of hypnosis, and here the attitude has persisted: medical hypnosis has never managed to isolate itself from its music hall association and its link with charlatans, mediums and the rest of the 'wake the dead' brigade. In fact hypnosis has serious applications both in conventional and fringe medicine. In conventional medicine its uses lie largely in psychiatry, where it is an important tool in penetrating the subconscious. In fringe medicine, hypnosis has been used, apparently effectively, to treat a wide range of stress related conditions, including headaches, obesity, lack of confidence, depression and many more. It has also produced some surprising, and largely unexplained, benefits in withdrawal-related disorders.

Hypnosis provides a sensation of tranquillity and calm both during and immediately following therapy. The treatment does not induce a state of unconsciousness, rather a state of altered awareness, not dissimilar to the effects of certain narcotic drugs. Like many areas of fringe medicine, hypnosis suffers from a mass of claims most of which are unsubstantiated by scientific evidence. Some patients do appear to benefit from hypnotic therapy, and some have certainly withdrawn from the harder addictions like tobacco and alcohol with its help. Whether this stems from the advice given during hypnosis or from some more deep-seated cause is not clear. This whole area perhaps deserves a more detailed examination, though whether this would be welcomed by the practitioners involved is uncertain.

Linked to hypnosis are the various forms of relaxation therapy which make up the third sector of alternative medicine. In one extension of relaxation therapy, patients are taught to hypnotise themselves, to produce a condition in which they are far more calm and relaxed. This auto-hypnosis, which typically lasts about twenty minutes, has been shown to help both in chronic pain and in several emotional and stress-related disorders. Although auto-hypnosis is a highly specific technique, it clearly has links with other areas of relaxation and meditation, where various changes in consciousness and awareness are sought as part of the overall method.

There are a wide range of relaxation methods now available, and they offer some of the most natural and effective ways to combat stress. The techniques range from long standing ones, like yoga, to modern, technically based ones like mechanised feedback therapy, where patients are able to study a range of autonomically mediated variables to see how well they are succeeding. Relaxation therapy is probably amongst the least controversial of the fringe medical techniques. It is also among the best researched. The relaxation response is highly specific to an individual, and is complex in biochemical terms, so the degree of change, and the nature of response brought about by therapy, may vary. The changes include:

* a decrease in oxygen intake and carbon dioxide excretion;
* a decreased heart and breathing rate;
* a reduction in blood cholesterol and lactate levels;
* a reduced flow of blood to the skeletal muscles;
* reductions in blood pressure and volume;
* increased galvanic skin resistance;
* changes in slow frequency alpha and theta brain waves;
* increased saliva output;
* increased gastric motility, coupled with the relaxation of the sphincter muscles of the rectum and bladder;
* dilation and improvement in blood flow in the vessels serving the salivary glands and the external genitalia.

All or any of these could be regarded as beneficial.

Modern relaxation therapy really began in the West in 1929 with the US physician Ed Jacobson. He emphasised, not that individuals should become free of stress, but that they should feel comfortable within themselves and alert to both their internal and external environments. A lot of false mystique now surrounds relaxation therapy, much of it imposed by those trying to sell courses or techniques, and much of it concentrating not on the therapy itself but on the unnecessary rituals which surround it. Not only does this debase the concept of relaxation, which has much to offer: it also deters many people from taking part. Let us be clear: relaxation needs no ritual, though a regular pattern of behaviour associated with relaxing may help. Neither need relaxation be associated with meditation or with quasi-religious groups. Stripped of its hype, relaxation needs:

* a quiet environment;
* a passive attitude;
* a comfortable position;
* a neutral object on which to concentrate.

If all these are available then anyone, with training, can benefit from relaxation therapy without the pseudo-Eastern nonsense which surrounds many techniques.

This should not be taken as criticism of the genuine Eastern mystics, followers of Yoga, Sufi, Zen and others. These often show the way in using meditation and relaxation to control bodily reactions, particularly the stress response. With rigorous training in diet, relaxation and gymnastic exercise, these people can gain a remarkable degree of control over breathing, heartbeat and other bodily functions. What we are criticising are the Western look-alikes who seek to cash in on the current interest in Eastern philosophy by producing courses with a largely meaningless mix of philosophy and relaxation. These typically lack both the depth and dedication needed to gain benefit from either the meditation or the relaxation, and are likely to do little good.

One genuine technique from which many have gained

benefit is transcendental meditation. This was introduced into the West in the 1960s, and by the early 1980s had over a million followers, half of them in the USA. Among the earliest was Hans Selye, generally regarded as the father of modern stress theory. The technique is simple, involving two lectures, an hour of training and a quaint initiation ceremony. Transcendental meditation requires two twenty minute sessions daily, during which the user repeats continually a short meaningless word [mantra] which concentrates the mind. What is surprising about transcendental meditation is not so much its effectiveness as its simplicity. Even with the short period of training the user experiences a reduction in oxygen use and lower lactate levels (a measure of stress), while blood pressure has been shown to decrease during the preliminary relaxation process.

Properly conducted the relaxation process linked with meditation can undoubtedly be beneficial to health: like all relaxation techniques it can help us recover from the effects of stress, and make us more resistant to the stress we meet in our daily lives. The problem is that many meditation techniques are also linked with religious philosophies or life styles which may be less acceptable. These, for example, are the eight precepts that would-be acolytes must accept before they attend a ten day course in Vipassa meditation:

* to abstain from killing;
* to abstain from stealing;
* to abstain from sexual activity;
* to abstain from telling lies;
* to abstain from intoxicants – drugs, alcohol, tobacco;
* to abstain from food after 12 noon;
* to abstain from sensual amusements and bodily decorations;
* to abstain from using high and luxurious beds.

Some of these requirements are desirable, but others are less explicable. As we have seen, in terms of bodily stress, long periods without food are not advisable, as they disrupt the body's natural rhythms. Also undesirable are the sexual recommendations, which apply even to married couples. These smack of the curious preoccupation with celibacy which permeates many religions both in the East and the West. Certainly this book does not recommend sexual abstinence.

There is now a wide range of straightforward relaxation courses, of which we shall review some of the best known or most widely available. In choosing a form of relaxation therapy the individual should take into consideration both his own objectives and how a particular technique will fit in with his home and work life, even if this involves trying more than one technique. A technique with which he is comfortable is one with which he is likely to persist.

Many of the relaxation courses still make use of extensions of Jacobson's original theory on progressive relaxation, with the emphasis on learning to relax as a muscular skill. The main problem with Jacobson's method is that it is lengthy to learn, proceeding steadily through successive muscle groups. It does, however, offer good energy-conserving qualities and is effective in reducing both anxiety and our response to stress. Far easier is the simple physiological relaxation method. The process should be conducted in an environment which is quiet, warm and comfortable, and involves four basic elements:

* precise muscular movements, including moving joints out of the positions automatically adopted when we are under stress;
* natural breathing, with some emphasis on breathing slowly;
* the mental regulation and control of joint position;
* the free flow of thought on a pleasant theme.

The aim is to concentrate on relaxing antagonist (opposite) muscle groups. In this way the muscles which are tense or under stress are automatically relaxed as the body seeks to restore equilibrium.

One modern technique gaining wide acceptance particularly in the US is Benson's relaxation response. This makes use of some of the techniques used in established meditation procedures. Benson's methods require a quiet environment, a positive attitude, a comfortable position and a repetitive device on which to focus attention. Typically the procedure needs to be carried out in two twenty minute sessions daily, during which a decrease in sympathetic nervous activity like that seen in meditation can be achieved. Overall Benson's techniques appear to be effective: they combine the benefits of relaxation and meditation without some of the more extreme ritualistic aspects, and have been shown to produce most of the beneficial changes listed earlier. Again, if the mechanisms by which relaxation and meditation induce such changes are not always fully understood, then we must defer to the end results – all of which are desirable in reducing our body's exposure to stress.

A feature of alternative medicine, and of relaxation therapy, is the way one technique will draw upon the experiences of others. One example is the relaxation techniques developed by Schultz, which emerged largely out of hypnotic techniques used in the 1920s. Known rather extravagantly as autogenic training, Schultz's techniques involve the user inducing something close to a self-hypnotic trance in quiet, warm surroundings. In a supine position the person concentrates on such thoughts as 'I am at peace', and on producing a sensation of heaviness and calm throughout the body. It is easy to poke fun at systems like autogenic training, but for devotees they do work. They bring about exactly the relaxation effects which we know are important in our ability to combat stress. The main problem with autogenic training is that it is akin to a ritual and may be difficult for businessmen to fit into their day-to-day work patterns.

Modern relaxation therapy concentrates heavily on anxiety management training. In many cases this is particularly suited both to the business world and to company health education programmes. Such training schemes vary but usually include:

* re-educating the individual about the importance of general health in determining our response to stress;
* teaching relaxation, including some background on how the therapy may help moderate our response to stress;
* teaching coping behaviour – both through visualisation and role playing – designed to reduce the effects of exposure to stress.

Such courses go well beyond simple relaxation therapy, though relaxation forms a crucial part. The aim is to ensure a positive response to stress, important when we consider how much more damaging stress can be when we take a negative approach to its presence.

Relaxation therapy used in association with other techniques has become a feature of the 1970s and 1980s. One such integrated system is Walpe's systematic sensitisation. This comprises three main elements:

* training in muscle relaxation techniques, using methods not unlike those originally conceived by Jacobson;
* each individual creates a list – and hierarchy – of those stimuli which are particularly stressful and anxiety-provoking;
* a gradual and progressive exposure, while in the relaxed state, to the stress stimuli causing most problems.

The aim of Walpe's system is not just to benefit from relaxation, but to steadily desensitise the individual to stressful stimuli through a form of pre-conditioning. How far we can go down this route is not clear, although we do know that various forms of pre-conditioning can help strengthen our response to stress.

It is impossible to give general recommendations on the effectiveness of relaxation therapy as a treatment for stress. The techniques vary widely, and so does our personal response to relaxation. A technique which helps one individual may be useless to another, particularly if ritual intrudes and makes him self-conscious and unable to dedicate himself completely. In general, relaxation invokes many bodily reactions which are helpful in supporting our response to stress, including the changes in respiration and heart rate already mentioned. Less predictable are changes in blood pressure. In one UK study, relaxation therapy in 192 patients was shown to lower blood pressure significantly, reduce overall cholesterol levels and – perhaps more surprisingly – help counter some of the worst effects of tobacco withdrawal. These results have not always been confirmed by other blood pressure studies, though many clinicians believe relaxation to be a useful adjunct to diet control and other therapies used in the treatment of mild hypertension.

We have concentrated here on the formal methods of seeking relaxation: these offer major advantages in their provision of feedback information by which the individual becomes aware that the technique is working. Many successfully develop their own form of relaxation. To this end, there is now a wide range of video and audio tapes which can prove effective, especially for those too shy or self-conscious to join relaxation therapy groups.

Most of us associate alternative remedies with traditional and time-honoured treatments. This is not necessarily the case: modern technology has been frequently linked with fringe medicine. We have already mentioned electro-acupuncture, and another fast-growing discipline involves the use of ionisation. This is linked with the incidence of 'witches' winds', like the Mistral, Sharav, Khamsin and Santa Ana, which have been shown to have an effect on behaviour and illness patterns, particularly in individuals who are weather-sensitive. The idea behind ionisation is the presence in the air of a mix of both negatively and positively charged ions. Witches' winds, and indeed much of our modern life-style, disrupt this ion balance causing disorders like headaches, asthma, anxiety and insomnia. In extreme cases, it is claimed, ion imbalance can also be linked to suicides, murder and other violent behaviour – all of which appear to rise statistically during the witches' winds. The examination of the 'ion effect' is in an early stage. It does appear to offer interesting possibilities, and some seem to benefit from the use of the ionisers now on sale. Whether further research will disprove the theory or open a new sphere of therapy remains to be seen.

So what is the place of alternative medicine in the treatment of stress-related conditions? Probably the least controversial recommendation is that relaxation therapy should have a central and most important role. Relaxation without doubt counters some of the most damaging effects of our response to stress. How well it does this varies from person to person, depending on how successful they become in switching off. Compared with all other therapies relaxation has one major advantage: it can do no harm. If relaxation therapy does not work for us, then all we have lost is time.

Outside relaxation the benefits of alternative medicine are more nebulous. Certainly many benefit from treatment provided by fringe medicine practitioners, even if the nature and origin of that benefit is not always understood. Virtually all fringe medicine disciplines pay great attention to close liaison between patient and practitioner, and the benefits of this should not be underestimated. Indeed, it is now being systematised in many medical areas both fringe and conventional. In the UK, ANAC [the Association for New Approaches to Cancer] offers a mix of techniques including meditation, relaxation and the laying on of hands. Its prime aim is to improve the quality of life of cancer sufferers, and to remove the damaging sense of hopelessness so closely linked with the disease. ANAC regards itself not as an alternative to conventional drugs and surgery, but as an important adjunct to all forms of therapy. It has proved very effective.

For anyone thinking of turning to fringe medicine, and indeed any author tempted to recommend its use, there remain problems. Alternative medicine is plagued by practitioners who use imprecise terminology and talk lavishly of poorly defined concepts and phenomena. This helps nobody and merely isolates fringe medicine from the main body of scientific research – not just from conventional medicine. Many alternative medical disciplines still have to put their own houses in order if their techniques are to be taken seriously in today's technically aware society. This means not just a closer analysis and verification of their techniques, but also the removal of the charlatans and hangers-on who seem to attach themselves to many fringe areas.

The authors believe that fringe medicine has much to offer in the treatment of stress. The treatments are simple and safe, and it is unfortunate that they are often considered only after conventional therapy has failed. Alternative medicine is also very good in the treatment of psychosomatic disorders, unlike conventional medicine. The attention paid to counselling, life style and diet is important to our handling and control of stress. The best recommendation may be to try alternative medicine, but to stick to practitioners who are recognised by the appropriate fringe professional bodies, and above all not to spend a fortune on therapy which does not appear to be working.

—14—

The way forward

By now it is evident that what we have reached is not the end but a new beginning. Although we already have a firm understanding of the way that stress causes some disease, this is only the tip of the iceberg. There is little evidence that stress in Western society is declining: if anything, the reverse is true. Our societies seem to grow ever more forceful, competitive and materialistic. As those in employment seek ever higher rewards, so the gulf widens between the employed and the unemployed, the old and the otherwise deprived. We build into our societies massive tensions which now appear inescapable. What we have created is a society for the fit and the able, but one which pushes even these to the point of breakdown. It is hardly surprising that stress-related disorders, even with the most limited of definitions, continue to grow at an alarming rate.

Had mankind set out to produce a model best designed to create stress, while inhibiting the body's natural defence mechanisms, it would have been hard pressed to do better. Change, we know, is a major cause of stress and change is a feature of our modern technology-based societies. Where past societies have evolved slowly, we now live in times of massive and rapid change. Technology can revolutionise how we work and play virtually overnight. Despite this we have failed to frame social and community structures which can help us to cope with rapid change. Where the eighteenth and nineteenth centuries saw the flood of workers to the cities, the twenty-first may yet see the creation of a highly decentralised information-dependent society in which huge conurbations are largely obsolete. This will place pressure both on those who work in decentralised locations, and those who remain in the decaying inner city areas. Although such change can be predicted, and is already happening in some cases, we still do little to frame more suitable social structures. Not only has technology frequently outstripped our legislative ability to find solutions to the problems it poses, it has also largely outstripped our social ability to cope with change.

More than any other profession, conventional medicine bears the brunt of this rise in tension and pressure. This is unfortunate because, as we have seen, conventional medicine is often ill-suited both philosophically and technically to handle stress-related disorders. With a heavy base in pathology correction, and a low emphasis on preventive techniques, much of conventional medicine can only be palliative. What we need is to turn medicine around and start identifying solutions before we are faced with the problems; to produce in fact medical structures designed to keep us well, not merely cope when we are ill. In this we must be clear in our reasoning. By the time stress-related medical conditions start to appear, we have already gone too far towards more serious problems. What we must try to do is to reduce stress in our society, pre-condition the individual to recognise its effects but above all to do what we can to raise our personal stress thresholds. To some extent this is already happening, though stress clinics and preventive medicine generally remain underfunded. Where we spend millions treating end-stage terminal illness, we spend only a fraction of this trying to prevent some of the commonest disorders we face. We also spend millions prescribing tranquillisers, while not doing enough to investigate the reasons

245

which prompt so many to dive for such apparently comfortable, easy solutions.

All this does not mean that conventional medicine does not have a substantial place in the treatment of stress-related conditions. The clinician, and particularly the general practitioner, remain of primary importance. What is less clear is who has the central responsibility for prevention. In the absence of any clear mandate much good, and indeed outstanding work in this area is done by general practitioners. This is not surprising: it is estimated that more than 30 per cent of all visits to general practitioners are linked to stress-related conditions, and this means conditions where the link is proven. Had these clinicians not accepted responsibility for the treatment of stress, then the situation could only have got far worse. But stress presents particular problems for general practice. It takes time to diagnose and to treat with counselling. Time is lacking in the busy general practitioner's surgery and the outcome is often drug therapy, which may relieve the immediate symptoms but does little to treat the underlying stress. It is therefore overdue that we acknowledge that, without help and support, general practitioners do not have the training and resources to tackle the current epidemic of stress-related conditions.

Drugs do have a place in the treatment of stress, but they often arrive on the scene far too early. This is not just the clinician's fault. As patients we have come to expect medication, not recognising that our doctor can often provide advice which is just as effective. In this area we must recognise the role of the psychiatrist and the psychotherapist – that they have not been given a wider role in this book stems from their failure to agree among themselves as to the way stress should be treated. Nevertheless with their emphasis on counselling, they will continue to fulfil a major role in helping those at risk.

Over the next few years medical advance seems certain to

modify some of the treatments for stress. Much of this advance will inevitably stem from our greater understanding of brain neurochemistry. Already we see the move towards drugs which are neurotransmitter specific. These have not so far had the impact which might have been expected – but it is early days. We also see the search for safer tranquillisers though here we must proceed with caution. For years existing tranquillisers, like the benzodiazepines, have been considered totally safe. Only now after some twenty years of use are we beginning to recognise some of the longer term problems of dependence and withdrawal. Even with a new generation of improved tranquillisers care will be needed. What is required here is education, and a society that does not believe that the solution to all its problems is found at the bottom of a pill bottle.

One solution to the problems of drug therapy may be the use of the body's own natural tranquillisers and opiates. If these can be harnessed and exploited then most, if not all, of the risks of side effects and dependence are eliminated. Considerable progress has been made in this area and some highly promising results are being achieved. One such technique, trans-cranial electrotherapy, uses controlled, low levels of electricity, often delivered via the traditional acupuncture points, to modify the secretion of neuromodulators like beta-endorphin. The two attractions of such treatment are its very wide application and the absence of any side effects. It has already been shown to be extremely effective in the treatment of chronic pain, which has been resistant to conventional drug therapy, and in the treatment of withdrawal symptoms in drug abuse patients. As we progress, this type of electrotherapy seems likely to have far wider applications, most of them associated with stress-related conditions or the treatment of addiction problems.

Conventional, advanced and fringe medical techniques all have a part to play in the treatment of stress, but a great deal is up to to the individual. As we have seen, life-style, attitude, fitness and conditioning all play a part in how well we react to stress. If stress does not diminish in our society, then we must find ways ourselves to minimise its adverse effects. As a society, we cannot continue to expect conventional medicine to provide all the answers, and to compensate as we undermine our health through lack of exercise, drug misuse, smoking, etc. Indeed, there are few medical conditions where the onus for treatment and prevention is so firmly on the individual.

Throughout, this book has concentrated on stress as it relates to the individual. Although certain factors like noise, chemical fumes and temperature may be considered universally stressful, what we find stressful is often extremely personal. In the context of stress in the business environment this causes difficulties: we can make a factory or office as clean, quiet and amenable as possible, but this does not eliminate all the causes of stress. Personal relationships are a major cause and these are often far harder to tackle. Stress may also be built into the political and adminstrative structure of an organisation, often not deliberately but out of a lack of sensitivity. In such cases the problems may appear almost immutable, particularly in large multinationals where people are remote geographically and functionally from the core of the company. We must also recognise that man does not work in isolation: pressure outside work may affect performance, even where stress at work is kept to a minimum.

Over recent years we have seen the growth of various techniques in industry which have at their heart the control of stress. These include job enrichment programmes and improvements in job design generally. Where these originally concentrated on control of the physical aspects of stress, many are now more ambitious. In some Swedish companies, a great deal of job design is left to the individual worker. This, it is claimed, produces more effective working patterns, and allows for the optimum fit between an individual and the job. How far we can follow this is not clear, though the Swedish experience has proved highly promising, with company goals still being achieved within a very flexible working structure. Here we must make a plea for egalitarianism. Too many job design and selection programmes concentrate on middle or senior management. Where these are extended to more junior and shop floor grades, they are often surprisingly effective. As we have seen stress is not found purely in the senior or executive grades: if we are to deal effectively with stress in the workplace we must recognise that everyone is at risk.

Stress usually begins at the top. This may stem from such administrative factors as unclear objectives, lack of job definition or unrealistic work loads to the outright refusal to recognise that stress itself could be a problem. Indeed a lack of sensitivity on the part of top management is one of the problems faced by those seeking to introduce stress management programmes. For many managers there is still a certain stigma attached to the concept of stress. They feel they have somehow failed if they acknowledge stress to be present in their organisation, an unrealistic attitude because stress is an ever present, and indeed essential, part of our daily working lives.

Studies in the UK and the USA have shown that top managers are resistant to stress, and have typically developed good mechanisms for the control of the pressure they face. This may be one of the reasons they achieve their high status, though we should avoid any idea that top managers are some form of stress-resistant superstars. Once they have reached the top they are also relieved, by secretaries and assistants, of some of the stressors which face lesser mortals. Stress-related disease patterns show that the top manager is less vulnerable than middle and junior staff. This could in part account for the top manager's lack of sympathy, and the fact that many who are not vulnerable to such disorders still regard stress-related conditions as a sign of weakness.

The key to the relief of stress in industry is in the hands of top management. If this area is sensitive to the problems then we are more likely to see a considered approach to stress control generally, either through formal techniques or through better management practice. Sadly, many managers still seek to achieve their own objectives by stressing both themselves and their staff. Work by ordeal and pressure is seen as an archaic but desirable quality in too much of our manufacturing industry. Many managers also use their staff as an outlet for their own tensions and frustration: a manager may relieve his own stress by shouting at a member of staff, but it does little to ease the stress of the latter.

The need to reduce stress is clear and vital if we are to maintain a healthy, interested and motivated work-force. Recession, mergers and takeovers have created a very dynamic industrial environment in most Western countries. This is more unsettling for the work-force than some recognise, and undoubtedly lies behind the increased militancy seen in traditionally moderate industry sectors. In the face of high unemployment levels, redundancy is now far more feared than ten or fifteen years ago when the labour market was more fluid and open. Despite this it is amazing how badly many experienced companies handle the process of redundancy. Some appear through incompetence to do nothing more than add stress to an already unhappy situation. Poor communication, rumour and innuendo feature in the way even major multinationals handle what might be called the terminal stage of employment, even when they have a good record in other areas of management and labour relations.

Fortunately, a more sensitive approach to stress control is

now emerging in many areas. Where industry is concerned, most progress has been made in the USA and Scandinavia, with the rest of Western Europe lagging behind. Industry is becoming more prepared to recognise stress and take steps to limit its effects. This involves not just formal stress and management training programmes but also efforts to improve such factors as job definition and communication which can lead to job insecurity and uncertainty. Many stress management and control programmes have had an effect far more spectacular than even the most committed had predicted. They have improved the health levels of the staff involved, reduced sickness absence significantly, and have provided a useful forum through which stress within the organisation can be identified and reduced. The courses have also been successful in even the most harshly costed cost-effective terms.

A wide range of such programmes have now been tried by industry both in the USA and Europe. These concentrate on identifying the type of management problems mentioned earlier, but also contain key elements specific to stress, and around which the courses are constructed. These elements include:

* the identification and recognition of stress within the work-place;
* stress management techniques – including the importance of support, counselling and information;
* coping mechanisms to raise stress thresholds, and this includes advice on life style;
* the creation of help groups and networks.

In most cases the effects of stress management courses are not immediate. Stress training and re-education take time, and we must recognise that coping with stress is a lifelong requirement. Despite this, many companies report a surprisingly rapid response, with the mere fact that the course has been established having an early and very positive effect.

Companies establishing stress control programmes must decide whether such courses should be orientated to the individual or the company. To gain maximum effect both sectors will require adjustment, although changing the organisation may prove more difficult. This is unfortunate, because unless we can tackle the root cause of stress, any benefit to the individual will be limited. It also means that, even if courses are individually orientated, they must include some [anonymous] feedback which allows the company to treat the causes of stress.

All stress management courses place a high emphasis on information. This is not just a vital part of understanding: people cope far better if they are fully aware of what is happening. In the medical field this applies even in terminal cases, where the worst prognosis has followed long periods of doubt and uncertainty. In terms of stress, recognising its presence and health implications can strengthen both our mental and physical resilience. By learning to recognise and face up to stress, we are in fact learning the most simple coping mechanism of all. It makes us more able to adjust, and less likely to turn to outside agents to supplement our body's natural defence. Stress courses are still not available to all at risk. Neither should we allow ourselves to become too dependent on formalised courses: stress control is also the responsibility of the individual. Courses, books and medical advice may help, but their effect is limited if our own attitude is wrong: a positive, almost aggressive approach is vital. We also need to be clear about our own place in society and what we want from life. Self-analysis enables us to identify our objectives, and prevents us striving for goals which are beyond our abilities, or which will only make us unhappy if we reach them. It is amazing how many businessmen spend unhappy lives striving for a position which in the end only makes them miserable, or ruins their health. If we can learn to accept what we are, and what we want from life, then we are happier and our stress levels are automatically diminished.

We are not advocating dropping out: on the contrary, we are trying to prevent an increase in the significant number of senior executives who now drop out every year while at the height of their powers. Many – if not most – of such cases are closely linked with an inability to cope with stress. Indeed, for the highly stressed executive in mid-career who is unable to cope, only three options may appear available:

* to withdraw from the work-place through ill health or dropping out;
* a hostile and aggressive attitude;
* sublimation, by seeking outside activities which reduce the place of work as the central interest in life.

In industrial terms none of these is acceptable. Dropping out is costly, both for the individual and the company. In Europe and the US, we lose hundreds if not thousands of skilled and highly trained staff in this way each year. There is no doubt that with help and training much of this loss could be avoided.

The second option, aggression and hostility, is also out of place in the work environment. Angry, unsettled staff at any level increase the stress faced by those around them. They are destructive both to themselves and to others. There is no doubt that the new, harsh unionism shown by many white collar workers has stress and uncertainty at its base. These groups are no longer secure in their position as computerisation and office automation make inroads into areas once considered inviolate. Also growing is the need for white collar staff and executives to find their satisfaction in life from areas outside work. Even in senior positions much modern work is repetitive and unfulfilling. This means many senior staff are following the pattern of their blue collar colleagues, and finding their most meaningful experiences outside work. Industry itself is largely to blame: if we fail to give job satisfaction, even to senior staff, then we can hardly expect the degree of dedication once taken for granted.

In considering aggression and hostility it is appropriate to mention recent work done on limiting the effects of Type A behaviour. In the past many have tried to link Type A behaviour with performance, suggesting it is somehow a prerequisite for successful managers. Were this true, it would be a major cause for concern: Type A individuals are damaging both to themselves and to those around them. For this reason, it is important to note that the recent successful work done on limiting Type A behaviour has not been accompanied by any apparent drop in professional perform-ance. Much of this work concentrated on patients with an existing history of cardiovascular disorders. This is signifi-cant because, as we have shown, Type A behaviour is linked with a higher than average incidence of heart disease. Various techniques have been used to counter Type A behaviour, including relaxation therapy, drug treatments [typically beta blockers] and cognitive [behavioural] coun-selling. Although relaxation therapy has some effects, by far the most outstanding results have been achieved by cognitive psychotherapy. Here in 25 per cent of cases Type A behav-iour was modified, an excellent result given the fact that many psychologists have believed for years that Type A behaviour patterns were impossible to change. More import-antly for those suffering from a prior history of heart disease, Type A patients receiving cognitive therapy were four times less likely to suffer a recurrence of their disorder than the untreated control group. Such results look highly promising although this work is still in an early stage. In the UK, a comprehensive study covering 11,000 civil servants is now under way. When this is complete, we will know just how successful we are likely to be in moderating the behaviour of extreme Type A individuals.

The main objective of this book is to help managers to recognise the implications of stress, both for themselves and the workers in their charge. In the past, too much emphasis was placed on executive stress, as if this were the only group subject to pressure and tension. We now know that this is far from the case: some of the highest rates for stress-related disease are experienced by manual or non-skilled workers. Many other books and articles have tried to quantify stress as it relates to individual jobs and careers. This is a path we have deliberately eschewed. In statistical terms, it may be interesting and significant to link stress-related disease to certain career groups, but it tells us little about the individual. In this book we are primarily concerned not with what job an individual may do, but what effect that job has on the individual. Many jobs are undoubtedly more stressful than others, but what is significant is how well the individual develops mechanisms to cope with that stress. It is also clear that even the least stressful occupation may cause problems for an unsuitable incumbent.

The effect of stress on the individual must form a vital part of future therapy, and be catered for in training and stress control programmes. While global facts and surveys are interesting and indicative, stress and its effects remain intensely specific. This was recognised by Hans Selye thirty or forty years ago, when he began to lay down guidelines by which the individual might seek to minimise the effects of stress. Many of Selye's recommendations are just as valid today, and they include:

* know yourself, do not seek to play the role of another;
* learn to recognise the early symptoms of stress, and relax when you feel these coming on;
* balance work and play;
* when worried seek a harmless diversion;
* learn good sleeping habits;
* live in harmony with natural laws: do not seek to dig too deeply into bodily reserves;
* pursue excellence;
* pursue a philosophy of altruistic egoism: love others and treat them with goodwill, trust and respect;
* focus on something greater than yourself, be it God, the Universe or something else, and your troubles will shrink in proportion.

If some of Selye's approach and language now seems quaint, the lucidity and depth of his recommendations shine through. Despite our heightened knowledge of brain neuro-chemistry this remains an outstanding profile of how the individual can tackle stress and live at harmony with the world. Above all, it indicates the importance of the individual, which must emerge if stress therapy is not to become merely another anonymous, impersonal – and indeed stressful – part of medical therapy.

Selye's distinction between positive stress (eustress) and stress which is harmful or damaging (distress) also remains valid. Although this book has concentrated on the deleterious effects of excessive stress, we should be clear that stress is an essential part of our daily lives. Without it we achieve nothing: it provides the pressure and drive by which we create and advance our lives. What is harmful is excessive and prolonged stress, and stress which begins to affect the body's ability to adapt. From this it is a short step to saying that we should modify the current interventionist approach, where stress is to be avoided, to an approach which concentrates on raising our individual thresholds to stress. In fact such an approach is simplistic: the best stress programmes will concentrate on avoiding unnecessary stress, while attempting to raise thresholds of tolerance to stressors we cannot, and indeed should not, avoid.

So what of the future? The answer seems to be a combination of advances in medicine, changing attitudes in industry and an increased role on the part of the individual. One area where technology will prove significant is in the creation of better stress markers. In physiological terms better measurement criteria seem an essential aid to future stress therapy. Much current measurement is based on endocrine activity, and while this is useful it presents problems because it is essentially transient, and requires the drawing of a blood sample.

Much recent research concentrates on measuring stress's effect on the immune system. This is useful because it not only measures the presence of stress, it also indicates what damage it may be doing. Any measurement of the immune system's activity is however extremely complex, not least because we still have a hazy understanding of how stress acts on the immune system. Much current attention is concentrating on the immunoglobulins [IgG and IgA], substances which we know are influenced by stress but have the advantage of being relatively stable. Research is in an early stage, though it does give long-term promise of diagnostic kits for use by clinicians or even individuals. Such kits could be useful because much of the onus for stress control will remain in the hands of the patient.

Outside more precise diagnosis, advances in medical technology will undoubtedly play a major part in both the understanding and treatment of stress. Already we have seen advances in our knowledge of brain neurochemistry which bring promise of new drugs and radical new therapies. Despite this progress, we must acknowledge that our understanding of brain biochemistry is still limited. Much remains to be discovered, and this will fundamentally influence our understanding and treatment of stress. It will also have a major effect on common disorders like depression, schizophrenia and senility. Indeed if one research area offers the promise of new futures for both the sick and the old, that area must be brain neurochemistry.

Fundamental research is not the only area which will improve stress treatment. As we gain a better understanding of stress, we can devise procedures by which its worst effects can be avoided. We have reviewed many of the simple techniques which can raise our resistance thresholds, but new and exciting techniques are also emerging. Behavioural psychologists are doing outstanding work in teaching problem-solving skills which aim to translate seemingly insurmountable worries into a series of problems which can be tackled and solved logically. In many cases these techniques have been shown to be effective in countering stress-related disorders, though much evaluative work is still to be done.

Although advances in medical knowledge remain vital, we must avoid becoming too dependent on medicine for our treatment of stress. Modern medicine is not omniscient, a fact readily acknowledged by medical practitioners themselves. As individuals we must take more responsibility for our own health, not accept dysfunction as a natural and inevitable part of life, and above all not expect clinicians to put right what we have spent years making wrong. Increased responsibility for our own health is the only practical and possible way the vast rise in stress-related disease can be tackled.

We have concentrated in this book on simple techniques which raise our individual tolerance to stress. This seems a more positive approach than merely trying to avoid the stressors around us. We place a high emphasis on relaxation:

the stressed businessman must learn to set aside time for relaxation, be it a formal or personal technique. Many believe, though it is not yet proved, that relaxation brings a more integrated functioning to the brain's right and left hemispheres. If this is true, it can only enhance perception and thought and make us more intellectually productive. Many stressed businessmen admit they have their most creative thoughts while lying in the bath. It is not surprising. It is probably the only time they give themselves to relax, and is anyway exactly the sort of quiet, warm and comfortable place in which relaxation becomes possible.

Outside relaxation, good working practices generally can help us cope with stress: these include regular breaks, weekends and above all holidays. Executives who boast of not having had a holiday in ten years are a menace, both to themselves and their company. Status is an important part of our working lives, and many of us like to feel we are indispensable. However, well-chosen holidays make us more – not less – effective, giving the body a chance to restore a balance. Holidays need not involve travel: for the marketing executive who spends months travelling, what could be more relaxing than two or three weeks spent quietly at home? We need above all to choose holidays which are not stressful in themselves but satisfy our own needs and objectives.

In this book, we place great emphasis on choosing our own pleasures, because it is clear that many are influenced by the opinions of others. We are encouraged to go on holiday to places we do not want to visit because they are trendy or because others thrust their advice forcefully upon us. In many cases tired businessmen, who would like nothing better than to spend time at home, go away on holiday for no other reason than that their peer group expects it. Similarly we must pay attention to those with whom we elect to go on holiday: group holidays can introduce friction and rivalry. Peer group pressure, either open or covert, not only affects our choice of holidays. Many businessmen would undoubtedly enrol in relaxation classes were it not for what others would think. The answer is not to avoid relaxation altogether, but to find courses which do not embarrass us, or which we feel we must hide from our colleagues. It is strange that some are more prepared to be seen playing with executive toys, than taking part in relaxation classes which are both wholesome and harmless.

It is strange too, how patient some of us are with irritating or time-wasting relationships. The boring and disillusioned are a major cause of stress in those around them. In our private lives we can – and should – cut back on personal relationships which are stressful, although this may be more difficult at work. We can learn cut off techniques but these may be hard to implement if, as often seems the case, the problem is a senior member of staff. Above all, we should not underestimate the ability of others to cause us stress. Although we can – and should – listen to others, and in so doing help with their stress problems, such conversations must be two-sided. If we allow a one-way tirade to develop, the other person may feel better, but we will feel worse. To some extent this problem has already been recognised in Tokyo by the opening of a grudge telephone service. This allows people to phone with an outburst about their wife, boss or mother-in-law. What effect this has on the stress levels of those who take the calls is not clear. The lines have however quickly reached a high level of use, suggesting that some problems show no national boundaries.

Our objective has been to place the facts in front of the reader so that he can adjust his individual life style to become more resistant to stress. As with any self-help issue, motivation is the key. If we wish to be fit, productive and resistant to stress, we must make sacrifices. Above all we must recognise that stress-related disease grows out of conflict and imbalance. If we reduce the conflict, and live sensibly, then our body has an innate ability to restore the balance. This it can do, in the vast majority of cases, without the need for outside intervention by drugs or other therapy. We must learn to live with ourselves – and with what we have. Constant striving for impossible targets is the most potent stressor of all. If we strive only for the top job, then we are unhappy and discontented no matter how successful we have been in real terms. Similarly, if we worry too much over issues we cannot influence, we add unnecessarily to our stress levels. The next few years will see no drop in the amount of stress we face. Unless we are to suffer disease, and a drastic drop in the quality of life, we must find ways to handle the pressures we face. The answer – we believe – lies largely with ourselves.

Glossary

Aetiology agonists Associating the cause with a condition/disease. Synthetic [usually] substances which act in a manner similar to, or increase the action of, a natural substance [especially neurotransmitters].

Amino acids Substances present in the diet, or synthesised in the body, amino acids combine in chains to form proteins. A number of amino acids have essential roles as neurotransmitters.

Antagonists [The opposite of agonist]. Substances which decrease or inhibit the action of another substance – especially neurotransmitters.

Arteriosclerosis Hardening of the arteries. There are essentially three types, the most relevant here being intimal sclerosis or atherosclerosis where soft, non-cellular lipid material is deposited in plaques often in the inner coat of the blood vessel.

Autonomic nervous system That part of the nervous system which regulates the functions of some organs independently of will power. It is divided into the sympathetic [stress response] and parasympathetic [pleasurable response] systems.

Avogadro's number [Or Avogadro's constant]. Is the number of atoms in one mole of a substance [6×10^{23} mol^{-1}].

Axon The projection via which one nerve cell conducts its

impulse to the receiving terminal [dendron] of another
nerve cell.

Biogenic amines Neurotransmitters which are biosynthesised
from the dietary amino acids. These include serotonin
[from tryptophan] and noradrenalin and dopamine [both
from tyrosine].

Blood–brain barrier Due to the unusually high number of
lipid-rich cells in the brain, ionised or water soluble
substances diffuse through the brain only with difficulty.
In contrast lipid soluble substances penetrate readily.
Once considered of greater structural importance, the
blood–brain barrier presents a quantitative rather than
a qualitative difference in capillary permeability when
compared to other tissues. In the study of stress it remains
important not least because of the implications it has for
the penetration of drugs to the brain.

Catalyst An agent which speeds up a reaction while itself
remaining unchanged.

Cell mediated immune response When an antigen [foreign
protein] enters the body, sensitised lymphocytes [special-
ised blood cells] are produced which serve to attack the
invading protein or organism. Artificially induced, by
an attenuated [harmless] vaccine, this is the mechanism
through which immunisation by vaccination is achieved.
Less happily it is also the mechanism by which skin grafts
– and other transplants – are rejected.

Cognitive therapy The restructuring of attitudes by psychological behaviour which is totally alien to the character so
is normally conducted in the form of special exercises. An
example might be inducing a Type A character to eat
slowly or listen carefully to other people without interrup-
tion.

Corticosteroids Steroid hormones secreted from the adrenal
gland especially in response to stressful stimuli. These all
have a basic cortisol structure, and synthetic drugs of this

type are used to treat a wide range of inflammatory conditions.

Dendrites [Also dendron]. The short terminal process of a nerve cell which receives impulses from the axon of another nerve cell. Although a nerve cell only has one axon it has many dendrites and is therefore capable of receiving simultaneously impulses from a number of nerve cells.

Dilation The expansion in volume of a closed space or area, usually resulting from the relaxation of muscles which otherwise constrict the area as in the case of the blood vessels and the heart.

Distress In the context of this book, and after Selye, distress is negative stress which produces a hopeless, defeated response – or a sense of arousal which impairs performance and [eventually] health.

Endogenous opiates Naturally occurring chemicals, like beta-endorphin, which bind to the same receptors as the poppy-derived opium family of drugs, to give a sense of comfort and well being.

Enzymes Highly efficient biochemical catalysts which perform all the metabolic interconversions in the body. Because they govern the speed with which these reactions occur their control provides the means by which all metabolic reactions in organisms may be co-ordinated and regulated.

Epiphyte A vegetable parasite which attaches to other trees and plants. The best known example is mistletoe.

Eustress Positive stress [after Selye].

Fatty acids The basic chemical units of which fats [lipids] are comprised. Although forming an important energy store, they are less suitable for this purpose than carbohydrates so as a general rule the synthesis of lipid stores from fatty acids only occurs when excess energy is available.

Glossary

Holistic medicine The concept of treating a patient as a whole being and not directing attention purely at the disease symptoms.

Homeostasis Maintaining the level of essential substances like nutrients and electrolytes within a narrow range to provide the body with balance and equilibrium.

Hormones Unique biochemicals which co-ordinate the action of all the tissues of the body. Thus, during periods of stress, homones like adrenaline increase blood sugar and fatty acids from stores in the liver so that it is available when needed for muscle use.

Humoural immune response The synthesis and release of free antibody into the blood, and other body fluids, to form a coat around invading bacteria so enhancing their destruction by the white blood cells.

Hyperperistalsis Peristalsis is the contricting/relaxing process which facilitates the movement of food within the intestine. Hyperperistalsis is the 'over activity' of this function which leads to intestinal discomfort.

Hypertension High blood pressure.

Immunoglobulins A number of molecules function as antibodies – or substances which attack for antigens (see: cell mediated immune response). These substances are now generally known as the immunoglobulins and are classified according to their structure.

Infarction The changes which occur in an organ as the result of a blockage caused by an embolism or thrombosis.

Labile Unstable.

Lipoproteins Polarised lipids associated with certain special proteins in the blood, which act to transport cholesterol – and other lipids – from the intestine to the liver, and then from the liver on to fat deposits.

Microsomes Sub-cellular particles formed on disruption of the cells. Their primary functions in intact cells includes protein synthesis and the metabolism of drugs and other xenobiotics.

Neuroendocrine Hormones emanating from – or controlling – the central nervous system.

Neuroleptics Substances – usually here drugs – which act on the autonomic nervous system.

Neuromodulator A nerve-originating chemical which does not fulfil all the criteria necessary for a neurotransmitter because when it binds to its receptor it does not generate an impulse but alters the action of other neurotransmitters so exerting a moderating influence on their activity.

Neuropeptide Until recently, most of the neurotransmitters, known or suspected, were relatively small in [chemical] size. More recently a whole group of substances which function as neurotransmitters and neuromodulators but are proteins [peptides] containing a number of amino acid sub units have been discovered. These are the neuropeptides – which have been found to be widely distributed throughout the brain and the gut.

Neurone The nerve cell.

Neurotransmitter The projections between connection nerve cells are not in physical contact with the gap between them being known as the synapse. To relay an impulse across the synapse a chemical neurotransmitter is released. This neurotransmitter is enzymically degraded after the impulse has been passed – so allowing another impulse to be transmitted.

Opiate The family of drugs originally prepared from the opium poppy.

Oxidation In the sense used here, the chemical combination – or utilisation – with oxygen.

Pain gate theory A hypothesis put forward to account for the sensory mechanisms of pain – and in particular how less significant pain or trivial pain caused by acupuncture or

TENS devices can raise the sensation threshold for more serious pain.

Pharmacological From the Greek pharmakon – a drug. Is used here to refer to drug-based properties and remedies.

Platelets [Also thrombocytes]. Small, spherical bodies in the blood – with up to 300,000 being present in each cubic millilitre. Platelets play an essential role in the clotting process following injury.

Potentiate To extend and enhance. In combination many drugs (and alcohol) create a synergistic effect. This gives a total (and dangerous) effect which exceeds the sum of the elements of the substances when taken separately.

Precursor The starting material from which another substance is synthesied. An example is serotonin, the precursor to which is tryptophan.

Psychoneurotic Involving a functional disorder of the nervous system.

Psychosomatic Diseases where the physical manifestations are due, at least in part, to emotional or mental factors.

Psychotic Relating to a serious disorder of the mind, insane.

Somatic Relating to the physiology of the body [vegetative] – and not involving the mind.

Synapse The gap between the transmitting axon of a nerve and the receiving dendron of another across which the nerve impulse must be transmitted.

Teratogenic Toxicologically damaging to the foetus.

Vesicles Here, the small sacs at the endings of the axons where the neurotransmitter substance is stored prior to its release into the synaptic cleft.

Xenobiotics From the Greek, meaning strange or foreign. Here it refers to alien substances not normally part of the natural metabolic interconversions in the body. The xenobiotics are rendered soluble by the action of enzymes – in which form they can be excreted by the body.

Reading list

ANTONOVSKY, A. *Health, stress and coping; new perspectives on mental and physical well being*. New York, Jossey-Bass. 1979.

BENSON, H. and KLIPPER, M. Z. *The relaxation response*. New York, Avon, and London, Collins. 1976.

DIAGRAM GROUP. *The brain: a user's manual*. New York, Berkeley Publishing Company. 1982.

HENRY, J. P. and STEPHENS, P. M. *Stress, health and the social environment*. New York, Springer Verlag. 1977.

LANDY, F. J. *The psychology of work behavior*. New York, Dorsey Press. 1985.

LAWRENCE, F. *Additives: your complete survival guide*. London, Hutchinson Publishing Group. 1986.

REISER, MORTON F. *Mind, brain, body*. New York, Basic Books. 1984.

Selye's guide to stress research. New York, Van Nostrand Reinhold. 3 vols 1980 to 1983. [particularly volume I pages 131–167]

STANWAY, A. *Alternative medicine; a guide to natural therapies*. Middx., UK, Penguin. 1986.

Index